THE F

Also by Gerald Brenan

The Spanish Labyrinth
The Literature of the Spanish People
South from Grenada

Gerald Brenan

THE FACE
OF SPAIN

THE ECCO PRESS

TO GAMEL

Copyright © 1956 by Farrar, Straus & Cudahy
All rights reserved

THE ECCO PRESS
100 West Broad Street
Hopewell, New Jersey 08525

Printed in the United States of America
This edition published by arrangement with
Farrar, Straus & Giroux
Library of Congress Cataloging-in-Publication Data
Face of Spain / Brenan, Gerald
I. Travel
57-5548
ISBN 0-88001-463-6

9 8 7 6 5 4 3 2 1

FIRST ECCO EDITION

MILES

Author's route........

STRAITS OF GIBRALTAR

Contents

Preface

THIS book is an account of a journey which my wife and I made in the central and southern regions of Spain. The ground we covered was not entirely new to either of us. In my youth I had spent some six or seven years in Andalusia. When I married we bought a house near Málaga and from it we watched the confusion and horror of the opening phases of the Civil War. Then, on our return to England, my wife wrote an account of our experiences, while I produced two large books—one on Spanish history and politics and the other on Spanish literature. But thirteen years is a long time, enough to make one wonder if one knows or remembers anything, and when we went back to Spain my mind was full of questions. What was Spain really like? What was the character of Spanish culture and civilization? How did it compare with the French and English? To answer these questions I decided to keep a diary in which I would record my everyday experiences and impressions. I did so, and it is out of this diary that the present book has been made.

But Franco Spain, it will be said, has a special interest. The democracies have been calling it names in the press for many years, but few people beyond the Pyrenees have any idea of what it feels like to live in it. To throw some light on that might be valuable. However, it was by no means part of my original plan to do this. I was tired of politics, especially of the hopeless politics of the Peninsula, and wished to give my attention to the more permanent and characteristic features of the country. Regimes, I said to myself, come and go, but what is really important in Spain never changes. It was with a certain dismay therefore that I was to find that such an attitude was impossible.

For this is what happened: From the moment of our arrival in Spain to the moment of our leaving it we were besieged by people who wished to talk to us about the political situation. Never have I been in a country whose citizens were so anxious to express their views on their government. And since many of these conversations got into my diary, I have passed on a selection of them to the reader—a sufficient number, I think, to give him a fair idea of how ordinary Spaniards feel and think at the present time. I leave it to him to draw his own conclusions from them.

Finally, I would like to add a word to the person who is meditating a trip to Southern Europe. The Spaniards are a remarkable people, and their country is one of the most beautiful in the world. Travel is easy and pleasant, hotels are excellent, the food in them is plentiful and good, and the prices are reasonable. Above all, the foreigner will find everywhere kindness and hospitality, and even the Falangists, who have no liking for democratic countries, will put on a pleasant face. The impression that abides from my visit is of how little, after all the vicissitudes of the last thirteen years, the character of the people has changed, and this, to anyone who knew Spain before the Civil War, will be the best recommendation. To those who did not, let me say that there is something about this country and its way of life which makes a unique impression. For centuries a mixing bowl of the cultures of Europe, Asia, and North Africa, Spain today gives off a note which is unlike any other—a sharp, penetrating, *agridulce* strain, both harsh and nostalgic like that of its guitar music, which no one who has once heard will ever forget. The northerner in search of new sensations has every reason for going there.

MADRID

We left Northolt airport just before sunrise and flew under a ceiling of grey clouds. Caen, Bordeaux, Saint Jean de Luz. Then, passing above a fringe of white, stationary breakers, we crossed into the air of Spain. At once the map spread out below us became harsh and menacing. Iron-grey ridges, iron-grey valleys, few roads or fields or signs of habitation. Soon we saw the young Ebro curling and twisting below us and the desolation became worse. We were flying over a dark, silver-grey plateau, scattered with loose rocks and spotted with snow—the Sierra de la Demanda. Immediately below us I picked out a small tarn which I took to be the scene where the body was buried in Antonio Machado's great poem *Alvargonzález*. The grey smoke-colored clouds drifted across, the earth with its rocks and stones was lost to sight and, when the geography lesson began again, we were flying over the bright red soil of the province of Guadalajara.

Flying induces a mood of religious scepticism. One realizes the fallacy of supposing that God can be "up above" and can "look down" on us. For the view of the observer up above is necessarily one of indifference. One sees a man bicycling, one sees a little farm with its stream and bridge, and they have nothing human about them. One does not wish to help the man on his road or to drop a blessing on the little house. To feel well or ill-disposed toward them one must see them horizontally, on the human level. Man can only be man to those who walk on the earth beside him. We landed at Barajas airport and got into the bus. This drive into Madrid is extraordinary. The bare ocherous earth, laid out flatly in a succession of mesas or tables, quite bare except for a few whiskers of dry rushes, suddenly lifts itself up into a cement house, a black spidery almond tree, a cluster of umbrella pines. Then we come to larger buildings hatted with red tiles, to white, blotched walls, to those incoherent spaces which the French call *terrains vagues*, to gaunt, bare villas and withered gardens; and so gradually the city begins, not scarring and antagonizing the landscape as in the approaches to English cities, but blending with it in color because it is made of materials that first came out of it and have then been reduced by the devouring heat and light to the same tonality. And always far above is the sky—high, whitish grey, spreading from horizon to horizon like the wings of a hovering vulture: a vulture whose feathers have some of the luminosity of the dove's. In Spanish skies one sees the reflected face of the Spanish continent.

The hotel where we are staying is in the Gran Vía, that vulgar and blatant street of dwarfed skyscrapers that cuts through an old quarter. It is new and run on modern lines. We have a bedroom and private bathroom with excellent and lavish food for fifteen shillings a day each and a view from the window of the distant mountains.

February 11

THE number of waiters in this hotel astonishes me. In the dining room there are fourteen, dressed in white jackets at lunch and in evening dress at dinner, but with various additions of insignia to show their waiterly rank. Upstairs there are not only the *valets de chambre* who bring breakfast, but the *camareros de piso* who carry other meals to one's room if they are required. In addition to these there are also of course the various chambermaids, each with her different hours and functions, the washer-women who occupy the roof, and the lift boys who are learning English. Every time we go up or down we give them a lesson. Really this relatively modest hotel—there are a dozen larger and more expensive in Madrid—is organized with the same lavishness of personnel and attention to hierarchy as the old houses of the nobility.

The Spanish waiters make up one of the most striking and representative types in the country. With their thick eyebrows and erect, stylized posture they have the air of bullfighters *manqués,* of *toreros* who wisely prefer the white napkin to the red cloth and the pacific diner to the charging bull. They move with the same litheness and ballet dancer's precision and put a certain solemn operatic air into every gesture. How refreshing to see people doing the supposedly humdrum and mechanical things with artistic relish and gusto! It is something that the Englishman, accustomed to the utilitarian outlook of his countrymen, to their mixture of sloppiness and Puritan philistinism, can hardly understand. It makes one realize the price we have had to pay for Locke's and John Stuart Mill's philosophy. We can hardly conceive of our dinner as a waiter's ballet—quick, yet with the gravity and seriousness generally to be expected of Spanish things. Yet that is what in this country it may easily be.

But what about the food? Spanish cooking, it must be admitted, has no claims to compete with French. It consists of little more than a selection of the peasant dishes of the various provinces, with a few supplements from other countries. But the materials are good and trouble is taken in their preparation. The only defect I find is that of monotony. Spaniards think of a meal as of a religious service. Just as the introit leads up to the gradual, so the soup introduces the omelet, the omelet paves the way for the fish—in which there is about as much variety as there is between one collect and another—and the fish ushers in the clinching part of the meal—the veal cutlet or beefsteak. But an Englishman will find absolutely no cause for grumbling till he has been living in a Spanish hotel for at least a month. And in the excellent but expensive restaurants of Madrid he will get all the variety that he needs.

February 12

I HAVE had to stay in bed for a couple of days with a touch of flu. The seclusion and rest have been rather pleasant. Our room is on the eighth floor and commands a wide view to the north. In the foreground is the Royal Palace, that vast eighteenth-century edifice which is the most imposing thing in Madrid, and beyond it lies the bare yellow plain that rises from the river Manzanares and stretches to the snow-covered Guadarrama. The sky is blue, but scattered with white clouds. None of these clouds could belong to any country except Castile: they carry their passports with them on their faces.

The *valet de chambre* stopped this morning to have a talk with me. He belongs to a type and profession that was common in Europe a hundred years ago, but is almost extinct today. That is to say he has acted as valet and *hombre de confianza* to a number of titled people. His stories were interesting and had a pleasant eighteenth-century air: the young marquis ruining himself at cards or by absurd extravagances, the old duke who preferred to lose money on his estates rather than to spend a penny on them, the love affairs in which he acted as intermediary. He was an attractive man, this valet—sensible, serviceable, without envy of the people he worked for and well able to maintain his own self-esteem and dignity. He had been caught by the Civil War in Madrid, where his sympathies had lain with the Nationalists, yet the picture he painted of present conditions was somber in the extreme. The black market, he declared, was the only business in the country that was flourishing. Everyone from the highest authorities down was in it. All the new money in the country came out of it. Yet the injustice of the land was such that though none of the big men were ever caught, the poor man who had hired a mule to go out foraging in the villages was often fined and imprisoned. As he waited at the police post, he would see lorries belonging to the Army or the Falange, packed with black market goods, pass without stopping.

"Spain," he went on, "is finished. Everyone who can leave is doing so. If the frontiers were opened tomorrow, half the population would walk out. If you could find me a job in London, I would be deeply grateful."

Like everyone else he complained of the cost of living.

Actually the prices in Madrid shops do not seem higher than those in English ones, and hotels are cheap. But wages and salaries are a fraction of what they are with us. There has been a severe inflation and everyone except the land-owners and *nouveaux riches* are finding it hard to make two ends meet. Many middle-class families, I'm told, can only afford to eat once a day, although, since the standard of dress has gone up, they turn themselves out well. If they did not, they would lose their jobs.

One of the sights of Madrid are the new American cars. I should say that there are more of these than in any capital in Europe. Most of them, I'm told, belong to government officials, but rich people can also get permission to import them if they are prepared to pay what is asked. They cost anything from £3,000 to £5,000. In contrast with these cars is the number of cripples; every few yards one meets a one-armed or one-legged man. Some have no legs at all and creep along on all fours, wearing a sort of boot on their hands. I am told that many of these cripples are *mutilados de guerra*, but not all. For example, a chambermaid in our hotel tells me that she is a widow who supports her three children and both her parents. Her father cannot work be-cause he has no legs. "I suppose he lost them in the war," I said. Not a bit of it. He was a railwayman and an engine ran over them. This seems to me typical. Spaniards are very careless of their safety and shed their limbs with the fa-cility of crabs. But what is really shocking is that, although foreign exchange is freely used to buy the most expensive cars, none is spent on artificial limbs. I am told that only those who get permission to go abroad can buy them, and certainly one sees well-dressed men and even women hobbling along painfully on wooden stumps.

We had wished to go over the Royal Palace, the scene of that superb novel by Pérez Galdós, *La de Bringas,* which my wife is translating, but we failed to get permission in time. (Galdós, by the way, is one of the greatest of European novelists, a Spanish Balzac whose books have some of the raciness of Dickens as well as the psychological profundity and interest in abnormal states of mind shown by Dostoevski. Owing to the indifference shown to Spanish things during the last century, none of his mature works have ever been translated out of Spanish.) We found our way instead therefore to the church of Nuestra Señora de Almudena, which is one of the three churches that have claims to be the cathedral church of Madrid. It is a large, ugly, modern edifice, still unfinished, designed to act as a mausoleum for the aristocracy of Castile. But money speaks even in a place such as this, and several rich men of plebeian descent have been buried here. It had cost them quite a bit: first they had had to buy a chapel—for this they put down £3,000—and then they had to decorate it. In all they would scarcely spend less than £10,000. The whole place stank of money and vulgarity.

The guide pointed to a gold crown made last autumn for the Virgin of Almudena at a cost of three million pesetas. And only a few hundred yards away, he added, men and women are dying of starvation.

This story, I imagine, is part of the daily conversation of every poor family in the city. It helps to fan that hatred of the Church which is often much greater than that for the

Falange. Of this nothing is expected, but the Church after all professes Christian ideals. Is there not something about the rich and the poor in the New Testament? What makes this particular act all the more foolish is that, although the Virgin of Almudena is one of the oldest cult images in Spain, dating back to the capture of the city from the Arabs in 1083, she is not a popular one, but has been appropriated entirely by the very rich.

Our guide, a grey-haired man with a hoarse voice and a fierce, bright eye, who as a sailor had known foreign countries, spoke with all the bitterness of the defeated:

"Though the churches are well attended today," he said, "nine out of ten people who visit them do so merely to be seen and to get a good name. When they ask me why I don't go too, I say to them, 'I neither bother God nor offend him.' You see, I imagine the world as a ship sailing through space; it is likely that the ship has a captain, but I don't know him."

However I do not think it is true that most of those who attend Mass do so for effect. One has only to go into one of the city churches to find it full of women, with a fair sprinkling of men, whose devotion is evident. Nor is the Church here entirely neglecting the poor. The impression I get is that though it is doing little for the adults, who are probably irreclaimable, it is making an effort to feed and bring up the children.

We decided today to walk out to the Prado de San Isidro, beyond the Manzanares, the scene of the annual festival of the patron saint of the city, which Goya has painted in one of his gayest pictures. The sun was hot and the wind cold, and, as we trudged along the bare road beyond the Puente de Toledo, eddies of dust blew round us and filled our mouths and eyes. Above us on the left were the three cemeteries, planted with cypresses, where the better families of Madrid are buried; on the right the flat, dusty valley bottom, still scarred with trenches, where the fair used to be held. Since many people, especially priests, were shot here during the Civil War, it is now held elsewhere and consequently has fallen off greatly. The view of the city, pale buff and ocher, clustered together on the plateau beyond the dismal valley, had its beauty, though the confinement of the river between concrete banks and a confused mesh of electric pylons have destroyed the foreground.

We climbed to the oldest cemetery, that of San Isidro, to see the grave of Goya. He is buried in one tomb with three famous writers—the insipid poet Meléndez Valdés, the brilliant playwright Leandro Fernández de Moratín, and the too emphatic Catholic polemicist, Donoso Cortés. Meléndez Valdés and Moratín died in exile because, like Goya, they held Liberal views, while Donoso Cortés was banished because he was a Carlist. Here, however, a symbol of Spain's agitated, inconclusive history, the three heretics and their mortal enemy lie cheek by jowl.

Battling through the dust storms we made our way to the lower cemetery of San Justo to see the graves of Larra and Bécquer. This cemetery, which has a special area reserved for great writers, is divided by high walls into a bewildering number of *plazas* or enclosures. Along these walls were the niches, set neatly one above another like drawers, while in the open space, among cypresses and evergreen shrubs, were the white marble tombs of those who preferred this more expensive form of burial. It was as though the spirits of the dead had been given their choice between country villas and city flats.

Cemeteries tell one much about what people really feel about death, as opposed to what they are supposed to believe and feel. Thus most of the inscriptions put up since 1880 began with the words *Subió al cielo*—Rose to heaven —neglecting entirely the intermediary stage of purgatory, while others had nothing at all but a pathetic exclamation —*Hija mía! Carmencita mía! ! !, Angelita!*—that in their naive expressions of grief reminded one of the pagan tombstones in Italy. I did not see a single religious text and often there was no sign whatever of religious belief, not even a cross. Yet the cemeteries are Church property.

One of the things that most astonishes me in Madrid is the amount of building that has been done since the Civil War. Everywhere one sees new blocks of flats, business premises, ministries, mostly of a very large size. On the outskirts of the city whole new suburbs of five- or six-story buildings have grown up. One has to search hard to find any trace of the ruins of the war. When one thinks of the small progress made in England, with her huge resources, one is impressed, though it is only fair to remember that labor costs in Spain are low.

Some of these new buildings are ugly, but others are handsome and add to the dignity of this well-built and orderly city; this is particularly the case when the lovely yellowish rose brick which is baked in the neighborhood has been left uncovered. But not all these buildings are

useful. Look for example at that vast quadrangular edifice
that has been erected on the site of the model prison. It
has more than a thousand windows facing outward and
must have as many again opening onto inner courtyards.
Ask what it is and one is told with a smile that it is the new
Air Ministry, built for a nation that has not a single modern plane. One may well admire the passion for size and
magnificence in architecture which the Spaniards have always shown, and yet see that the real intention behind this
Escurial-like pile was to provide several thousand salaried
jobs which the rest of the country would have to pay for.
This is simply the latest installment of the old system by
which the middle classes are sheltered from competitive
work and given a stake in the regime. As they know there
will be a general scramble if it is turned out, they support it.

One cannot contemplate the size of Madrid nor the scale
of life that prevails in it without some misgivings. Here is
a city of nearly a million and a quarter inhabitants built in
a wilderness and manufacturing next to nothing. Philip II
chose the site for no other reason than that it was at the
geographic center of Spain, the point to which you would
have to attach the string if you hung its cardboard replica
horizontally from the ceiling. As a friend of mine once remarked, it was designed as the observation point in a cen-
trally organized prison. Today, however, it is the daydream
residence of almost every person in the country, for Spaniards, unlike English people, are city dwellers by instinct
and Madrid—like Paris but unlike London—has all the
attractions of a great capital. And it is growing rapidly.

The fall of real wages in the country is driving the agricultural laborers into the towns, while the new money made out of the black market is pouring in to spend itself, in Spanish fashion, in dissipation and luxury. To these additions must be added the increase in the numbers of the bureaucracy.

Now surely, one would think, such a dead weight must be more than the rest of this by no means wealthy country can carry with safety. The weight is all the more felt because Madrid is emotionally and intellectually cut off from the processes of agriculture and manufacture that maintain the nation. The backwardness of Spanish agriculture and the really shocking neglect of the condition of the land workers are due in part to the fact that most Madrileños know nothing of country life and would care nothing if they did know. Not only the landowners, but the politicians and administrators too, are absentees from the sources of their wealth. And this is not true merely of the present regime; it was equally true of the Republic and of the Monarchy. Only Primo de Rivera's government showed itself aware of the importance of food growing.

Meanwhile the city spreads. One may remember that one of the chief causes of the decline of the Roman Empire was the excessive load which the overhead expenses of city life threw on the agricultural community. When Rome fell, it was the country-dwelling peoples, the barbarians, who took up the power she had dropped. The farm with its manure heap superseded the forum with its theater and baths, though the feudal castle had to be built to protect it. The chief need of Spain today is therefore, I would say, the revitalization of its countryside.

The Spanish press makes a curious study. The first thing one notices is that there is scarcely any news given in the Madrid papers about Spain. One is not told, for example, that the factories in Barcelona are working only two days a week because the shortage of water has reduced the hydroelectric power. Yet the lack of rainfall this winter can surely not be put down as one of the sins of the regime. Nor is any encouragement given by describing the progress of the various plans that are under way for building new hydroelectric plants and for re-equipping the country generally. The foreigner casting his eye over the press might well suppose that nothing happens in the Peninsula except football matches, religious ceremonies, and bullfights. Even when some politician makes a speech, it is merely to reaffirm that Spain is great, glorious, and triumphant and that it is due to some unaccountable streak of malice that other nations do not understand her.

On the other hand the interest shown in foreign affairs is limitless. Every part of the world is surveyed, from Peru to Cochin China, and English, French, and North American affairs are reported and discussed at length. These reports, especially in the *A.B.C.*, are often intelligent and objective, but they have usually been doctored at the end by stressing some point that is favorable to the regime. Most amusing are the veiled allusions to Spanish corruption and black marketeering. Falangist papers will headline some trifling case of malversation of municipal funds in England, while

the *A.B.C.*, which is Monarchist, devotes a leader to the
bottomless corruption of the Chiang Kai-shek government,
making it a transparent description of what is happening
much closer home.

But the thing that most strikes one about the Spanish
press is its obsession with Communism. It is interested in
nothing else. Every paper gives the impression that war is
imminent and that the whole of Europe down to the Pyrenees will be overrun by Russian armies. I do not think that
this is due to nervousness. Spaniards are remarkably smug
by nature and do not easily imagine that anything that
happens outside Spain can seriously affect themselves. The
real purpose of this anti-Red ballyhoo is that it helps to
keep the two parties on which the regime depends, the
Monarchists and the Falangists, together. But for the wide-
spread fear of Communism left by the Civil War and by
the advance of the Russians westward, Franco would have
left long ago. He remains because he is thought to be the
best man to deal with a crisis, having proved himself both
as a general who could command the obedience of the
Army and as a politician who could deal prudently with
foreign nations.

In no other country in Europe does one find such a
passion for the cinema. Madrid, which has very few
churches, has over seventy film theaters. There are also a
large number of ordinary theaters which cater to playgo-
ers. But the drama is in a bad way. It is not for lack of
actors, for these are as good as one could find anywhere
and rather above the English standard. It is because Spanish audiences will only tolerate new plays. So they were in

the seventeenth century and so they are today, and the
thinness and air of improvisation that weakens the Spanish classical drama, alive and vivid though it often is, are
the consequence of this passion for novelty. Since at present there are no good dramatists, for all the creative arts
went down in the Civil War, one has to content oneself
with going to the *zarzuela,* or musical comedy, which has
its attractions, or visiting a rather remote theater to see a
revival of the Quintero brothers. Here we saw that delicious comedy, *Puebla de las Mujeres,* splendidly acted,
with the part of Concha Puerto taken by Ana Adamuz, a
very accomplished and subtle actress. We also saw two bad
plays by Benavente (his recent work has gone off) and—I
would like to print this in red ink—a performance by those
greatest of Andalusian dancers, Rosario and Antonio. A
long visit to America has not corrupted their gypsy in-
tegrity or weakened their superb technique: the somber,
tragic power of their dancing and the passion that their
bodies conveyed, as they advanced toward or receded from
one another, transcended anything I have seen before,
even in Diaghilev's time. It made the Sadler's Wells Ballet,
excellent though it is, seem pale and superficial by comparison. Unfortunately we could not see them a second
time, as we left Madrid the next day.

CORDOVA

In our carriage, as we traveled slowly southward, there were three other people besides ourselves. One was a fat man with a large white head like an egg and two little, plumply lidded eyes set transversely in it. As soon as the train had started, he put on a soft traveling cap, spread a handkerchief over his face, and went to sleep. Next to him sat a lean, nervous man in the middle thirties, with one of those thin, eyebrow-like moustaches often worn by Fascists, and his pretty wife. They talked in monosyllables, while the man kept taking up and putting down his newspaper and moving restlessly from one side of the carriage to the other. Since he avoided my eye, it was obvious that he did not wish for conversation.

We passed Aranjuez with its tall elms, silent in the morning light, and entered the dreary, reddish yellow steppe that prepares the way for the equally dreary plain of La Mancha. At a station the fat man woke up suddenly and got out. Through the window I could see him cross the platform and climb into a diminutive horse bus, which apparently connected the station with the town. Where it could lie was a mystery, for we could see for miles in every direction.

My wife had started a conversation with the smiling woman who sat opposite her, and I joined in. Her husband listened in a moody silence. The conversation languished. Then Valdepeñas came and we decided to have lunch. The

hotel had provided a lavish four-course meal and we pressed
our companions to share it. They yielded, and over a cold
omelet, red mullet, and a bottle of wine the man's hostility
broke down and he began to talk.

He had plenty to say for himself. He was a doctor who,
while still a *practicante* or medical assistant (a rank we do
not have in England) had joined the Blue Brigade and
gone to Russia. Here he had spent two years. He said that
he liked the Russians: they were a good-natured, simple
people, easily imposed on by their rulers and at bottom
more sympathetic than the Germans. But their standard
of life was terribly low. The Ukrainians, who lived rather
better, hated Communism and for that reason had deserted
in large numbers. When the brigade returned to Spain
many of them had begged to come with them; we should
find two or three in Málaga. I asked him how he had liked
the Germans. Not much, he said. They were too technical
and too fanatical. That was why they had failed, in spite
of their many great qualities.

He questioned me about England. Like all the other
Spaniards I had met, he was full of curiosity to know what
the conditions of life were in our country. But there was
resentment mingled with his rather grudging admiration.
Why had we outlawed Spain? I said that we had no wish to
outlaw Spain (it is odd how when traveling abroad one
becomes the official spokesman of one's country), but that
it was impossible for us to have close or friendly relations
with its present regime. Our foreign policy was governed
by the political struggle with Russia and if we admitted
General Franco's government to the union of West Euro-

pean nations, many people in France and Italy who at present supported that union would give their votes to the Communists. We could not afford to make such a gift to Russian propaganda.

This was a point of view that seemed entirely new to him and he sat brooding over it for a few moments in silence. But when I added that if a monarchy were to come in in Spain, we might feel that the position had altered, he became very excited.

"This Don Juan," he said, "with his talk of elections and of friendship with Prieto will never rule in this country. Never—you may take my word for it. For if he were to, in a few years' time we would be back where we were in 1936 and all the work of the Liberation would have to be done over again. That would mean another Civil War."

As we talked, we were passing out of the flat tableland of La Mancha into a different region. Round sage-green hills, topped by whitish rocks, began to collect round us—at first in ones and twos and at some little distance from the track, as if to prepare us for the change that was coming, then crowding close about us in massed formations. In the brittle air the rocks glittered faintly and patches of broom, which the Spanish peasants call *novia de los pastores*, or shepherds' sweetheart, made yellow smears upon the grey-green hillsides. All at once, as we crawled up a little pass, the train began to move faster and looking out we saw that we were racing down a steep grassy valley; jagged cliffs and rock pinnacles sprouting ilex and umbrella pine stood up on either side, rising above one another in distant recession. In an instant the whole scene had changed from the motionless and classical to the picturesque and romantic. We were in the Pass of Despeñaperros, the only breach in the three-hundred-mile wall of the Sierra Morena.

I went out into the corridor to look at the view and the doctor joined me.

"Is it true," I asked, "that there are bandits in the Sierra?"

"You bet there are," he replied. "All those rocks and peaks you see are full of them. Some people call them the Maquis, but you can take my word for it that they are nothing else but bandits and murderers. When they want food, they come down from the mountains to raid farms and then they shoot everyone they see. They spare no one. If, as they pretend, they sought out their personal and political enemies, I should respect them. One knows where one is with people who fight for their ideals; either you kill them or they kill you, but the fight is pure. But these people—no. They have no ideals, they just kill for money and love of bloodshed."

"Are there many of them?"

"Their numbers vary. Sometimes there are only a few, at other times there are thousands. When the police press them in one place, they move to another. They travel where they like and the towns are full of them. While they are in the mountains they live in caves and fire from behind bushes at the civil guards who try to close with them. Then they raid the farms and villages and carry off the cattle and pigs. As they kill any landowners or bailiffs they can catch, the estates are not supervised and agriculture suffers. The whole of the river valley above Cordova is terrorized by them."

"This is the classical region of Spanish brigandage," I remarked. "José María made himself famous here a century ago."

"Yes, but these are not *caballeros* like José María," the doctor insisted. "They kill, kill, kill. And they don't defend the poor against the rich as he did. They rob for their own pockets."

We had come out of the pass into a rolling country planted with olives. Soon we saw on our left a slow, muddy stream bordered with tamarisks and oleanders; it was one of the headwaters of the Guadalquivir. Periwinkles and yellow marigolds were in flower in the hedges and the farmhouses we passed looked white and clean with their pots of geraniums and their iron *rejas*. Everywhere we saw horses, mules, asses, and ragged children. There was no need to be told we were in Andalusia.

We began to talk of the conditions on the land.

"They are not good," my fellow traveler said. "It's the old, old story—the landowners won't pay a living wage. We do all we can to press them in the syndicates, but they refuse to budge. Yet they are some of the richest people in the country. Look at Espejo, for example. The whole town and all the country round it are owned by the Duchess of Osuna, yet the workers on her estates are starving. The Reds ought to have shot those people."

I told him that at Málaga, where I had been living when the Civil War began, the Reds had not shot the landlords, but only the industrialists and the small people.

"That's just it," he said, very excited. "The Reds didn't shoot the right people. They left the landowners alone, and now we have to pay the price for it."

The train drew up at Andújar and a crowd of miserable, starving creatures, dressed in rags, stood on the platform.

"Did you see Russians who were poorer than that?" I asked.

He admitted that he had not, but added that whereas all the Russians in the country districts were miserable, except the commissars, only a few people in Spain were undernourished.

"It's what I'm telling you," he went on. "This is the fault of the landlords. They pay wages that no family can live on. And for half the year they pay no wages at all."

"But why can't you do something about it?" I asked. "After all, Spain is a dictatorship. Franco can do anything he pleases."

"Ah, Franco!" he broke out. "Don't talk to me of Franco! He's the best man Spain ever had. He's a saint, that man is. He's so good his image ought to be on all the altars. If anyone ever had a heart of gold, it's he. But he doesn't know what's going on round him. Poor man, he's always surrounded by his guards, has to travel in a bulletproof car and see Spain from hoardings and balconies. If only he could step just once into a bar or café and listen to what people were saying, the country would change overnight. And then he's so unjustly blamed. If it doesn't rain and the crops fail, they say '—It's Franco's fault. It's all because of Franco. If we had a king, we should be better off—' Is that fair?"

"No," I said. "But they do say that some of the people round him are robbing the country."

"And so they are. Look at X." (He named a well-known political figure.) "He made a pile by pure swindling, ran off to America and lived there for a year. Yet now he's back again and more influential than ever. But Franco doesn't know this. He is *muy caballero,* a very great gentleman and trusts the people round him. And this is how they repay his confidence!"

The train drew into Cordova and we got out. The doctor shook hands and gave me his card. From it I could see that he was one of the leading figures in the Falange of the province. Something neurotic in his bearing told me that during the Civil War he had been responsible for many disagreeable things, and this impression was confirmed later. Yet I left him with a feeling of respect for his honesty and frankness, as well as with pity for the disillusion he had suffered. It is strange that fanatics, because they live tragically, should often be more likeable than reasonable and balanced people.

I have been carried away this evening by the beauty of Cordova. Our hotel is an eighteenth-century house in the middle of the city, built like all old houses in Cordova round a patio. It is quite a modest place—we pay only 40 pesetas a day—and bears the time-honored name of the Hotel de Cuatro Naciones. From the moment when I went upstairs to the corridor and bedroom and smelled the sour smell of washed tile floors that is so characteristic of Andalusian *fondas,* I felt completely at home here. This was the Spain that I knew.

Our window opens onto the fretted stone balustrade of the Romanesque church of San Miguel, built toward 1240, immediately after the Reconquest. Yellow moldering walls, yellow peeling wash, for yellow is the prevailing color of this city. Its harsh, jangling bell, angry and hurried like a bird's alarm chatter and lasting only a few moments, is calling the devout to evening service.

After a coffee in the plaza we went for a stroll in the warm air given off by the houses. The sun was just setting and we let ourselves be carried by the crowd down one of the narrow, winding streets that lead to the river. Soon we came to the mosque with its long blank walls of yellow stone and its lovely Renaissance minaret. Beyond it lay the river. *O gran río, gran rey de Andalucía,* as Góngora addressed it: the river of Tartessos, whose roots, said the Greek poet Stesichorus, lie among silver. Here, below the stone parapet, it rolled slowly by, a brownish yellow current spotted with white bubbles, and beyond it a low sandy shore, scattered with washerwomen and donkeys and girls carrying pitchers; further off still, the white village of the Campo de la Verdad.

February 19

THE Mosque of Cordova is certainly the first building in Spain—the most original and the most beautiful. From the moment of entering the great court planted with orange trees, one gets a feeling of peace and harmony which is quite different from the mood of religious holiness and austerity imparted by Christian cloisters. The small reddish oranges cluster among the dark green leaves, butterflies chase one another, birds flit about and chirp, and the great marble cistern for ablutions seems to be there to say that the warmth and richness of Nature and the instinctive life of Man are also pure because they have been willed by God.

When one enters the mosque itself one is likely to suffer at first from conflicting impressions. The Renaissance choir built in the center disturbs one's view of the forest of columns; some of the restorations, especially the rather garish painting on the ceiling, clash with the warm color of the stone and marble; and then the double horseshoe arches, striped buff-white and brick-rose, arrest one by their strangeness and novelty. One has to visit the building several times to allow its magic to sink into one.

This mosque is surely a first rate example of the adage, so true of all the arts, that necessity is the mother of invention. The Arabs, when in 785 they began to build it, had no style of their own. They wished to make use of the Roman and Visigothic columns that littered the city and, since these were too slight to support the heavy pieces of masonry that would be needed to continue them if the roof was to be raised to a sufficient elevation they were compelled to strengthen the arches by inserting above the abaci a second lower range of arches to act as buttresses. This contrivance—so clumsy structurally but so beautiful in effect—paved the way for the later invention of the wonderful intersecting arches of Al-Hakam's *maqsurah*, which is the crowning glory of the building. A new style, put together from the syllables of a Byzantine idiom, had come into existence.

No two modes of architecture could well be more different from one another than the Moslem and the West Christian. West Christian architecture in its early phase is filled with the craving for weight and massiveness; and in its second phase, the Gothic, for a spectacular liberation from that weight in a skyward ascent. In both cases there is an emphasis on the tremendousness of the force of gravity, either in the form of great masses of stone weighing downward, or of lofty columns springing up like trees in defiance of the downpull. The load of original sin that oppresses the human conscience and seeks to drag the world back into the savagery of the Dark Ages is expressed in a load of stone. The sense of duration, too, the confidence in man's firm establishment on the earth is emphasized: the Universal Church has been built on a rock and will last forever, and, while it lasts, it will interpret history in terms of moral profit and loss, as the Old Testament has taught it to do.

Moslem architecture is quite the opposite. A mosque is to be a court, a square, a market place, lightly built to hold a large concourse of people. Allah is so great that nothing human can vie with Him in strength or endurance, and in a society where the harem system complicates the line of descent, the pride or *orgullo* of the feudal ages—which comes from their association of land tenure with family and from the vista of the long line of descendants—is out of place. (In the feudal ages a man thought of his line as

stretching forward into the future; in the aristocratic ages
he thought of it as stretching back into the past.) Even the
Moslem castles, large though they are, give the effect of being light and insubstantial. But a mosque is also a place
for the contemplation of the Oneness of Allah. How can
this better be done than by giving the eyes a maze of
geometric patterns to brood over? The state aimed at is a
sort of semi-trance. The mind contemplates the patterns,
knows that they can be unraveled and yet does not unravel
them. It rests therefore on what it sees, and the delicate
color, the variations of light and shade add a sensuous
tinge to the pleasure of certainty made visible. This, at all
events, is the only explanation I can give of the strange
state of mind set up by Al-Hakam's *maqsurah* and *mihrab*.

Another building not to be missed in Cordova is the
synagogue. Though erected as late as 1315—that is to say,
after the Christian occupation—its arabesque plaster designs are in the purest Moslem style. Close by lived Maimonides, the great Jewish poet and philosopher, whose
tomb is still shown at Damascus. A square near by has
been renamed after him.

This old Jewish quarter of the city is particularly lovely.
The characteristic feature of Cordova, as everyone who has
been there knows, is the two-storied house built round a
patio. These patios with their pots of ferns and flowers and
their fountain in the center have an irresistible charm and
since the street doors are left open, one gets a glimpse into
them as one passes. The plan of these houses is Roman, but
none are older than the sixteenth century and most of

them were put up after 1700. A large part of the area of the present city was occupied by ruins and gardens until well on in the nineteenth century.

February 20

THIS afternoon we set off to see the famous hermitages in the Sierra. To do this one takes the bus a couple of miles as far as Brillante, a garden city built since the war, and then walks. As we got out of the bus, a man came up and offered to show us the way. He was a pleasant, eager little fellow who was enchanted at the idea of speaking to two English people, because he was a regular listener to the Spanish program of the B.B.C. Very soon his history came out. During the war he had been a sergeant on the Nationalist side; then he had been appointed schoolmaster of a village in the Sierra, but, finding the pay insufficient to support him, he had put in a local man as locum tenens and opened a small business in Cordova. He regretted having had to do this because he liked teaching and had a strong sense of its importance.

We were walking up a broad track between limestone boulders and evergreen oaks. Clumps of asphodels with their glossy leaves and elegant, starry flowers were scattered about and among them, under the trees, sat parties of picnickers, dressed in their gayest Sunday clothes, with bottles and slices of ham and cold sausages spread out on napkins. This was the Quinta de Arrizafa, where the caliphs once had their summer place.

Our friend talked a great deal, holding forth on politics

and religion. His politics were Monarchist, his religion a sort of liberal Catholicism, tinged with mystical adumbrations. He believed in goodness. The steepness of the climb was alleviated by the frequent pauses he made to gesticulate and explain his views. But when I told him of the Falangist doctor I had met in the train, he stopped short in his tracks and dropped his voice. It is remarkable what a fear these Falangist extremists set up in some people, in spite of the fact that they have today lost most of their power. People dry up when they discover that you know them. One only begins to understand it when one remembers the fantastic number of people that they are supposed to have killed in and after the war; here in the province of Cordova rumor credits them with having shot 28,000. However our friend soon brightened up again and, in answer to my inquiries, told me that the picture that the doctor had drawn of the brigands in the Sierra Morena was greatly exaggerated: they had been a nuisance some time before, but were now of very little consequence. And they rarely killed anyone. They were all of them political men—Socialists or Communists on the run.

The schoolmaster turned back after a mile and we went on alone. The road climbed slowly in long hairpin curves, so we took a short cut. This led us past the mouth of a little cave or rock shelter, whose entrance had been blocked with a few household chattels. Behind these we discovered a woman lying on some sacks, who, when she saw us, got up and came out. She was a woman of under thirty, dressed in a very old and ragged black dress which showed her naked body through its rents. She had been ill, she told us, after the birth of a child, which had died because her milk had dried up. Her husband had been employed on an estate near by, but as the work had come to an end and they could not pay their rent, they had left and come here. Now she could not leave because her clothes were not decent. She was obviously starving, but she did not complain, or ask for money and, when I gave her some, appeared surprised. "Times are bad," she said with resignation. "Let us hope they will soon take a better turn."

We arrived at the hermitage that crowns the rocky hill. Grey rocks, grey trees, white jonquils and asphodels, and no sound but the tinkling of goat bells. Far below we could see the white city, spread out like a patch of bird droppings by its brown river, and beyond it the red and green *campiña*, flowing in bright Van Gogh-like undulations. The hermits strike me as being museum pieces rather than examples of a serious contemplative life. There are ten of them, each occupying his own snug little hermitage, each dressed in a long brown robe and decorated with a bushy white beard that flows down over his chest in the true Carolingian manner. On Sundays they are on view and, as we walked down the path to the chapel, we passed one of them, seated on a chair under an ancient oak tree and reading from a calf-bound folio with the aid of a prodigious pair of cows' horn spectacles. It was obvious that he was fully aware of his own picturesqueness.

These hermits own the mountain on which their cells are built and employ a man to look after their goats; otherwise they depend for their subsistence on alms, which are never wanting. I imagine that this is the oldest colony of hermits in Europe, for they have been here continuously since Visigothic times. But the age is hostile to the sentiment *O solitudo, O beatitudo* and when I praised the beauty and seclusion of this spot to the hermit who was showing us over the chapel, he grunted and said, "*Es mucha soledad*. It's very lonely."

The people of Cordova are exceedingly proud of their city. If, for example, one happens to mention wine, they tell one that the wine of Cordova (which is unknown anywhere else) is the best in Spain. "You have only to carry a bottle of Montilla across the river and it improves at once, and when you take it back again, it gets worse." Yet they know very little about the famous men their city has produced: Seneca they have heard of, but Góngora to them is just the name of a street and no one knows where his house stands. I had spoken about this to our schoolmaster acquaintance, who has a certain liking for poetry, and he promised that he would help me find it. We met therefore by arrangement at a café.

Our first step was to visit the Instituto de Segunda Enseñanza or secondary school in search of the city archivist. This school was housed in a magnificent building with a large interior court. All the children in it were well dressed and came from middle-class families, so I asked our companion whether any working-class children found their way here.

"Very rarely," he replied. "These children all come from the primary schools run by the Church. In most of these one has to pay something, but one gets a fine education. The state primary schools are today so neglected that the

children who go to them make no progress. This suits
everyone: the Church sees its schools well sought after and
the ruling classes are pleased to have the poor kept in their
place. Most of the children of the poor grow up without
learning how to read or write."

We found the archivist, who gave us the address of
Góngora's house and promised to show us other sites connected with him when we returned to Cordova in a month's
time. Then we adjourned to a tavern to taste, not Cordovan, but the far better Montilla wine. We discussed bullfights and, after that, religion.

"Yes," said the schoolmaster, "there has been a genuine
revival. But you must bear in mind that the Church in
Spain is like an old, old tree, some of whose branches have
fallen and lie rotting on the ground. Not all the people
you see dressed as Catholics are Catholic inside."

He is a pleasant little man, combining gaiety with genuine kindness and a rather ineffectual enthusiasm for the
things of the mind. A man with middle of the road opinions. How many there are of them in this country, in spite
of the Spaniards' reputation for fanaticism! Yet how little
effect they have had!

February 21

THIS morning we took a taxi to visit Medina al
Zahra. This was the palace which the first and greatest of
the Spanish caliphs, Abd-er-Rahman III, began to build in
936 and which his successors enlarged and completed. The
accounts given of it by the Moslem historians show it as

being possibly the largest and certainly the most luxurious palace ever built in any age. Four thousand marble columns were used in its construction and the quantity of gold, bronze and silver employed in decorating it were fabulous. The whole Mediterranean region as far as Constantinople was ransacked for precious materials.

The most splendid of its apartments was the so-called Chamber of the Caliphs, a vast room entered by thirty-two doors, each decorated with gold and ivory and resting on pillars of transparent crystal. The roof was made of sheets of variously colored marble cut so thin as to let the light through, while the walls were of marble, inlaid with gold and silver. But the most astonishing feature of this apartment was the great basin, or perhaps fountain, which stood in the center. It was filled with mercury instead of water and when set in motion it dazzled the onlooker with the flashes of light and colors which it set up.

Thirteen thousand male servants lived in this palace, not to speak of the harem and their attendants, whose numbers could scarcely be counted. The fish in the garden tanks alone consumed 12,000 loaves every day. The quantities required for the human inhabitants can be left to the imagination. And what became of this superb edifice? In the year 1010 the Berbers, who were besieging Cordova, wrecked and looted it, and so complete was its destruction in the course of the ensuing ages that till a few years ago its very site was unknown, and wild bulls pastured and fought one another where once the most beautiful women in the world had yawned on their solitary beds and stuffed themselves with sweets and pastries.

The excavations lie some four miles to the west of the city, on the lower slopes of the long grey-green line of the Sierra. The situation is beautiful. Ilexes and lotus trees stand around in solemn dignity and under them grow daisies, asphodels and that flower of piercing blue—the dwarf iris. The ruins are scarcely worth seeing, since all the stones have been carried off to build a monastery on the hill above, though there are plenty of fragments of stucco arabesques, mostly of acanthus patterns and showing a strong Byzantine influence. The museum contains some interesting pottery with designs of birds, fishes, and animals in pale green. However only a small area of the palace has yet been excavated; beyond it stretch acres of formless mounds, covered with creeping acanthus leaves and low-growing mandrakes and the dried stalks of fennel. The cormorant and the bittern, the screech owl and the satyr still have the place pretty well to themselves.

As we left, the new civil governor of Cordova drove up in his car. I remarked to the chauffeur that he was said to be an energetic man who would attack abuses. But the chauffeur, an ex-sergeant of the Air Force, was a cynic.

"If that's so," he replied, "he won't be here for long. A few years ago we had one who quadrupled the ration by seizing the stores the syndicates were keeping for their black market operations. This allowed the poor to eat, which on the present scale of rationing they can't do. So they got rid of him."

One cannot walk about the streets of Cordova without being horrified by the poverty. The standard of life has always been very low among the agricultural workers of

this part of Spain, but this is worse, far, far worse than anything known within living memory. One sees men and
women whose faces and bodies are coated with dirt because
they are too weak or too sunk in despair to wash in water.
One sees children of ten with wizened faces, women of
thirty who are already hags, wearing that frown of anxiety
which perpetual hunger and uncertainty about the future
give. I have never seen such sheer misery before; even the
lepers of Marrakesh and Taroudant look less wretched, because, besides being better nourished, they are resigned to
their fate. It presents one too at every step with a personal
problem: what right has one to eat meals, to drink coffee,
to buy pastries when people are starving all round one? No
right at all, and yet, being selfish by nature, I could not
help doing so.

Most dreadful are those who creep about the streets without arms or legs. The government provides a small pension for persons who lost their limbs on their side, but
those who were involved with the Reds, even if they are
women or children, get nothing. They ought to have been
living in some other place when the war broke out! The insurance scheme only caters to those workmen who have
regular employment. Agricultural laborers, small shopkeepers, street vendors, bootblacks get nothing. If they fall
ill, they will not even be taken into a hospital unless they
can pay. A bootblack said to me:

"When the Civil War broke out, I had some money
saved up. Then, after the Nationalist victory, all the cur-
rency in the Red zone was annulled and I lost it. Now I
am getting old. I have no children and if I fall ill there is

nothing left for me but to die of starvation. So I mean to try to get to France, where they treat people more humanely."

The middle-class Cordovans tell one that most of the destitute one sees in the streets are from other provinces. "From all over Andalusia they collect here." But this is their local pride speaking; the truth is that they are unemployed agricultural laborers from the large estates of the *campiña*. The system in use on these large estates is to keep a handful of men on the payroll all the year round and to take on the rest for short spells as the season requires. For every ten that are permanently employed, a hundred will be at the mercy of casual labor. This means that, even in a good year, an agricultural laborer will have to support his family for twelve months on what he earns in six or eight. Before the Civil War it was just possible for him to get along in this way when the season was not too bad, but now, owing to the inflation, the value of wages has fallen considerably. To make matters worse, this has been an exceptionally bad year. The olive crop last Christmas was very poor—and it is on the money made by olive picking that a family dresses itself—while the drought has held up the spring hoeing. The consequence is a famine—a famine too which cannot be mentioned in the press and which the possessing classes shut their eyes to.

A bad mark for the Franco regime? Yes, certainly—but let us in fairness remember that every other regime, including the Republican, refused to grapple with this problem. What is needed is a complete reorganization of the system of cultivating the land, coupled with a severe pressure applied to the landowners. And this is something that the present government, weak and discredited as it is and fearful of making more enemies, cannot do.

I had wished to visit the dungeons of the Inquisition, which are still apparently to be seen in the medieval Alcázar, adjoining the Arab one. This, however, was not possible because the buildings have been converted to military use. Nor were my inquiries very well received. Spaniards are still chary of speaking of this once revered institution and, when a foreigner puts some question about it, profess ignorance.

Its proceedings at Cordova were particularly revolting, or perhaps it would be better to say that we are particularly well informed about them. Take for example the case of Lucero. In 1499 a canon of Cadiz Cathedral called Rodríguez Lucero was appointed Inquisitor of the Tribunal of Cordova, and at once set to work to arrest and burn all persons of Jewish descent against whom allegations of doubtful faith could, rightly or wrongly, be made. When evidence was lacking, he employed professional perjurers. No objections were raised to this by the people at large, for such acts were in the ordinary line of inquisitorial business and the *conversos* were unpopular. But finding that the thoroughness of his operations was exhausting this field, he began to extend them to persons of Old Christian descent, obtaining the evidence he needed by torturing their dependents. The object was money: the property of persons convicted of heresy was confiscated and paid into the Crown, who returned part of it to the Holy Office. Besides this there were the sums obtained by selling dispensations and imposing fines (termed penances), which went straight into the coffers of the Inquisitors, not to speak of what could be got by squeeze and blackmail. Few criminals have ever had greater opportunities.

Of course in arresting persons of impeccable orthodoxy and Christian descent there were certain risks, because the Inquisition had only recently been established and the country was not entirely cowed by it. However *poderoso caballero es Don Dinero*—money speaks—so that by buying one of King Ferdinand's secretaries and, when the need arose, other important dignitaries, not excluding a cardinal, Lucero made sure of his position, and soon the reign of terror he set up was such that no one in the south of Spain was safe. Eminent ecclesiastics were especially attacked, because during their incarceration the income from their benefices was paid into the Inquisition funds, and a moment came when even the saintly Archbishop of Granada, who had been Queen Isabella's confessor and was now eighty years old, was on the point of being arrested.

There is no knowing how far this diabolical man might have gone had not an accident intervened. In 1506 Philip the Fair landed in Castile and, anxious to exert some act of sovereignty, listened to the appeals of the clergy and municipality of Cordova, which both Ferdinand and the Inquisitor General, who had a pecuniary interest in Lucero's extortions, had refused to hear, and suspended him. In the trial that followed two years later his guilt was fully established, in spite of the fact that he had had time to burn most of the hostile witnesses, and he was therefore dismissed to his canonry at Seville (for an inquisitor could not be punished) where he spent the rest of his days in comfort on the proceeds of the money he had accumulated. This is the only case recorded of an inquisitor being either dismissed or brought to trial.

I have mentioned this episode, which is related at length in Lea's abundantly documented *History*, because it has become the fashion of late to whitewash the Inquisition. Both its principles and its methods, it is asserted, were in accordance with the spirit of the age; it was slow in making charges, scrupulously fair in its prosecutions, just in its sentences, and so forth. But whatever may be said of its procedure in other countries, this was not the way in which it operated in Spain. In the lush and fertile soil of the Peninsula, this institution not only reached the extremes of fanaticism and cruelty (we read, for example, of children of ten being prosecuted and imprisoned for life), but those of the most sordid corruption as well. And what is one to say of those scenes in underground chambers where elderly priests looked on while naked women and girls were tortured? Of all the rackets recorded in history, the Spanish Inquisition, during the first hundred years of its career, was perhaps the most mean and repulsive.

This evening we walked to the hermitage church of Nuestra Señora de Fuensanta, on the eastern edge of the town. On the way we passed a convent where two nuns, dressed in white starched caps, were distributing bowls of soup to the poor. A queue of some three hundred people stretched down the road outside. These nuns belong to an order which is confined to the city of Cordova, and those

who have the state of the poor on their conscience con-
tribute to their fund.

The church we were looking for stands in a large open
space on the edge of the fields. An avenue of plane trees led
down to it and the sunlight flooded their grey trunks and
lace-like branches, dotted with little red buds that would
soon be bursting into leaf. A cantankerous looking fig tree,
growing among heaps of rubbish, filled the air around it
with its dense, sticky smell, as if to show that it too was
feeling the effects of spring and poetry. Entering the courtyard, we came to a long portico hung with ex-votos. Some
of these consisted of crutches or tresses of hair, others of
little figures cut out in tin and representing limbs, others
again of crude paintings or miracles performed by the
Virgin, which often had the charm and freshness of children's drawings. There was also a narwhal's tusk and a
stuffed crocodile, formerly esteemed for their aphrodisiac
properties, though why hung here I cannot say. Possibly
the crocodile, which recalls that to be seen in the porch of
Seville Cathedral, was at one time regarded as a maiden-
eating dragon which some chivalrous saint of the type of
St. George had slain.

Passing through into the church, we found its interior
cool and dark. The whole of one end was taken up by a vast
gilt *retablo,* carved and scrolled and ornamented, in the
center of which—an insignificant doll-like figure—stood
the miracle-working Virgin. We made our genuflections
and whispered our desires, then walked back by the warm
evening light along the river.

HILL TOWNS *of* ANDALUSIA

This morning we took the train to Aguilar de la Frontera, a small town that lies some thirty miles to the south of Cordova on the edge of the *campiña*. This bare rolling country is beautiful. Its whitish soil blushing to red and rose seems well cultivated and the wheat is strong and green in spite of the lack of rainfall. I especially liked the small river we crossed, with its yellow water running lazily in a sandy bed, overhung by red-branched tamarisks and tufts of pampas grass. Herds of bulls grazed along it or stood pensively under a line of white-barked poplars. As we rattled past, the eye was caught by small stabs of intense blue—the dwarf iris.

Aguilar is a town of some fifteen thousand inhabitants standing on a low spur that juts out over the *campiña*. Its houses are white with brown-tiled roofs, looking like seagulls with russet-colored wings, and all around them is air and sunlight. At the end of the spur, on a slight rocky elevation, stand the remains of its once famous castle, the Castillo de Polai. Little is left of it, but from its emplacement one gets a wide view, north, south and west, over the empty country. This castle provides the explanation of why Aguilar is a name in history. After the reconquest of Cordova in 1236, it became one of the principal fortresses protecting the lands of the Christians from the raids of the Moorish cavalry. For this reason it figures in various ballads, while its counts were second only to the Counts of Cabra in the ranks of the Andalusian nobility.

At the inn where we went for lunch—it had the strange name of the Fonda de las Moscas or Fly Inn—a sad-faced elderly woman was sitting over a round table which had under it a brazier of *orujo* or olive pressings. She did not rise when we entered, but motioned to us to sit down beside her.

"The air is cold," she said. "Warm yourselves."

We asked her how things were.

"Bad, "she said. "Very bad. No trade, no work, no bread. We are just rotting away. We have nothing to do but wait for the gravediggers to come and bury us."

"How's that?" I asked.

"Why, there's no work. Everyone is starving. The rations we get aren't enough to keep a dog alive and who but the rich can afford to buy on the black market? Even when there *is* work, look at the wages they give—12 pesetas! How can a man keep his family alive on that? I tell you, the people in this town are dying."

She crouched over the brazier in the little darkened room, while the maid, a lusty girl of fifteen, stuffed so tightly into her dress that it had to be held together with safety pins, stood wiping her nose on the back of her hand and staring at us.

"And who cares?" she went on in her angry voice. "Not the rich, who live in their palaces and marble courts. Who ever saw one of them give a piece of bread to a hungry man? Yet all their money comes out of the pockets of the working man, doesn't it?"

To change the subject, I asked her what had happened here when the Movement began.

"The Reds held part of the town for a day, then the Nationalists won it. That's what happened. The Reds shot one man, so the others had to shoot a hundred. Now we're paying for it. The olive crops fail, the rot gets the potatoes, the heavens won't give rain. You see, up above there's justice."

"Were you a Socialist," I asked, "or a Syndicalist?"

"I? What makes you think I was one of them? I am a Falangist like my husband. We were the first to join the Falange here."

And it seemed that her husband was indeed a Falangist and what is more, one of the leading ones in the town. But her brother, a Socialist, had been shot.

We had lunch, not a bad meal, and went to the café. *Radio Sevilla* blaring out its jazzed *flamenco*, colored posters showing bullfighters and women with roses in their hair, a noisy group of cardplayers, old and young men staring into vacancy. All the boring life of the small town, where nothing ever happens but deaths and marriages and good and bad olive years. No wonder politics is such a passion in this country; they take to it as they take to gaming, all the more furiously when, as the Civil War has shown, the stakes are high.

We were sipping our coffee when the driver of the town bus came in and sat down beside us. He was a small man with a hard, round head and a pair of oversized steel-rimmed glasses that covered his sharp little eyes like pieces of scaffolding. A scruff of grey hair grew untidily down his neck and his hands were brown with motor oil.

"Yes, things are in a bad way here," he said. "It hasn't rained, so there's no hoeing to be done. Two weeks ago the municipality was providing work on the roads, but now its funds have run out. I don't know what will happen."

He took us out to show us the town. We passed a convent where the nuns were educating the children of the *fusilados*, that is, of the Reds who had been shot. There were seventy of them and they each got a bowl of soup at midday. Then we saw a fine new house that had just been put up. On asking what it was, we were told that a rich widow had built it and endowed it for twelve poor married couples. She had also built a home for old people at the other end of the town. So there were after all some landowners who had a social conscience! Had we not passed this house and inquired what it was, we should not have been told of it. I got the impression that little gratitude was felt for this act of benevolence and even that there existed a certain resentment against rich people who belied the general reputation of their kind for being screws and misers. For is not generosity too a luxury?

We returned through the poorer quarter of the town. Its streets were clean and pleasant, but one had only to glance at the rags worn by the women to realize their poverty. Except in the smallest villages, Spaniards have always preferred to tighten their belts rather than to dress badly. These people could neither eat nor dress themselves.

"This is a wretched place," said the bus driver. "Nothing but poverty and hunger. Why, it's *más feo que Dios*, uglier

than God. You ought to go to Cabra. Ah, that's a town!
Fine streets, fine houses and lovely women! See Cabra and
you'll say it's like a silver cup set among olive trees. Beautiful all over! I come from Cabra and I curse the day I ever
left it."

We explained that we intended to go there, but that we
would visit Priego first.

"Ah, that's a fine place too. You'll see the Fuente del
Rey. In the whole of France and Europe there's nothing to
equal that. But still, taken all round, Priego doesn't compare with Cabra."

The bus for Priego left toward sunset. We took our
seats in it. In a Giovanni Bellini sky, with the red light
coloring the white town and throwing long glimmers upon
the drooping, feminine olive trees, we drove into the growing darkness.

Priego is a town of the sierra, built high up in a circuit
of rocky peaks and overlooking a valley. We awoke therefore with the sound of running water in our ears and a
good appetite. After a breakfast of hot *churros,* or *tejer-
ingos* as they are called here—those excellent flour fritters
fried in olive oil—we went up the street to see the famous
fountain, the Fuente del Rey, which is the pride of the
place. Soon we came to it—a long marble trough of green
water into which little streams poured through a hundred
and thirty stone *bocas* or spouts. A sculptured Neptune (he
was the *Rey*) rode his car through it under the shade—except in summer—of nine immense planes that lifted up
their network of branches into the light. At the bottom of

the water a few brown leaves lay spread out, like botanical specimens in a green album.

Some dozen steps above this basin was the head fountain or spring where the water welled up from the depths of the rock. Looking down into it, one saw the long, green water-weeds that grew out of it, waving with an undulating movement that suggested a naiad's hair. And there above in a rusticated niche sat the naiad herself, the Virgin of the Spring, the rock wall about her plastered with gilt trinkets, locks of hair and framed photographs, the gifts of the people who had been cured by her therapeutic powers. She seemed far from primitive, this Virgin. She had in fact a smug and hypocritical look, as though she remembered her Iberian origins as a water sprite and was endeavoring to conceal them under a mask of respectability. At all events the people of Priego had lost none of their devotion to her. As we stood there, women came up and crossed themselves in the Andalusian manner, which ends with a resounding kiss on the thumb, and muttered a few *Ave Marias*, while no men passed near the place without raising their hats. On asking her name, I received the answer: "She is the *Virgen de la Salud*" (an ambiguous word signifying both health and salvation) "*y es muy milagrosa.*"

We sat down on the marble edge of the cistern, while the water made a pleasant sound in the ears and the small birds twittered. In the milky light of early morning—for the sun had not yet dissolved the mists—the white trunks and branches of the plane trees looked as holy and virgin-born as the spring. There was a crisp smell of burning *orujo* or olive pulp, and behind us, only a few hundred yards away pressed between two cliffs of white houses, a pale lavender mountain rose abruptly, as in a Japanese color print, into the sky.

After a little we set out up the hill toward a chapel and calvary that dominate the town. The rocky hillside was littered with rusted iron crosses and with a various assemblage of small flowers, among which we picked out marigolds, daisies, blue irises and red anemones. Below lay a jumble of box-like houses and beyond them, the deep, terraced valley and hills planted with olive trees. All around, a circuit of jagged, sunlit mountains. I observed, standing up from the valley, a number of small factory chimneys. The sacristan, who had come out of his house to talk to us, said that there were over thirty small cloth factories in the district as well as a hat factory. A new quarter had been built since the war and the town was growing. These factories, with the plots of irrigated land and the lack of large estates, gave the place considerable prosperity.

We descended to the streets again. One of the sights of Priego is the *adarve*, a walk some five hundred yards long along the edge of a precipice that skirts the town. Below, irrigated terraces and slopes falling to the river. What a wonderful situation this for a primitive city, with its abundance of water and its natural fortifications! Priego must have existed before Athens or Syracuse, and its Virgin be older than the nymph Arethusa. But where are the myths about her, the poetry and the scandal of primitive legends? Probably there were none. The Iberians lacked the myth-making imagination and their gods were as dim and featureless as the Roman ones. The Spaniards have inherited this blankness of mind, for their saints and Virgins are the dullest in Europe—numb, larval creatures who have never put out wings—and the only theological doctrine they have taken up and made their own has been that of the Immaculate Conception. Religion in Spain, except during the brief period of the Carmelite mystics, has been an affair of ritual and observance, heavy with taboos and seeking neither intellectual nor imaginative expression.

Sealing the end of the *adarve* is the castle, a handsome square edifice with a large inner court in which three very serious little boys were spinning esparto rope on a primitive ropewalk. From here we went to look at the parish church. It is a medieval building, completely transformed inside during the seventeenth century. Like most of these Spanish baroque churches, the first effect it produces is one of astonishment at its richness and luxury. Compelling ourselves to consider it in detail, we admired its plaster-faced columns and capitals, with a design based on a familiar Moorish motif of flat plaques. The Moorish and the baroque style fused in Spain very successfully. There was also a fine plaster ceiling with complex decorations, a richly carved *retablo,* handsome choir stalls and an elegant rococo chapel.

Everywhere the eye rested, it found movement and color. In the pains they took to remodel the inner surfaces of the churches they decorated, to the point of concealing the Gothic columns under plaster casings, the baroque architects spared themselves no expense to achieve unity of design.

Another church that is worth a visit is San Francisco. Later in date than the parish church, it strikes the note of elegance. Its white plaster walls and ceiling with their floral decorations suggest the aristocratic *salon,* and make an effective contrast to the heavy barbaric gold of the side chapels with their twisting *retablos* and *rejas,* and the absurd but charming bric-à-brac on the altars. One cannot think of anything that St. Francis would have liked less.

Baroque art, as Werner Weisbach has said in his admirable book on it, is the art of propaganda. The Church was no longer universal and had lost much of its previous self-confidence. It therefore felt the need to excite, impress, dazzle, and overwhelm the people. Its master art was architecture, but in its church interiors, which are where one must seek its principal triumphs, it summoned all the visual arts to collaborate in producing grandiose theatrical effects of luxury, mystery, and drama. Just as at this time music, poetic drama, and scenery were combining in the new art form of opera, so painting, architecture, and sculpture were being taught to come together and lend something to one another.

The talents required of a baroque architect were therefore great powers of fanciful invention in several media combined with a firm grasp which should hold together all the various flowing, twisting, colored, discordant parts. He had to be a sort of impresario in wood and stone and to have a strong sense for stage effect. The Spaniards showed a remarkable aptitude for this. It fitted in with their tradition of Arab and Mudejar craftsmanship in devising complicated linear patterns and with their fondness for organiz-

ing elaborate religious ceremonies and processions. Still
more it suited their native craving—African, one might
call it—for extracting every drop of emotion out of a situation, for carrying every feeling and especially every painful feeling to the point of orgasm. Hence those brainless,
ecstatic faces of Zurbarán's monks, so different to the intellectual gravity of El Greco's; hence the delight in suffering
depicted in the wood sculptures of Montañés and Pedro de
Mena. And hence too the concentration of the architects
and church decorators on creating in the mind of the worshipper a mood of awe and mystery, in which he will lose
his sense of his own personality and be unable to think
critically or with detachment on any subject. Let me, to
make this plainer, quote from Roger Fry's *A Sampler of
Castile*, which, brief though it is, is by far the most mas-
terly essay ever written on Spanish art:

> The architecture, the sculpture and painting in a
> Spanish church are all accessory to the purely dramatic
> art—the religious dance, if you like—of the Mass. By
> the very superfluity and confusion of so much gold and
> glitter, guessed at through the dim atmosphere, the
> mind is exalted and spellbound. The spectator is not
> invited to look and understand, he is asked to be pas-
> sive and receptive: he is reduced to a hypnoidal condi-
> tion. How different from this is the early Gothic of
> France or the Renaissance of Italy! In those all is
> luminous, clear-cut, objective. The mind is drawn out
> of itself to the active contemplation of forms and
> colors. Those arts are precisely *expressive* of aesthetic

ideas—the Spanish is *impressive* by reason of its want of clearness. Its effect is cumulative: it allows of one art mixing with another and all together producing a state which is quite other than that of aesthetic comprehension.

It is for this reason, I think, that Spanish baroque has a power of stirring the emotions and putting the mind into a state of confused exaltation and astonishment that is not given by the more intellectual and classically rooted baroque of Italy. Since these qualities are precisely what baroque art was aiming at, it seems only reasonable to call it more perfect. But whether such an art can be regarded as a great one is another matter.

I had formed the impression that the standard of living in Priego was distinctly higher than in the other towns of the province that we had visited. In its poorer quarters one saw only the old familiar poverty of Southern Spain, not that new excruciating sort which we had come across in Cordova and Aguilar. However a shopkeeper with whom we got into conversation would not hear of this. Inviting us into his garden, he poured out his heart to us on the state of the country.

"English people," he declared, "are coming out here and saying that everything is magnificent. I met one in Granada who, on being shown one of the gypsy caves, said it was as good as an English palace. It's so easy to lead foreigners by the nose. But you speak Spanish. Go and see things for yourself and then you'll be able to tell your countrymen that life here is impossible and that the working classes are dying of hunger. You've only to look at the wages they get and the amount of the ration to see that this is true. Even when they have work for every day in the year—and how many of them have that?—they cannot feed their families."

This of course is true. The ration consists of a small roll of bread a day, a quarter of a liter of olive oil, and three ounces of sugar a week, with minute quantities of chick peas and rice, very irregularly distributed. Even these rations are not always honored. And on the black market bread is 12 pesetas the kilo—just about the average daily wage. When one remembers that the staple food of an agricultural laborer consists of bread and olive oil, with a little salad and vinegar and some cheap sort of fish, one will understand what straits he is put to.

In the evening we took a car to Cabra, retracing the road we had traveled in the darkness from Aguilar. For a time we kept up a little valley, terraced for irrigation and planted with walnuts and olive trees. Women washing clothes and spreading them on bushes to dry, small boys herding black goats, a watermill with its horizontal wheel, sulphur butterflies. Then we climbed up past a grove of ancient ilexes to the summit of a pass and saw on our right the white limestone cone of the Sierra de Cabra with the hermitage of its Virgin, *La Serrana* or Hill Maiden, gleaming on the summit. The Balcony of Andalusia, this mountain is called, because west of it there are only low hills and plains. From here we dropped down and presently saw Cabra lying white and clean—"like a silver cup," as the bus driver of Aguilar had said—among its grey olive groves.

Cabra—the Igabrum of the Romans—is a place of various associations. In 192 B.C., as Livy relates, Caius Flaminius captured it with its king Corribilius. It was then a walled city, rich in vines. After this we do not hear much of it till 1080, when the Cid took it from García Ordoñez, a Castilian *ricohombre* or nobleman who was holding it for the Moorish king of Granada. He not only imprisoned García Ordoñez but insulted him in the genial manner of the times by pulling his beard. This episode formed the opening passage (now lost) of the *Poema del Cid,* and out of it devolves the long tale of rivalry and ambition which that great *cantar de gesta* relates.

Another literary association is provided by the fact that Cabra was the home town of Mocádem, a blind Arabic-speaking poet or jongleur who flourished about the year 900. The peculiar interest of Mocádem lies in his having been the first person to compose verses in a measure which he borrowed from the local romance (i.e. Spanish) folk song and which is known as the *muwassaha* or *zéjel.* These verses, which were imitated by a succession of later poets, achieved an extraordinary popularity throughout the Arabic-speaking world, from Seville as far as Samarkand, producing on the audience (for they were sung, not recited, and with an admixture of Spanish words) the sort of effect that Negro spirituals do on us. But the *zéjel* has a history in Spanish literature too. Under the name *villancico* it became the popular dance song of the Middle Ages, and when taken up by court poets at the close of that period, gave rise to some of the most lovely and delicate poetry in the song-books. Its descendants live on today, both in the popular *copla,* which is an abbreviated form of it, and in the revivals of contemporary poets.

We had not, however, gone to Cabra in the hope of catching some lingering aura either of Mocádem or of the Cid, but because it was the birthplace of Juan Valera and the scene of most of his novels. One cannot understand a novelist fully till one has visited his country, and Valera is, one might say, the Spanish Jane Austen. With this in mind we called on Don Juan Soza, who is the secretary of the Club of the Friends of Valera and also the town librarian. We found him in the excellent library and reading room put up during the Republic and he was kind enough to answer my questions about Valera and to give me a book about him which is now out of print. He showed us too the house that had once belonged to Pepita Jiménez, the most famous of Valera's heroines; it disappointed me by being entirely different from what I had expected.

Cabra is a pleasant, clean little town set in a pleasant, neat little countryside of hills, vineyards, and olive groves. If only a few cypresses had been planted, we should have fancied ourselves in Umbria. There is some irrigation, the waters issuing from another sacred spring, also presided over by its naiad, a rather dejected damsel who suffers from the competition of the more famous oread on the mountain top; the land is fairly well divided and there seems to be little extreme poverty. It is a town too with a quiet Liberal tradition. The parish priest, Don Antonio Peña, who courteously showed us the sights, was an excellent person who in his spare time collected fossils—"dating from the flood of Noah," as he said to me with a sly expres-

sion—as well as Iberian coins and pottery. There was a
marquesa who read memoirs and a town clerk who had a
taste for history. Even the Falange seems to have been un-
dermined by the Liberal spirit, for when the movement
broke out, it shot only fifty people.

Looking down on the square is the castle of the Condes
de Cabra, a rambling edifice with a large square tower,
built in Moorish times. The late Conde put it up for
auction some thirty years ago to pay his gambling debts,
but it fetched only 20,000 pesetas. The purchasers were the
Escolapian nuns, who turned it into a school. Next to it is
the parish church, which was once a cathedral and before
that a mosque; in its present form it dates from about 1630.
The interior is very impressive. Colonnades of stilted
arches, sustained on yellow marble columns, divide the
building into four equal naves in the manner of a Moslem
mosque, while the roofs are barrel-vaulted and decorated
with plaster moldings of a Moorish baroque design. The
general effect is both original and beautiful and bears out
my previous experience that one never knows what one
will find when one enters an Andalusian church. There is
also a polychrome statue by Pedro de Mena and another
by the same sculptor in the church of the Augustinian
nuns. As one re-enters the town one crosses the square, an
empty irregular area made alive by a few street vendors'
stalls; here the blind Mocádem must have sat cross-legged
to sing his *muwassahas,* while two musicians accompanied
him on the lute and *rabel* and a dancing girl did her stuff.
One can more easily picture such a scene than one can the
visit of the Cid, buttoned up to the neck in his chain

hauberk, with his long sword Tizón hanging by his side, his dragon shield and his blinkered and caparisoned barb (height 14 hands) ambling under him.

Our next stage was to Lucena, a town of some twenty-five thousand inhabitants, lying four miles away in a plain planted with olive trees. To reach it one leaves the sierra with its running waters and descends to the *campiña*. Lucena is known for its Jewish associations. During the Moslem period it was populated entirely by Jews, till the fanatical Berber dynasty of the Almohades drove them out. They then settled in Christian territory, where their learning and industry made them welcome. But in the end their wealth excited envy and in 1391 the inevitable pogroms began.

Lucena is much larger than either Cabra or Priego and much poorer. From the moment of entering it we were struck by its look of rot and decay and by the miserable, starved appearance of its inhabitants. The hotel was a run-down sort of place, kept by a slovenly Jewish looking man with a week's growth of beard on his face, who spent his time poring over forms and accounts and waving his hands ineffectually whenever the women of the house interrupted him: the type of Jew who lacks the talent of his race and so is always struggling, always lost, always late. Going out, we found the streets filled with gaunt, dejected men, standing silent against the walls and staring in front of them. In the market were crowds of women with set, lined faces, bargaining for shreds of fish or vegetables that were sold cheap because they were beginning to turn; wherever we went, we were followed by swarms of begging children, who pestered us with their whining voices, tugged at our coat sleeves, and could not be got rid of.

Why such abysmal poverty? Lucena, it seems, is a town of agricultural laborers, dependent on the vicissitudes of the weather and the olive crop; the estates are large, there is no irrigation and few industries. Almost everyone therefore was unemployed and the municipality, faced with a problem that exceeded its small resources, had thrown its hands up. Neither the convents nor the Falange were providing assistance.

Finding this atmosphere unendurable, we decided to make an expedition into the country. The obvious place to choose was the shrine of Nuestra Señora de Araceli, which stands on a hilltop some way beyond the town. Toward three o'clock we set off.

For a couple of miles we climbed slowly through terraced olive groves. Then we came out on a spur and saw the white sanctuary standing some eight hundred feet above us on the summit of a conical hill. The road wound round it in a spiral and as we trudged up it a wide view unrolled, from the cruel, jagged Sierra de Rute close at hand to the more distant coastal range and the far-off, snow-covered Serranía de Ronda. Immediately below us, a bowl of grey-green olive groves, gently undulating and studded with small white cottages—the *cortijos de labor*.

The sun was hot and we lay down under a solitary stone pine to rest. The wind murmured faintly in its branches and the short, grey herbs gave off an aromatic smell. Before us the great expanse of air. Then we cut up through the stiff asphodels and reached the summit and its sanctuary.

On ringing the bell, a woman with a baby in her arms appeared and let us in.

The chapel is seventeenth-century baroque and very charming. Baroque too the miraculous Virgin and her blue and silver dress and long train. On her head she wears the gold crown with which she was presented last October—four bishops took part in the ceremony—while the Child Jesus on her lap sports a little straw hat and waves a toy sword in his hand. The inner chapel or shrine in which she sits in state glows with gilt scrolls and volutes and complex floral decorations, while the outer body of the building, conceived in a more rococo style, is in blue, white, and rose, with many cornucopias and mirrors and a multitude of little cherubs' heads peeping out from behind capital and cornice. Surely a prettier dolls' house was never seen!

The Virgin of Araceli lives on her hilltop for nine months of the year. Then in May she is carried down to the town for her festival and remains there till the harvest is in. These journeys are the great moments in her otherwise solitary and uneventful life. Crowds of devout admirers climb the hill to accompany her and the whole town turns out to fire off rockets and shotguns when she enters the streets. Then, after an equally vociferous return journey, the silence gathers round her and she must spend the long winter months in voluntary seclusion and self-absorption to gather sufficient strength and *baraka* (as the Moors call it) for her great work of influencing the next year's harvest. How important this retreat is for her psychic processes is shown by the fact that the excitement of her recent coronation destroyed her potency and led to the worst olive crop and drought that had been known for decades.

These Virgins of the hilltops are as much a feature of Andalusia as are the Virgins of the springs. (In Estremadura the Virgins are dryads and live in the oak trees.) Traditionally they go back to the discovery of a sacred image or the appearance of the Virgin to a shepherd at some date following closely on the Reconquest. But almost certainly their cult is more ancient. The situations of their shrines closely recall those of the Iberian sanctuaries with their abundant ex-votos, which have recently been discovered in the hills and caves of the Sierra Morena and near Baza. Some day perhaps excavations will be made on the sites of these hermitages to determine their origin.

The woman who looked after the chapel—*santera* is the proper term—chatted away cheerfully as she showed us round. She told us that she got 3 pesetas a day for scrubbing and cleaning and that her husband, a cobbler, earned 15 pesetas when he had work. They also got their house rent free and had the use of a donkey to fetch food and water. But how could one bring up four children on that? They only managed to do so by neglecting their clothes, and here she lowered her eyes to her thin black dress, which certainly seemed to be on its last legs. Few women of the working classes, she said, could attend Mass because they could not carry out the prescriptions of the Church about covering the body.

On her invitation we went into the kitchen, which opened off the chapel, to see her family. Her husband was sewing a pair of long shooting boots by the light of the

window; the little boy—he was barely four—was playing
with the baby. Spanish boys seem very devoted to their
smaller brothers and sisters: one never meets with the false
shame one finds in England. We sat down to smoke a cigarette and to talk—of England, of Spain, of children, of the
winds that howled round the hilltop in winter—while outside the donkey stood patiently in the courtyard and, across
a great space of air, a jagged crest of mountain, like a
gigantic ebullition of coral, glowed lavender and rose in
the sunlight.

On the way back we stopped at a *cortijo* or farm to ask
for a glass of water. While a woman brought it, her husband, a jovial *labrador,* who gave the impression of having
walked straight out of one of the Quinteros' plays, began a
conversation.

"You are foreigners?" he asked.

"Yes, we are English."

"Well, I'm pleased to meet you. I have never met one of
your nation before. They tell me that the English are a
people who travel all over the world to laugh at other
countries. That's fine. I thoroughly approve of it. I hope
you are having a good laugh at us."

I told him I found very little to laugh at.

"Well, I do," he answered. "I do. I find things to laugh at
all day long."

"Is that sanctuary very old?" I asked, as I handed back
the glass.

"Old? Why, I should say so. Very old indeed. Immensely
so. Why, I am forty and when I first remember anything, it
was standing there."

In the *fonda* at Lucena dinner was not served till half past ten. The smaller and more wretched the place, the later and more fashionable the hour. We wandered about the town, depressed by the awful poverty and misery. The women in particular horrified us. In all the side streets one could see them, dressed in rags that had never been women's clothes—potato sacks, scraps of Army blanket, moldering remains of soldiers' greatcoats—with their legs and faces caked in dirt which they no longer troubled to wash off. The babies they carried were pinched and emaciated and even the young marriageable girls were in no better way, but walked the streets in the same strips of cloth fastened together with safety pins which the married women wore. Were these Spaniards? we asked. Were these members of that proud and modest race for whom twelve years ago even a stockingless leg was regarded as an iniquity? No, they were a pariah class, though the family of ordinary day laborers, a class who, I was told, never entered a church or married or baptized their children because they could not either pay the priest's fees or cover their bodies sufficiently. Yet in the town there was a monastery of Franciscans!

This Belsen atmosphere depressed us so much that next morning we took the train for Málaga.

MÁLAGA

THE little engine, giving off prodigious puffs of smoke as though the three carriages it was pulling were really thirty, clanked slowly along between the olive groves. Great vistas of plain and pastureland opened out, falling gently to a wall of rugged mountains. Gnarled ilex trees, shallow meres, moldering castles, herds of cattle and horses, flocks of large winged birds moved across the windows. Then the train entered a gorge. Walls of rock on either side, palmetto scrub and oleander, tunnels and more tunnels, and we emerged, still descending rapidly and with long frightened whistles, into the broad valley which is known as the Hoya of Málaga. Now we could see the frontal aspect of the coastal range. The northern scarp had been all calcareous rock and crag, sharp and precipitous. These southern foothills were of rose-colored shale, their contours rounded and eroded and gathered up in folds like heaps of crumpled cloth. Only their height— some four thousand feet—surprised me. Pricked out on their surface was a design of little spidery markings, the almond trees, and a faint green haze suffused them, for these almond trees had dropped their flowers and were coming into leaf.

Málaga! We had left it in the autumn of 1936, a couple of months after the outbreak of the Civil War. We had seen its fine villa quarter go up in smoke, its streets seeth-

ing with armed mobs, corpses curled up like wax dolls by
the roadside, red-flagged lorries filled with excited militia-
men. All the stir and frenzy of a proletarian revolution. I
had—with some mental reserves—sympathized with the
Republican cause and had written a book of a social-his-
torical sort on the events that led up to the military rising.
Later, during the European War, I had broadcast to Spain
in a somewhat belligerent fashion. Now I was going to find
out what sort of reception awaited me. And above all I was
going to discover what had become of the house, garden,
books, possessions—all the personal accumulations of a
lifetime—which we had abandoned in such a hurry.

We took a room in a hotel looking onto the main street,
then went out to see the town. Yes, it had altered. The
buildings that had been burned had been rebuilt, but
many shops that I remembered were no longer there.
There were fewer cafés than before, fewer barber shops
and more banks. Also there was a change of tone that I
could not define exactly. As we sat in a café, I noticed that
the customers no longer clapped their hands to call the attention of the waiter. I asked one of them about this. "That
is one of the bad customs of the old times," he replied. "Today only people without *ilustración* venture to clap." This
suggested something that has since been fully confirmed.
The social change that has swept over Europe since the war
has had repercussions here too, though only among the
white collar workers. Like everyone else except the landlords and the black marketeers, they are worse off eco-
nomically, but in compensation have acquired an increase
of dignity. And women have more liberty.

Common sense suggested that we should hurry off next morning to our house at Churriana, a few miles outside the city, since this was the dream we had been nursing for so many years. But, when it came to the point, a certain fear held us back. Supposing we should find everything there in ruinous condition, the books mold-eaten, the flower garden uprooted, and the furniture splintered and soiled by rampaging tenants? We decided to postpone our visit for a day or two and to spend this time in paying a few visits. Then in the afternoon we went out to explore the city.

Walking rather aimlessly through the narrow, crowded streets, we came to the Plaza de Riego. It is a handsome square, named after the Liberal hero who overturned the autocratic government of Ferdinand VII in 1823, and in the center of it there stands an obelisk put up to the memory of General Torrijos, another Liberal who led an unsuccessful rising against Ferdinand in 1831. He had been lured from Gibraltar by a particularly base act of treachery on the part of Moreno, the Governor of Málaga, and shot with forty-nine of his companions on the sea shore. One of the victims was an Englishman, Robert Boyd, and it was only an accident that the poet Tennyson was not another. He had intended to join the expedition with his friends Hallam and Trench, but at the last moment the British government prevented their sailing. To our surprise we found that, although the name of the square has been changed, the monument has not been pulled down and in the Town Hall there still hangs the famous picture of the shooting of the Liberal martyrs. It is sad to reflect that if deaths by the firing squad were still to be commemorated in this way, not all the public buildings in the country would provide enough wall space.

From the Plaza de Riego we went to the Cathedral. It is a huge, monumental structure—one of the first churches to be put up in Spain in the Renaissance style—and though it does not give the sense of unity and inevitability required of great architecture, it is undoubtedly impressive. It made me feel once more how much I prefer the rounded arch to the ogival. Here, as in only the very largest Catholic cathedrals—St. Peter's or Seville—one gets the feeling of being in a sort of factory or market in which the whole life and business of a religion is carried on. Thus, while at the principal altar we saw High Mass being celebrated and a sermon preached, at one of the side chapels a Low Mass attended by some hundreds of people was being conducted in an undertone, and nearly all the other chapels had their knots of kneeling figures and the confessionals their queues of visitants. In the great aisles circulated a slowly moving stream of men and women who were so small in comparison to the height of columns and the width of the vaulting that they looked like mice, while all round flowed the space and air in their different gradations of light and color. When this building was erected, Málaga had a tiny population, nearly all of them very poor: no wonder that it took a hundred years to build and that one of its twin towers was never finished.

We listened to the sermon, which was on the importance of preserving an interior solitude (what a Spanish subject!) and went out. Immediately above rises the hill, a thousand feet high, of the Gibralfaro, crowned by its Moorish castle.

We started to climb it. Before the war this hill was an ugly lump of rock and shale without vegetation. Now it has been planted with stone pines and a garden laid out on the summit. The work was done by Republican prisoners and it has been done well. The crumbling walls have been tactfully restored, the area enclosed by the outer circumvallation has been set with flowering shrubs and cypresses, and a restaurant built for those who can afford its prices.

A violent wind got up as we reached the summit and a grey veil of dust rose between us and the sky. The sea below broke into white waves. Making our way down to it, we came to a line of newly quarried boulders, deposited along what used to be the sandy beach. This, when it is finished, will be the two-mile long esplanade which, it is claimed, will transform Málaga into a Nice or Brighton. But work on it has stopped, because the credits are exhausted. To construct this esplanade two popular bathing establishments have been swept away and also a little wooden restaurant where one sat under a canopy and ate excellent sepia and red mullet. To bathe, it will now be necessary to wait half an hour in a queue to take one of the hopelessly overcrowded tramcars to the Baños del Carmen, two miles away—unless of course one is the lucky owner of a new American car. But the whole point of these changes is that Málaga is being turned into a city for people who own American cars. A new plutocracy has arisen, demanding the luxuries that in the past used to be provided by France. But how long, in this half bankrupt country, is this class likely to maintain itself?

We returned to our hotel by the avenue of plane trees

and palms known as the Parque. On our left was the port,
half empty. English ships, once such regular callers, never
put in now except during the orange season; trade with
Germany and the Baltic ports is at a standstill. As a result
the City Council has no money to spend on its ambitious
projects. One speaks of the wealthy classes in Spain, yet
how few in number they are!

March 2

WE set out this morning with many fears and
premonitions to visit our house at Churriana. After buying
some lengths of cloth as presents for the servants, we took
the Torremolinos bus and, at the turning off to the village,
got out to do the last mile on foot. It was a lovely morning.
All around us lay the broad, flat, richly cultivated fields,
spreading like a lake of green water to the edges of the
mountains. A team of oxen was ploughing and from far
away a boy's voice, carried in gusts by the wind, could be
heard singing one of those deep, richly *appoggiatura* d
songs that are peculiar to this country. A Vergilian scene,
taken from a time when the world was young and poetical
and the word Mediterranean meant civilization as well as
culture.

We came to the village, which stands upon a little ter-
race above the plain, and climbed its long central street.
There at the far end was our house, a tall white building
rising directly from the roadway. We knocked at the door
of the gardener's lodge, and there was Rosario.

Here I must offer an explanation. Till 1934 we used to

live in a remote mountain village in the province of Granada. Then we bought this house and brought down with us from the village three people—Antonio to be the gardener, his wife Rosario to act as cook, and her widowed sister María to be general servant and housekeeper. When the Civil War broke out and we returned to England, we left Antonio in charge with the authority to let the house as best he could, use the rent to pay the taxes, and keep whatever was left over as wages. This he had done, reserving the lodge and garden for his own use and letting the house, first to a large landowner and then to a number of different families, who divided it between them. All this we knew from letters—now we were to see the reality.

Rosario opened the door and fell into my wife's arms. Tears rolled down her cheeks and her heart beat so fast that she had to sit down heaving and panting on a chair. Andalusians are an emotional people. A moment later her two children, girls of ten and sixteen, came in. They were nicely dressed, so that we could see at a glance that the family was prosperous. Then, when the ejaculations were over, a long, breathless conversation began; all the difficult, painful history of the past twelve years began to pour out in confused snatches.

Rosario is a stout, handsome woman of a little past forty —warm, sensual, emotional and very capable and clever. She has a bold aquiline nose, large, lively eyes and a very decided way of speaking. It is she who rules in her family. Before long her husband, who had been sent for, arrived— a simple, transparently honest man, not a Southern type at all but large boned and fair complexioned like a Northerner. One would say a regular peasant. We went out in a body to look at the garden.

The garden! We had forgotten what a garden we had. The long path hedged with box bushes, the orange and lemon trees, the Japanese medlars with their fish-shaped leaves and thick snake-like branches, the grove of Burmese canes, the pecans and avocado pears and jacaranda—two acres and more enclosed by high white walls and irrigated from a raised tank in front of the central patio. The flower garden had been planned as an eighteenth-century parterre, with beds of various shapes enclosed by edgings of some dwarf shrub-like plant, sometimes trimmed in fancy designs. The roses, which here flower at Christmas, were over, but the arum lilies and freesias were in full bloom and along the outer wall bushes of heliotrope gave out a faint, delicious smell. We walked about in a sort of enchantment, amazed that this wonderful garden, with its wealth of flowers and handsome trees, should be ours. It had even improved during our absence. Knowing that there was a shortage of food in Spain, we had told Antonio to pull up the flowers and plant vegetables for his own use. But he had not done so. On the contrary, the flower garden had spread into the vegetables and had been better tended and looked after than ever before.

We went into the house. One wing, that of the *mirador* or tower, had been set aside for our books and furniture. They were in perfect order. The rest of the building was filled with tenants—there were five families of them—but they had done no damage. I found it hard to express what I felt. This country had gone through a Civil War, a revolu-

tion and a famine, had been half occupied by the Germans
and the Italians, had been brought to the verge of war
with England, and yet Antonio and Rosario had quietly
continued to carry out their role of trustees of our interests
and to expect our return. Such fidelity to a foreigner was
deeply touching and I wondered if under similar circumstances an English laborer's family would have given it to
Spaniards.

We had scarcely seen over the house before Rosario's
sister, María, turned up with her twenty-year-old daughter,
Isabel. María is a very different sort of person from her
sister. In the first place she is plain, with a snub nose, dark
button eyes, a yellow complexion, and straight black hair
plastered down on her head. Her character is different too.
Fundamentally timid and unsure of herself, she has developed a dignified air and a severe, ironic way of speaking,
which is partly contradicted by her humorous, good-natured expression. Much of her conversation consists in re-
partees and home truths, of which we naturally come in
for our full share. But honesty and loyalty are written all
over her plain face.

Her career since we last saw her has been remarkable.
Forced by our departure to find a new way of earning her
living, she took to selling vegetables in the market place
and by sheer hard work and saving habits earned enough to
set up a shop for vegetables and groceries which has done
extremely well. Today she is prosperous, but the grind has
been hard and she is looking forward to the easier life that
will come for her at the end of the year. Her daughter will
then marry and take over the shop, while she will accept

the hand of a person who has long been courting her: a man of forty-five who is the agent to a large estate and is addressed in the village by the title of *Don*.

"To think," said Rosario, laughing, "that this sister of mine who could never leave the house after dusk because of her fear of ghosts and who, till you took pity on her, had no other prospect but hoeing in the fields, should have risen to this eminence!"

María smiled with ironic self-satisfaction.

"It's because I was brought up in the mountains," she said, "where people know what work is. Here they think of nothing but pleasure, and every penny they earn goes straight to vice and drink and luxury."

But in reality María's case is only one among thousands. The Civil War, the famine, and the black market have led to a social revolution in which, all over Spain, people of energy and determination have risen out of poverty to affluence. One must hope that some day the good effects of this infusion of new blood will show themselves.

We returned to Málaga in a happy frame of mind, after promising to come back as soon as our business in the town was completed and stay in Antonio's cottage. The evening promenade was in full swing as we walked up the main street. The sun had just set, long scarlet cloud streamers were draped across the sky, and the whole broad thorough-fare was choked with men and women pacing slowly up and down. Beyond it the crowd extended its tentacles into the narrower streets and alleys that led toward the center of the city, as well as off to the left toward the market place. Smiles, scents, flash of eyes and teeth, thick, black, hanging

tresses passed in bewildering frequency. If Spanish girls
dress poorly, no English girl can compare with them for
the care with which they make up their faces or brush and
set their magnificent, glossy hair. Then in the narrower
streets leading westward off the Calle Larios one comes to
the abode of the black market. Young neatly dressed girls,
carrying baskets of white rolls under their arms, keep up a
continual scream of *pan a contrabando*, contraband bread,
while with equal vociferation young men and boys offer
packets of American cigarettes, which have been smuggled
out of Gibraltar under the skirts and bodices of the wives
of the coast guards, who naturally would not be so ungen-
tlemanly as to search them. The police stand by and look
on, for why should they interfere with a traffic which provides so much employment and besides is necessary to
maintain the standard of living of the middle classes? Ration bread, though I found it as good as much English
bread, is detested, while Spanish state-manufactured cigarettes, once excellent, are today unsmokeable.

A few yards further on one comes to the taverns, crowded
with soldiers, sailors, and the less monastic sort of prostitute,
while the long narrow street on the right, which connects
the market place with the popular quarter, is given up to
houses of assignation. These have greatly helped to spread
extra-marital relations between the sexes, since all a young
woman has to do is to step sideways into an open doorway,
where she will find her lover awaiting her and a bedroom at
their disposal for a trifling sum. As if this were not easy
enough, there are innumerable bawds, both professional
and amateur, to act as go-betweens, seeking out the men

who have money to spare and the women who are in need of it and charitably bringing them together. The poverty and straitened circumstances to be found among almost all classes has weakened female morality and increased the number of persons who prey on it. I was told that one or two of these professional bawds met every bus and train on its arrival in order to make arrangements with their country clients. Rosario even pointed out one of them to me.

However, vice or no vice, the general impression made by this city in its hours of leisure is one of expansiveness and vitality. The Englishman, fresh from the dull hurry of London streets and from their sea of pudding faces—faces which often seem to have known no greater grief than that of having arrived too late in the chocolate or cake queue—feels recharged and revitalized when he bathes himself in this river. For it is not only the Spanish pulse that he is feeling here: it is that of the great ports of the Mediterranean and the Levant. Before becoming a Moorish city, Málaga was Carthaginian, and coins with a Carthaginian inscription continued to be minted here for many centuries after the Roman Conquest. This Carthage, money-making, pleasure-loving, easygoing—in short Levantine—is still the preponderating influence.

During the last few days we have heard a good deal about the bandits in the Sierra de Ronda. From their caves and mountain fastnesses they dominate large areas, including many villages. The whole Serranía is cordoned off by police, who, however, show little anxiety to risk their lives by attacking them. And the bandits, for their part, remain quiet and give few signs of their existence. Only from time to time they kidnap a wealthy man and hold him for ransom, and with the money they obtain in this way replenish their supplies.

Their most famous exploit in recent times has been the holding up of S., the owner of a large drapers' store in Málaga. He was spending the week end at his country house not far from the city when two men dressed as sportsmen approached him and asked for a light. While he was fumbling for it, they said, "We are Reds from the Sierra and we must have half a million pesetas within three days. Until it is paid, you will come with us." S.'s nephew, who was with him, pleaded that his uncle was too old to go with them and offered to take his place. The bandits agreed to this and carried him off instead. They treated him well, feasted him on the best food and wine, and every evening ordered him to say his prayers.

"We have our principles," they said, "and you have yours. If you wish us to respect you, you must live up to them."

The money was paid and he was released.

Another story that we have heard from several people concerns the bandits of the Sierra Nevada. A rich and much hated landowner was sitting in a café in Granada when a well-dressed man came up and sat down beside him. Suddenly he lowered his voice and said, "I am a Red from the mountains and I want so many thousand pesetas in compensation for the prison and beatings you gave my wife. I shall be here at this hour tomorrow to receive them. Mind you bring them and tell no one."

The man, however, told the authorities and when the

next day came the whole street was filled with plain-clothes police. Presently a large new car drove up and a captain of the Civil Guard got out. Walking up to the table where the landowner was sitting, "I think I have caught your fellow," he said. "Do you mind coming with me to police headquarters to identify him." They left the café together and the car drove off. It drove straight into the country and as the last house had been left behind, the police captain said, "I am the comrade of the Red who spoke to you yesterday. Hand over the money or you're a dead man." The man handed it over and was left by the side of the road.

Whether this story is true or not I cannot say, but it is told all over Andalusia. It shows the popularity of the brigands. The country people protect them and even their official enemies often have a sneaking affection for them. No Spaniard can help respecting a man who is brave and who successfully defies authority.

The paper this evening contained an amusing specimen of Falangist oratory. The Minister for Labor, Sr. Girón, was unveiling a monument in honor of Onesimo Redondo, the leader of the Castilian Falangists, who was killed in the war. "There was a man!" he said. "The whole of his life was an austere lesson in intransigence, in intimate discipline, in iron will power. What is more, this attitude of intransigence was projected outward into his public and private life, against the lies of half truths, in the burning fanaticism with which he defended his convictions, in his implacable demeanor toward the importers of smuggled ideas and the cultivators of liberaloid techniques."

Yet, as everyone knows, all the leading Falangists, who before the war had nothing, are today rich men with houses and broad estates. Corruption is one of the great civilizing factors because it saps the pride of the powerful, and the fanaticism of the Falange is at present confined to their oratory. They are feared only for what they have done in the past.

March 4

THIS afternoon we decided to call on our old friend, Don Carlos. A word of explanation is here needed. It was from Don Carlos that we had bought our house at Churriana. When, a couple of years later, the Civil War began, he was living with his wife and five children close to the airport, and bombs began to fall near by. We therefore invited him and his family to come and stay in his former house with us. But Don Carlos was a man of the Right and, though I did not know this at the time, a Falangist. Since the working-class syndicates held the town, he was in great danger and we were obliged, every time armed lorries entered the village, to conceal him in a secret cavity in the roof of the bathroom. Eventually, after considerable risk and anxiety to all of us, I obtained a pass for him and put him on a British destroyer.

My wife, Gamel Woolsey, has told the story at length in her book *Death's Other Kingdom*, which came out in 1939. I shall not repeat it here. But the drama of the situation will be apparent when I say that, while I took the Republican side and was outraged by the ferocity with which the Fascist rising was conducted, Don Carlos was the head of the Falangist secret police for the province. He knew my opinion, because I did not conceal it. However, even in revolutionary times, men are men before they are political partisans and I never lost my warm regard for his personal qualities or my admiration for the courage and gaiety he showed when he was in the most horrible danger. His wife, Doña María Luisa, was one of the noblest and warmest hearted women I have ever known and his children were delightful.

We found Don Carlos' family installed in a small, rather dingy flat at the top of an unfashionable building. Although he was working in the Food Office of the municipality, an organization which has an unsavory reputation, he had evidently not done well out of it. One of his sons opened the door, and then we saw, through the half darkness of the curtained sitting room, his tall figure coming toward us, and recognized the high bald head, bold aquiline nose and small tight mouth with its somewhat forced smile. He welcomed us at first with a rather uneasy cordiality; then his wife and one of his daughters came in and at once the atmosphere became affectionate and intimate. All the things that we had lived through together during those terrible weeks came back to our minds and we went over them together. I saw that I had been forgiven for having saved his life.

Don Carlos, though he had English blood in his veins, was a very Andalusian—one might say, very Irish—character. A man of good family, related to the Larios and the

Heredias, he had long ago spent the little money he had
inherited and lived in a descending scale, first farming in
Tierra del Fuego, then running a car agency, then a
chicken farm and finally landing up in a municipal job.
He was optimistic, scheming, irresponsible, always taking
up new projects and having his hands full of petty affairs—
in short, a Micawber, but with a streak of hardness and, I
suspect, cruelty in his buoyant disposition. His family life
was perfect, for parents and children all adored one another, in spite of the fact that his business enterprises invariably ended in failure. As for his conversation, it was in
the Malagueño vein of lighthearted and rather fantastic
irony, with a certain boyish thread of braggadocio running
through it. He used to say that I was an Andalusian too,
because, when I talk Spanish, a manner of this sort comes
easily to me.

I soon found that he had turned the episode of his con-
cealment in our house into a magnificent story, in which
we all came out as heroes; he had told it, he said, to a
French woman journalist who had been so struck by it
that she had published it in the *Revue des Deux Mondes*.
The painful episodes, as when, disgusted by General
Queipo de Llano's broadcasts and by the horrifying things
that were happening all over the country, I had forgotten
his position as my guest and broken out into a denuncia-
tion of the Nationalists, had been forgotten: I had always,
he said, been "the perfect gentleman." We went on to talk
of the changes that had occurred since that time; he had
lost one of his sons in Russia and his two daughters had
dedicated themselves to social service. One, the eldest, had

joined a newly founded nursing convent in which the nuns
slept on bare boards and ate the most meager food, going
out by day to nurse the poor and, when necessary, spending
the night also in their hovels. The other had enrolled as a
trained nurse in the Social Help Service of the Falange. All
the women in the family were deeply religious and, I think,
regarded these acts of self-abnegation as an expiation for
the terrible things that had been done during the Civil
War. One cannot live long in Spain without acquiring a
deep respect for Spanish women or observing how, in many
cases, their religion draws the best out of them.

The table was set and supper laid on it—a simple meal
of cheese, black ration bread, and sardines—and Don
Carlos proceeded to tell us what he had been doing. The
Civil Governor, as we know from the papers, had been
making an official tour of the villages of the Serranía de
Ronda, listening to complaints, promising reliefs and cajol-
ing the *alcaldes* and principal landowners. Don Carlos' job
had been to enter the villages on the day following the
Governor's visit and, in a very different spirit, to squeeze
the *alcaldes* and the landowners, so as to make them dis-
gorge the corn they had hidden away to sell at a higher
price on the black market. It had been Cervantes' job, I
told him: he had had serious trouble over it in the very
same district. But Don Carlos assured me that he had powers that the author of *Don Quixote* had never possessed. He
was a *fiscal*, armed with the authority of the secret police.
Acting on private denunciations, he could search houses,
arrest delinquents and impose fines without any legal
process or sanction. Such men, I knew, were much hated

and so I asked him what he did to protect himself against the brigands.

"Nothing," he said. "I refused even the police guard they offered me. These *rojos* never molest a person who has not plenty of money and, as they are informed about everything, they are well aware that I have not a cent and that no one would put up a hundred dollars to ransom me. So I felt quite safe."

Doña María Luisa sighed audibly.

"Quite safe," he repeated cheerfully. "There is a parish priest who goes from village to village to say Mass and they never interfere with him. He tells me they wave their hats when they see him. I saw them too several times and they just looked at me. They kill no one but the people who inform on them."

And he went on to talk of the various rich men who had been kidnapped and obliged to hand over large sums. If one refused one was shot, and if one paid one was stuck in jail by the authorities on the charge of collaborating with criminals. So men of means rarely left the city except by rail.

March 7

W E set off this morning to visit the ancient Greek site of the Peñón de Vélez, some sixteen miles to the east of the city. The easiest way of getting to it is to take the narrow-gauge railway that runs along the seashore. Warned to be early, we arrived at the station an hour before time in order to secure seats. We were none too soon.

The long carriage, fitted like the interior of a tram, with wooden seats facing the engine, was nearly full. Workmen in patched and dirty cotton clothes, old women with quince-colored faces in voluminous black, a few girls, two elderly civil guards, casting about them their heavy gummy eyes and lugubrious expressions. Baskets and bundles filled the luggage rack and were piled up on the floor, for nearly all the women were *estraperlistas*, engaged in black market traffic.

Through the carriage there passed a continual stream of street vendors of all ages, offering for sale bananas, nuts, pastries, sunflower seeds, sweets, lottery tickets, water. As they passed, they cried out their wares in loud, chanting voices—*Hay agua fresca, Tortas tiene buenas, Oye, las avellanas*. Among them, with a discouraged look, was a woman offering combs and pocketbooks, which no one bought. Then came a guitarist and played a few airs, collecting in our carriage a peseta, and after him a hunchback, with sharp, piercing eyes like acid berries, which he rolled round among his audience while he stroked his fiddle. Suddenly the engine gave a hoot and in a great hurry they all bundled out.

These scenes are no doubt one of the pleasures of travel in Southern countries: they stimulate the sense for life, by putting before one's eyes the spectacle of the struggle for existence. But what poverty they represent! There are, it seems to me, at least four times as many street sellers in Málaga as there used to be, and more than four times the number of beggars. One cannot sit in a café for ten minutes without a ragged boy coming in on all fours, so that the

waiters may not see him, to collect cigarette ends. Then
there are the armless and legless, the sick women carrying
sick children, the brigade of bootblacks and lottery vendors.
And how many more whom the police do not allow to show
themselves!

This search for food going on visibly under one's eyes
can be distressing, yet it is also, one must in honesty admit,
stimulating. It charges the air with real desires and crav-
ings. Perhaps it has more resemblance to the habits of birds
than to what in Northern countries one thinks of as the
settled routine of human life. To keep alive from day to
day these people must depend upon their wits, their cun-
ning, their familiarity with their environment. A mistake
or two, and they will die. Society does nothing for them. It
does not even provide rites for burying them. No prayers
are said over the dead, no ceremony carried out till 500
pesetas in cash have been put down. Lacking that, they go
like dogs into the common pit. For naturally the priest has
to live and can no more afford to say a prayer gratis than a
journalist can write an article for a periodical that does not
pay. Nor can they marry, these people, since the minimum
fee for this is 200 pesetas, nor in many cases attend church.
When I asked a woman who was struggling to keep a sick
husband and three children alive by her begging if she ever
went to Mass, she replied, "How can I in these clothes?"
Religion has become a luxury which only those in good
employment can afford.

But now the train has started, rattling along the narrow
strip of land between the hills and the sea. First we pass the
long garden suburb of Caleta with its expensive villas and

shady gardens. The pale lemons hang from their over-loaded branches, the smooth-trunked rubber trees spread out their glossy leaves, the pepper trees trail their feathery tendrils. From wall or balcony the bougainvillea falls in crimson or purple cascade. How pleasant, one thinks, it would be to live here the life of the lotus-eater, looking out on the unchanging sea and distant mountains. But in these houses there is a skeleton in every cupboard—the famished women, the child who will grow up rickety and tubercular through chronic undernourishment.

After Caleta we came out into a gay, lively country of little red, hat-shaped hills dotted with almond and locust trees, and above them were other red hills that were also dotted with trees, and above them still others. The highest range was planted with vineyards, and every one of these distant hills had a little white house like a cardboard box perched on its summit. Below, beside the rails, were irrigated plots of green alfalfa with fig trees standing among them and, on the other side, the beach. Stretched out at full length on this, their coats over their heads and their nets beside them, lay the fishermen, fast asleep. Every now and then we passed their shacks, each with a scarlet-flowered castor oil plant growing in its backyard and a row of ragged washing. Then at the stations there were eucalyptus trees, their low branches combed out by the wind, nostalgically dark against the bright, false glitter of the sea.

At Torre del Mar we got out of the train and walked back up the road. We were on a flat alluvial plain planted with sugar cane, that kept up a continual dry rustling in the wind. Soon we came to a river and climbed down the bank to eat our lunch beside it. There was not much water left in its bed, for the main flow had been drained off for irrigation. But the place seemed pleasant. On the bank facing us stood a row of straggling poplar trees, whose leaves danced in the sun and between them, some miles away, was an immense mountain. Greyish white, variegated by blue cloud shadows, quite bare, it seemed to float like an island of alabaster above the valley.

We sat there eating our fish and cold omelet among the periwinkles and grasses, while the water ran noisily by and the birds chirped to one another. An old man driving his black goats down the river bed saluted us and thanked us gravely when, as good manners required, we invited him to join our meal. An oxcart heaped with freshly cut canes passed slowly across the bridge. Three girls with white handkerchiefs tied round their heads leaned over it and laughed. That was all, and yet this is the moment of our three months' peregrination in Spain that stands out most persistently in my memory. The purpose of travel being to obtain ecstasy—that delight which one had as a child but lost later—I had it here. But I had it without knowing it. The realization only came to me months later. How am I to explain this? Except by repeating that we sat by the brown current of a stony river, with a line of ragged trees dividing the sky in front of us and a high mountain in the distance, I cannot do so.

After finishing our lunch we prepared to climb the hill known as the Peñón de Vélez, on whose summit the most westerly of all Greek settlements once stood. Here, toward 600 B.C., the Phocaeans from the Ionian coast founded a

city which they called Mainakē, to trade in gold and silver
with the neighboring tribes. The moment was propitious,
for the Phoenicians, who claimed the monopoly of these
Far Western waters, were just then in a decline, and a few
years later their city Tyre was captured by Nebuchadnez-
zar. However for all this the Greeks were not able to maintain themselves for long. When, toward the end of the sixth
century, Carthage took the place of Tyre as the chief mer-
cantile state of the Western Mediterranean and allied itself
with the new naval power of the Etruscans, Mainakē was
swept away and its site deserted. So impenetrable was the
curtain that then fell across these regions that we should
have no knowledge of its existence if an African proconsul,
by name Avienus, had not taken it into his head to trans-
late into bad Latin verse a Greek sailing book, written nine
hundred years before his time. In this poem, *Ora Maritima*,
which the archaeologist A. Schulten has recently un-
earthed, we find a description of the place as it was not
long before it was destroyed:

Before the city lies an island, ruled by the Tartes-
sians, and long ago dedicated by the natives to Her
who shines by night. Within this island is a marsh and
a safe port, and above it stands the town of Mainakē.
The country rises steeply from the sea and the Silurian
mountain swells up into lofty crests.

The aspect of the place has changed in the course of the
two and a half milleniums that have passed since then.
Today island, marsh, and harbor have all been swallowed

up by the advance of the land. Only the hill on which the city stood remains. It is a typically Greek site, consisting of a limestone outcrop—the only limestone to be found in a four-hundred-mile stretch of coast—and must have been chosen as much for the excellence of its building stone as for the natural harbor at its foot. At present the hill is used as a quarry, and a goatherd told me that last year a great wind blew down a piece of cliff and killed the workmen who were cutting stone below.

We climbed up over grey rocks and boulders, matted with asphodels, wild asparagus, and dwarf iris. The summit was flat and steeply scarped toward the sea; no signs of occupation remained except that, where a party of archaeologists had been at work, there were shards of rough pottery. But the view! On one side, where harbor and island had been, was a brilliant patchwork of greenish golden sugar cane and deep green alfalfa, spreading out to meet the white fringe of the sea, half a mile away. On the other side were the red earth hills of the coastal range, rising in rounded domes above one another and planted with almond trees, and beyond them the limestone massif of the Sierra de Tejares. Like a cloud it floated in the sky and I remembered that, when I had first come to Spain, thirty years before, I had watched the sun set from its summit and scrambled down its slopes in terror in the half darkness. I had not reached the *posada* till after midnight, my clothes torn and drenched in sweat. And then an army of bugs had kept me awake.

We retraced our steps down the hill and took a lane that led up the valley to the town of Vélez. Here all was semitropical Arcadia. The frogs croaked in the cisterns, the canes rustled, the pomegranate hedges were putting out red buds, the lemons hung like pale moons among their dark foliage, the banana leaves made vertical rivers of intense green. Now and then we overtook a loaded oxcart. Then, under a red conical hill, we passed a ruin overgrown with twisted locust trees, and felt down our backs the thrill of something sinister and treacherous underlying this immense luxuriance. When at last we reached Vélez, a white town sliding down a steep hill, we had barely time to drink a cup of coffee before the bus left.

Then the return journey. The jolting, roaring bus with its petrol fumes and broken windows—every Spanish bus is fit for the scrap heap; diagonal views of the pale, blue, oh much too nostalgic sea; glimpses of sun-drenched rocks and of trees soaking themselves in their own shade; fisher girls seated at the doorsteps of their shacks, singing the songs that, for the noise of the exhaust, would never be heard; the descent of evening.

> *C'est trop beau! c'est trop beau! mais c'est nécessaire*
> *Pour la Pêcheuse et la chanson du Corsaire,*
> *Et aussi puisque les derniers masques crurent*
> *Encore aux fêtes de nuit sur la mer pure!*

CHURRIANA

W<small>E</small> left Málaga yesterday for Churriana. Antonio and Rosario had prepared for us the best bedroom in their cottage and given us their small sitting room. Rosario's excellent cooking—she has learned to temper the monotony of the Spanish cuisine by a few simple French recipes—makes a welcome change. We eat less, but better.

The talk of the province during the past week has been the prophecy of an old *sabio* or wise man of Alhaurín (the next village up the road) that it was going to rain. The prolonged drought has been causing great despondency everywhere and so his prophecy has been seized on and given headlines in the local papers. Now, the day after our arrival, the sky is overcast and a few heavy drops fall. Toward night it begins to rain in earnest and when we wake up the patio is full of water. All morning the heavy drench continues. Then, soon after three o'clock, there is a cloudburst, with much thunder and lightning. The mountain above the house has a turban of mist and the whole vale bellies with dark purplish cloud. The villagers sit up all night in fear, muttering *Ave Maria*s.

So the *sabio* has been right and the drought has broken. His photograph comes out in all the papers—a little dried-up old man with as many wrinkles on his face as there are gullies in the mountains. A man too who knows his own mind: when they wanted to photograph him in a collar and tie, he refused to put them on, saying that he had never worn such things and that they must take him as he was or not at all. The Civil Governor sent for him to thank him and give him a present, and everyone is as pleased and grateful as if he had made the rain himself. I learned from a woman who knows him that he is a shepherd and lives in a small *casita* some way outside the village. His wife is blind and, as he sleeps badly, he is in the habit of spending much of the night wandering about the fields; thus he gets to know the signs and portents. The rain, I am told, began on the day he had predicted and stopped just when he had said it would.

Everyone has longed for this rain, yet the immediate effect has been unemployment. No work can be done on the fields for four or five days, so wages have stopped coming in and the day laborers' families—that is, more than half the population of the village—find themselves with nothing to eat. At once children and old people begin to appear at the door, asking for money for bread. What sort of an agriculture is this when a couple of days' rain reduces every laborer's family to such straits? Behind it lie centuries of bad organization and heartlessness.

From the moment of our moving into Antonio's cottage, we have been overwhelmed with visitors. Every hour or two some fresh person arrives. Among those who come expecting assistance, the most troublesome has been Frascillo. He is a man we used to know as the hanger-on of a friend of ours, Juan Navaja, village baker and political agent for the Catholic Conservative party, who was shot in the first weeks of the Civil War. Feckless, restless, with neither parents nor wife, he has now degenerated into a complete drunkard. In his alcoholic mind I have become the successor of his former patron, and I am told that he used to boast in the village that he had had letters from me. My arrival was therefore a great event for him, to be celebrated dramatically. Coming up to me in the street, he threw his long, drooping arms about me and thrust his red, bloodshot eyes and two weeks' growth of beard into my face. "Can it be true? Don Geraldo home again! My protector returned! Are these eyes of mine really seeing him in person?"

I gave him a few pesetas, which he hurried off to spend on wine, and after that he set up a perpetual guard at the door of our house, seizing my hand when I went out and mumbling to himself and weeping when I did not appear. One night he spent in a drunken slumber on the doorstep. He supports himself on wine, and for food eats only a crust of bread a day; when offered more, he refuses it.

Another visitor is a beggar woman called Marta, aged about thirty, and simple. She lives in a rock shelter by the cemetery, sleeping on a heap of straw and rags with a blind man much older than herself, who is said to beat her. In the spring and autumn they set out on long journeys, going as far as Seville and Cartagena. Marta is liked by everyone, for she has the goodness of very simple people, a gay disposition and quick tongue. The game is to tease her and ask smutty questions about what she does with her blind man; she makes a naïve or a witty answer, and is given a piece of bread or a penny.

It is extraordinary how much this country resembles

Russia before the Revolution. In a sense it is even more revolutionary in feeling than it was in 1936, because it is corrupt and rotten and conditions are so bad that everyone except for a few black marketeers wants a change. But no revolution can take place. The police and the Army see and will continue to see to that; they are the one solid and dependable thing in this ramshackle regime, in which bureaucratic interference with legitimate business is combined in the worst possible way with the *laissez-faire* economy of the black market. And they get the moral support they need, in the dread which everyone who has anything to lose feels of another civil war.

I have been surprised to find how friendly the whole village is to us. Smiles everywhere. This is because of the broadcasts I made against the regime during the war. But even the people who supported the military movement seem well disposed to me, partly for the reason that Antonio and Rosario have such a good reputation and partly because they are now thoroughly disillusioned. Even the leading Falangists, who by the way are excellent persons, send polite messages. One of these men is the brother-in-law of Juan Navaja, who, as I have said, was a great friend of mine. His mother, in her grief at his assassination, had blamed me for his death, because when he was on the run I refused to shelter him for more than a single night, knowing that if I did so the house would be searched and Don Carlos arrested. But I gave him advice, which if he had not been too besotted by fear to act on it, might have saved him.

One of my first acts, therefore, was to call on this brother-in-law. He received me well, though a little stiffly, and at once began to talk about the state of affairs.

"Things are much worse today than before the Civil War," he said. "The poverty is atrocious. Never has such poverty been known before. It is not safe to leave the main streets after dark, as hungry men will take any risk to get money. Yet Málaga is one of the richest towns in Spain."

Then suddenly he dried up; the words had burst out because he could not keep them in, but it was not for him to talk politics to a man who had backed the other side. When I saw him again, he was polite but distant. But I must record the fact that, though exposed as a baker to the worst temptations of the black market, he had the reputation of being honest. So, I think, are many of the local Falangists; the corruption in which their leaders are involved has not touched them.

March 12

WE set off today to visit our old friends, the Washbrooks, at Torremolinos. A beautiful walk, skirting the foot of the mountains: olive trees, carobs and a mile or two away the sea, throwing up its white arms against the long curved shore of the bay of Málaga. Clear air, the distant barking of dogs and silence.

Mr. Washbrook is a New Englander, thin, grey-haired, angular, with a harsh creaking voice and, in moments of excitement, a slight stutter; his wife is a handsome and vigorous Madrileña. When the Civil War broke out, they took the side of Franco and left the country, returning nine

months later with the victorious armies. Anything tinged
however lightly with Red was anathema to them and I was
therefore especially curious to learn their opinion of the
present state of affairs.

We had not been in their house five minutes before Mr.
Washbrook began to explode with indignation. The rob-
bery going on on all sides, he declared, was incredible. People started with a handful of dollars and in a couple of
years had made their fortunes; all they needed was a friend
in the government and a lack of shame. Then the condition
of the working classes was intolerable. Their wages were
barely sufficient to keep them alive and the moment they
lost their work, they starved. The folly of the government
at allowing such a state of affairs was unbelievable. But
then the government and the municipality scarcely existed.
This was not a dictatorship, but a free-for-all regime in
which no one thought of anything but feathering his own
nest. People did as they pleased and no one could stop
them. Not even Franco. If he tried to do so, they would
shoot him. Look at the position here! Numbers of men had
been thrown out of work because the landowners had
turned their corn lands into sugar cane, which required
very little labor. Although corn was short, the government
did nothing to stop this.

Mrs. Washbrook joined in in her vigorous way:

"Give the people enough bread and olive oil and you
would never hear a word of complaint. But they have
neither bread nor oil, so naturally they are all Communists.
If I were a workingman, I would be one too."

"That's it, that's it," broke in her husband, stammering

with excitement. "The people in power here seem to have no idea of what they are doing. We are living on a volcano. Everything is heading for a tremendous eruption."

"But unless the Russians come here," I said, "what eruption can there be?"

Mr. Washbrook waved his arms.

"No, no, I say. You can't go on like this forever. Something is bound to happen. And then we shall have to pack our bags and leave the country once more."

They took us out to show us their little property of two or three acres. They grow their own corn, grind it in a hand mill and bake it in an oven brought expressly from the United States.

"The bread here is poison," Mr. Washbrook declared. "There is no government inspection and the millers throw in any rubbish they like. If one wants wheat bread, one must buy on the black market."

"The bread in England is bad too," I said. "In fact I prefer Spanish ration bread."

But he wouldn't hear of this. The bread might be just eatable in some places, but wherever the miller was dishonest it was poison.

After tea we went out to look at the new villas that were springing up. Marbella, thirty miles to the west, has been turned into a fashionable *plage* and now this is happening in Torremolinos too. The new fortunes made since the Civil War demand new outlets. There is a municipal building scheme and land values have soared.

"Look at that house," our friend exclaimed, pointing to a very ordinary looking villa. "It belongs to the director of a bank and cost 1,500,000 pesetas, because it is built of steel and concrete, which can only be obtained at fantastic prices on the black market. Flats at controlled rents have been put up for the lower middle classes, but, would you believe me, not a single working-class house has been built either here or at Málaga. These people are living in a fool's paradise."

"The other day," said Mrs. Washbrook, "a man on the bus put the matter well. General Franco, he said, is a really great man. He is teaching Spaniards a wonderful thing—how to live without eating."

Darkness fell before we reached Churriana. We quickened our steps, remembering how often we had been told not to be caught out of the village after nightfall; the footpads are more dangerous than the brigands, as well as ten times more numerous. As we hurried along, the mountains loomed high above us. The crickets sang loudly from the moist earth of the wheat fields, the goat bells tinkled, the frogs kept up their amazing croaking. And so we came at length to the village, where Rosario was waiting for us.

The housing problem is certainly acute. In Churriana twenty working-class families are living in a barn divided up by cane partitions: each family has an area of some ten feet by ten to live, sleep, and cook in. The reason for this overcrowding is that, on present wages, no working-class family can pay an economic rent, and the government and municipality make no grant. They have, it is true, put up blocks of flats at controlled rents, but these are for the lower middle classes and their rents—1,000 pesetas a month —far exceed the total earnings of a working family. The

Falange may say what it will, but the people who govern Spain today could hardly do more than they are doing to show that the working classes are their enemies. The result is that no laborer does more work than he can help. As a man said to me, "It's as though one planted potatoes and then refused to hoe or manure them. Naturally one gets a bad crop."

Une cannot be long in this country without realizing that the sole thriving industry is the *estraperlo* or black market. Legitimate business is starved, throttled by forms and regulations and frowned on by the Falange and the authorities, whereas the black market moves on oiled wheels with the secret help and connivance of everyone.

Take for example the building trade. Cement, iron and wood are all rigidly controlled and one has to get a permit to buy anything at an ironmonger's. And these permits cost money. They are only granted on the payment of a substantial bribe and, if one refuses to pay this, one must buy on the black market. The controls originally had a sensible purpose—but their effective use today is simply to keep up black market prices. Rightly or wrongly, it is widely believed that the ministers who impose the controls are in the pay of the racketeers.

"How can one expect people to be honest," said the master builder who gave me this information, "when the men at the top are thieves? The flower of the country's manhood is either overseas or dead."

This man, who before the Civil War had built up a position for himself by hard work and shrewdness, was a Monarchist and a great admirer of Primo de Rivera.

"We need another dictatorship like his," he said. "A dictatorship of *pan y palo,* bread and the stick."

Now the motto of Franco's dictatorship is *pan y justicia,* bread and justice, and people say, "We have seen his justice and we don't like it, but we haven't seen his bread."

One evening the bailiff of a large estate in the Hoya, whom I had known slightly in 1935, called in to see me. He was a strong, athletic man in the prime of life, with clear blue eyes and a face redder than one usually meets with in Andalusia. Like most of these bailiffs, he was hardheaded, capable, and honest. I asked him how he was getting on.

"We farmers," he said, "carry the burden of everything. First of all there's the host of forms to be filled in: every year there are more of them. Then comes their presentation. Two or three times a week I go in to Málaga with a dispatch case full of them and dance attendance on the authorities. I stand in a queue at the various government and municipal offices, but they only open from eleven to one and then as likely as not the boss is out and my business cannot be attended to. For these officials can't do anything on their own: they have no training or technical knowledge, but are just *recommendados,* people who have got their jobs through personal influence. You can't believe their incompetence."

"But are they honest?"

"Honest? Not likely. How can they be on the salaries they get? The other day I asked permission to buy Seville potatoes at so much the ton—the current price. They agreed. But when the forms came to be filled in I found that I must pay an extra 10 per cent—as a tip, of course.

This made the potatoes too dear and I had to look for others. And the hours wasted!"

"Tell me how the black market works."

"Oh, in a thousand ways. A manufacturer of quince jelly writes to say that he has twenty tons of pulp. This entitles him to an equal weight of sugar. An inspector goes down, is feasted and wined and given a present; he enjoys himself so much that he fails to note that there are really only ten tons of pulp, and the manufacturer is able to sell half the sugar he gets on the black market. He makes much more out of this than he does out of his quince jelly."

"And is it true that this is done by the authorities too?"

"Of course. By them more than by anyone. Here's a case. Not long ago a ship arrived with 50,000 tons of artificial manure. Headlines in all the papers, smiles on the farmers' faces, for artificial manure is the new treasure of the Incas. I hurried down at once with particulars of my crop to claim my share. But this share turned out to be nothing—scarcely worth collecting. Then, hardly was I outside the office than I found I could buy all I wanted at double prices. The greater part of the cargo had been sold on the dock to the *estraperlistas*—sold, you understand, by the municipal authorities."

"That's bad," I said. "I wonder you manage to survive."

"Oh, we manage that all right," he replied. "All we have to do is turn the tables on them. They tell us, you know, what to plant, at what price we must sell, to whom and so forth. On paper every detail is controlled. But we are on the spot and they are in their offices and so, without their being able to stop it, we contrive to place a good part of our crop on the black market. If we didn't, we couldn't live."

"Many people don't live."

"That's true. The land has never been so well cultivated before, yet half the population is starving. And if you put an end to the black market, then the middle classes would starve also."

"So what do you suggest?"

"Oh don't ask me. I'm not a politician. But obviously the Falangist syndicates that work the controls will have to go and then a foreign loan will be needed to break the black market. It will have to be a large one."

The black market has, however, its better side. Like the industrial movement in Victorian England, it offers facilities to hard-working and enterprising persons of all classes to rise in the social scale. Very large numbers of poor people are engaged in it in a small way and many of them have succeeded in bettering themselves. For example there is a woman we know who has risen from absolutely nothing to be the owner of a neat little shop in Málaga and of some landed property. I asked her how she had managed this; entirely, she said, by very hard work. Every morning over many years she has risen early to take the train or bus to some distant village to buy from the peasants. She has not got back till late that evening or early on the following day, after a night spent uncomfortably on a bench in the railway waiting room. On every journey she has had to run the gantlet of the police with her boxes and baskets and to risk a considerable fine if she was caught. But she was never caught; according to her brother, her air of quiet respecta-

bility disarmed the civil guards, who were not out to en-
force the law but to keep up appearances. For everyone
realizes that without the black market life would simply
come to an end.

The most risky type of *estraperlo* is selling coffee. In the
buses and trains women place their bundle of coffee some
way from where they sit, and if it is discovered they do not
claim it. It becomes the policeman's perquisite. Barley
coffee is also on the forbidden list. Those who deal in this
get up at two or three in the morning to roast it, so that
the smell may not give them away, and then hawk it around
on hand carts or bicycles. Another secret trade is the making of macaroni on a portable machine. The white rolls
one buys are made at the ordinary bakeries, but their sale
is the monopoly of certain nice looking young girls, who
no doubt have their own ways of placating the police. At
all events they sell it under their eyes and are never arrested. In short the world of the *estraperlo* is vast and complicated and sometimes linked to other kinds of vice. To a
novelist such as Balzac or Pérez Galdós its investigation
would open up endless and fascinating possibilities.

The two forces in Spain that represent something more
than the money interest are the Church and the Falange;
they are naturally rivals and most people believe that the
Church is today the more powerful. The struggle between
them is especially acute in Málaga. This, I imagine, is because the Bishop, Dr. Angel Herrera, late editor of the
great daily paper *El Debate,* is a man of exceptional ability
and, what is more, has strong ideas on the part the Church
ought to play in the social question. Last year he used his

influence to get houses built for the fishermen of Palo and this year he has been canvassing a project for settling peasant families on the land. But the landowners have refused point-blank to have anything to do with it; in a recent meeting they denounced all such projects as Communism and had the audacity to request the Bishop to stop preaching on land reform and to put his ideas to them in private.

Not to be outdone by the Church, the Civil Governor, who is of course a Falangist, has also had his idea. Last week he produced a scheme by which the landowners should hand over a tenth part of their estates on long leases to small proprietors. But this has had to be dropped too. The only real power in Spain today is the power of money, and neither landowners nor *estraperlistas* see why they should make sacrifices for the sake of warding off a revolution that, so long as army and police stand firm, can never come. And why give a tenth part when nothing less than three-quarters would meet the need? They probably have the sense to see that the Church and the Falange are merely nibbling at the problem.

A Spanish friend of mine, who has lived many years abroad, poured scorn on all these projects. The main effort of the Church, he said, was devoted to getting everyone to do the Exercises of St. Ignatius. These were the panacea, and the Jesuits, who controlled Church policy, had little faith in land reform or in economic amelioration. The Catholic social organization, too, was hopelessly weak: just because it was Spanish, it was halfhearted and lethargic and did not compare with the drive and efficiency of the

Catholic institutions in the United States. However, he said, the seminaries were turning out a better and more idealistic type of priest and many women of the middle classes, appalled by the misery of the poor, were taking the veil in charitable orders. The worst symptom was that the young no longer had faith in anything—not even in common honesty.

One thing, however, may be said, and that is that as the shadows deepen over the Spanish scene, such idealism and enthusiasm as are still to be found tend to take a religious form. The wealthy give their money to the Church and new convents and schools spring up. Now, under the instigation of Dr. Herrera, a hundred acres of land has just been acquired by the Building Society of the Sacred Heart. On this a model village is to be built for working-class families, complete with church, dispensary, market, nursery and sports ground. If Dr. Herrera's influence were to spread —and it is said that he will be the next primate—the Church could do something to regain its former position. But how many bishops are there of this type? The last Bishop— he has now been promoted to the Archepiscopal See of Granada—was a very different sort of person. A characteristic story is told of his dealings with the fishermen of Palo. These men have a Virgin for whom they feel a great devotion because they depend on her to keep the sea calm when they go out. Every year they hold a fiesta in which they carry her from her sanctuary with rockets and frantic applause and dip her in the waves. The Bishop forbade this. To dip the Blessed Virgin in the water! That was highly disrespectful, and even to carry her across the beach was insulting to her purity, because from this beach women were accustomed to bathe. If they wished to take her to the edge of the sea, they must choose a portion of the beach where during the past fifty years no woman had taken off her clothes.

Such is the old rigid type of bishop, brought into being by the Liberals when they closed the chairs of theology in the universities. Educated in a narrow and poorly endowed seminary, nurtured on readings of the fathers and doctors of the Church, they know nothing of life or of the world. For them the whole duty of man may be summed up as death to the Liberals, suppression of sex and frequent attendance at divine service. The great discovery of the Jesuits—how to relate means to ends—has made no impression on them.

As for the Falange, it is simply the party of the Spanish lower middle class. From 1840 to 1920 this was the vocally discontented class in Spain and under its radical program it championed the politically uneducated working classes. But when these began to form trade unions and political parties of their own, the lower middle class became isolated. Liberalism had by this time died in the general stagnation of parliamentary politics, so that when the threat of revolutionary socialism began to develop, the lower middle class adopted in a hurry a program borrowed from Italy and Germany, whose chief merit was that it promised to give them power rapidly. But it is a gross oversimplification to say, as the Marxists do, that the Falange came into being to support the interests of the landowners and capitalists. On the contrary it is a genuinely revo-

lutionary party, both anticapitalist and anticlerical. Its
tragedy is that it has not been able to seize power. It finds
itself a prisoner of the landowners, the Army and the
Church and so unable to carry out any of the reforms that
it desires and to obtain which it has shed such rivers of
blood. Thus it has become disillusioned and cynical, and
its leaders, many of whom entered the party late and for
purely personal reasons, have allowed themselves to join
in the general wave of black marketeering and corruption
which has been brought about by the inflation. Disgruntled,
angry and suffering from a bad conscience, it is very much
on the defensive today.

One of the pleasures of living in Spain is the enlarged
sense one gets of the passage of time. In England the day is
broken up by a thousand little fences and obstacles, which
produce a feeling of frustration and worry. One passes
from breakfast to supper with struggle and effort, and
when night comes one feels one has not had a day at all.
Nothing of interest has happened, no taste or color has
been left to mark out that day from all others. But in Spain
time imitates the landscape. It is vast, untrammeled, featureless and every day gives the sensation of a week.

I write this after seeing from my diary that I have spent
nine days at Churriana. Already I feel rooted in this life
and house again, almost as though, thirteen years ago, I
had never left it. The fixed background, giving the mood
and tone, has been the garden. Every day we pace round it
a dozen times with Antonio or Rosario, touching, smelling,
admiring, commenting, breathing in the calm and happiness that only Southern gardens, bathed in perpetual sun-

light, can give. The orange buds come out, the goldfinches chase one another among the branches; the flower of the avocado pear tree gives off its summery smell, the datura its Cleopatra perfume. Then evening falls: every color becomes transparent, every shadow filled with light, while in the sky above long pink and scarlet trails of cloud act the charade of another garden overhead.

Night too has its intoxication. One walks out, and the smell of the warm, moist earth takes possession of one's nostrils. The great lotus tree, *Celtis australis,* a cousin of the elms that has borrowed the smooth, soaring trunk of the beech, seems to be suspended downward by its roots from the sky. So strong is the feeling that the fixed part of Nature lies above! Then one starts to grope forward between the shadows; here the canes give a faint rustle, there one sees or smells a white flower. At length, at the end of the box path, one climbs the platform built to give a view over the wall. Moon and the dark, towering mass of the sierra. Stars pulsating like organic bodies. Away across the valley are the lights of Málaga and its attendant villages and, more brilliant than these, the flares put up to guard the crops of the artichoke growers. Frogs raise their concert in the ditch, owls hoot, and from every farmyard in the plain comes the sound of dogs barking. Slowly and in an altered mood we turn and go back to the friendly faces and the fire of olive twigs.

One of the most frequent visitors during the past ten days has been a young priest called Don José, who is the confessor of a new convent of nuns that has been recently established here. He is a curious and original character.

Pale, slightly built, with clear-cut, feminine features, soft brown eyes which he scarcely ever raises from the floor and long, tapering hands, he seems to ooze out refinement with every pore of his body. He speaks in a slow, careful voice, articulating every syllable, as though language were a kind of music that required precise execution, and in everything he says there is a mixture of what, if it did not almost ring true, one would call affectation.

He had come to visit us, he said, because he had heard from Rosario that we were interested in literature. Poetry in his opinion was, after religion, the highest activity possible to our weak human nature; indeed it was itself a form of religious practice, the expression of man's adoration of the world in which he had so marvellously been placed. Did we, he wondered, like poetry? I assured him that we did and asked him with some curiosity what poets he liked best. Rubén Darío and Juan Ramón Jiménez, he answered —which for an English reader may be rendered as Swinburne, Verlaine and Yeats—and I replied that I admired them too and had recently been shown some letters written by Juan Ramón Jiménez from America.

"Juan Ramón!" he exclaimed, laying his long fingers on my sleeve and raising his eyes from the ground to give me one of his rare smiles. "But he is one of the most divine! And you do not have to tell me that his handwriting is as exquisite as his poetry. It must be so."

"Of course you write poetry yourself," I said.

"I confess that sometimes in my clumsy way I practice the art. At present I am engaged in copying out a few of my little efforts in a fine calligraphy. I have no ambition to publish, but the album in which I am collecting my verses will be left on my death to a friend. I would like to feel that, when I pass from this world, I shall leave something behind me, even though it is too worthless to interest posterity."

Don José has very delicate health. For this as well as for aesthetic reasons he is a vegetarian and a firm adherent of the Naturist clinic in Málaga, with its theories of opposites and harmonies in foods. (Vegetarianism has been a semi-religious cult in Andalusia since the beginning of the century.) It is in fact on account of his health that he is here. He is a Granadino by birth; the Archbishop sent him to Málaga because its climate is so mild and secured his appointment to a post in which, after he has said Mass at eight o'clock, he has no further duties.

"That is something," he said, "for which I cannot thank the Lord sufficiently. My spiritual health requires two things—complete leisure and the contemplation of beautiful landscapes. These are both things that I enjoy superabundantly here."

It seems, however, that the nuns of his convent think differently. They belong to an order which looks after the prisoners and the sick and they have many acres of land on which they try to grow the food they need. Although they give better wages than anyone round about, they understand nothing of estate management and so are imposed on and swindled by everyone who works for them. They therefore need a priest who can not only say Mass and give absolution, but act as their bailiff. This, of course, their poet confessor is unable to do.

Under his affected way of speaking Don José is a man of great simplicity. Rosario, a warmhearted but worldly woman who never enters a church, treats him as a child. She makes him salads and lets him walk about the garden, listening to his Don Quixotesque speeches with a scarcely concealed smile. Antonio, her husband, is after all another simpleton, though of a more Sanchoesque sort.

I use the word Quixotesque deliberately, for this priest is really an example of the Don Quixote type of man, in that he has incorporated himself completely into his idealistic philosophy. Every word, every gesture expresses the way of thinking he has adopted and the person he would like to be. Listen to his conversation. He is a mystic and a Nature mystic. He tells me in his slow, precise voice, with his eyes modestly lowered and his hands crossed in front of him, that he sees God in the plants and leaves and hills and butterflies. Yes, and in the beetles too. For Nature ought to be loved in many different ways on several different levels. One should love it immediately with one's eyes and ears and sense of taste and smell, then with one's imagination as the material of poetry, and last of all mystically, as a means of raising one to God.

As a first step one should accustom oneself to seeing everything under the aspect of poetry. Thus there should be poetry in one's eating, as when one sits down to a meal off fresh fruits of the earth. There should be poetry in the movements of one's body and in one's thoughts. Speaking of the country people, "They are virgin savages," he said. Uncultivated, but at bottom pure and good, like all human beings. *Bondad*, goodness, was the clay out of which God had made men, only with the process of time it had been corrupted. "But the world is created afresh," he said, "for every man who has a poet's imagination."

As we sat together on the platform of the wall, looking out over the green countryside, I thought how, on the surface at least, he resembled St. John of the Cross. But one thing was lacking—the interior struggle. He wore his creed, not as an obsession that filled him and tormented him, but as a fine suit of clothes. This made him in the long run a bore.

March 18

TODAY we had intended to climb the mountain above the house, but instead had to endure a merciless afternoon of visits. An engineer from Málaga and his wife, drawn by the prospect of airing their views to an Englishman, were the first to arrive. He was a shrewd, clever little man, who as a ship's engineer had traveled and seen the world, but he was an intolerable talker. He commenced his monologue by explaining to us at length what England and the English character were like—a common Spanish habit which my wife, who is American, tells me the English practice on her about her own country—and then in a rapid voice, hard as a machine gun's rattle, he held forth about world politics. The Russians, the Americans, the Russians, the English—olé, what maneuverings for position in preparation for the world war that would shortly break out! Easy to see what they wanted Spain for! Then, lowering his voice to a loud whisper, he began to speak about the

crimes of the Franco regime. I pretended to listen to the
furious, sibilant sounds that issued from his mouth, but
all the time I was watching the goldfinches in the orange
trees and the solitary mountain with its three dark pines.
What silence one would find there! But on he went and,
when at last he got up to go, it was to make a Russian farewell.

This monkey type of man is a common Mediterranean
species. Always too clever by half, they are sometimes good
and sometimes bad, but invariably crude and superficial in
their judgments. This one was better than most: his heavy
eyelids and large, liquid eyes showed sensibility, his wrinkled forehead the chronic anxiety of the neurotic. He lived,
like so many of his kind, the life of the addict, whose drug
is not sex, or morphia, but politics. But isn't that a poison
naturally secreted by the Spanish scene, with all its out-
rageous examples of injustice and misgovernment? This
man, I reminded myself, was a man of the Left, a Republican, living among people he could not confide in. If
he was so boring, it was because he had spent months stor-
ing up what he had to say, and then suddenly found the
chance of unloading it upon a person who came from an
almost mythical world of sanity and reasonableness.

The papers announced today a 40 per cent rise in the
pay of all Army officers and N.C.O.s. A bribe to keep the
Army faithful, a foreigner might remark. But in fact the
rise is a just one, because for a long time now it has been
almost impossible for a Spanish officer or N.C.O. to live
on his pay. As the hours in which they are employed are
few, they nearly always take on other jobs in commerce or

business, or supplement their earnings by selling Army
stores on the black market. This is not generally regarded
as dishonest. The rations provided are deliberately far
larger than can be consumed, and every officer and N.C.O.
has the privilege of selling his share of what is left. Yet
over every army and police barracks are written the words
Todo por la patria, All for the fatherland, and many feel
intensely the humiliation of being obliged to live in this
manner. I was told of one heroic lieutenant colonel who
refused to follow the usual practice and chose instead to
exist in an undignified poverty.

How do the working classes, who cannot afford to live on
the black market, manage to keep alive? One way is by
having extra ration books. New births are registered that
have not occurred, deaths are concealed and so forth. There
is even a trade in ration books and one wealthy man from
the Limonar, who was heard saying that he could not understand why people complained of a shortage of food, had
to admit that he had thirty-two. For this reason I cannot
help being sceptical of the statement put out in official
quarters that there has been a huge increase of population.
This statement is founded on the returns sent in by the
various provinces of the rations that they require, and such
returns cannot, I think, be taken very seriously.

I had been careful up to now to avoid making any con-
tacts with the Underground, or indeed seeking out anyone
who might have Left Wing opinions. If they came to me, I
listened and that was all. However when I was offered an
opportunity of meeting in Málaga a man who could tell
me how the Reds in the sierra were organized, my curiosity

was aroused and I accepted. My informant was an elderly
man who, as a Socialist, had spent many years in prison and
had come out maimed and scarred by the beatings he had
received. His native village was in the Serranía de Ronda
and he had left it because, as a man of the Left, he would be
held responsible by the police for any subversive actions
that took place in the vicinity. The Reds, he told me, were
composed of Socialists and Communists under Communist
direction. They were highly organized in regional commands and took their orders from code messages given out
by a foreign radio station. The effective unit was a group
of from five to ten men living in the sierra, and linked to
another group dispersed about the towns and villages
whose task was to provide information. At present they
were lying low and giving as little trouble as possible.

Until recently people suspected of Underground activity
had been arrested and court-martialed. But this had led to
an agitation in the foreign press and to the intervention of
ambassadors, so now a different procedure was adopted.
Suspects were either kept in prison without trial or taken
to some mountain district where police rule was absolute
and there left dead by the roadside. When their bodies
were discovered next morning, it was given out that they
were Reds who had been shot while trying to escape. Since
May 1947, when the Civil Guard was given full powers in
certain areas, this has been the usual method for getting
rid of unwanted people.

The enormous number of police of all kinds is, of course,
one of the things that first strikes the foreigner. In certain
districts, where the Reds are active, they give the impres-

sion of an army. But the civil guards, who form the flower of this force—if flower is the word to use in such a dismal connection—are not what they used to be. The visitor to Andalusia before 1936 will recollect the traditional type— grave, stern and monkish, planted in a hostile village like Knight Templars among infidels, and devoted to the tradition of their service and its code of honor. These men exist no longer: the civil guards of today are just civilians in uniform. Traveling about the country in buses, I have often been struck by their easygoing friendliness, without reflecting that this might imply a lack of discipline. In fact they are often corrupt and indolent, take their private toll off black marketeers and show little eagerness in risking their lives against the Reds. More serious than this is their tradition of brutality. Only two days ago some civil guards were passing down our street when they heard some young men laughing. Thinking quite wrongly that they were laughing at them, they went up to them and began beating them on the head. Apparently these sorts of incidents happen frequently; a man of the working classes has no defence and no protection. And, of course, anyone taken to the police station as a political suspect receives a good beating, simply as a matter of routine.

March 20

THE time had now come for us to leave Churriana. For the last time we walked round our garden, as Adam and Eve might have walked round theirs, before deserting it for the impersonal world, unwarmed by the friendly glow of ownership. The feeling of affection that can grow for a house and its corner of land is surely one of the more valuable kinds of piety that civilization has produced. When we pour scorn on the feudal spirit, we forget the frigid nomadism, the camping ground in the desert of flats and villas, with which we are replacing it. How is it that every step we take in the intellectual mastery of Nature leaves the world more uncongenial and unassimilable to our other faculties?

In Málaga we went to say goodbye to Don Carlos. He was sitting hunched up with a red muffler round his neck, his bald head rising steeply above it and his eyes gleaming, as he listened with the excitement of a schoolboy to the radio report of a football match. Cordova was playing Corunna and to his delight was one goal ahead.

"*Viva Andalucía,*" he said. "We'll show these Gallegos we can beat them."

And we had to sit down and wait patiently for the end of the match.

Then his wife and daughters came in, some refreshments were produced and we drew up to the table to eat them.

"You're leaving us very soon," said Doña María Luisa. "Are you tired of Málaga already?"

I protested vehemently. Málaga, I said, was an earthly paradise.

"Aha," said Don Carlos, laughing, "you know the saying *paraiso habitado por demonios,* a paradise inhabited by devils. That describes us completely. When you're with Malagueños, keep your eyes open."

Before long the conversation drifted on to politics. Here

Don Carlos had a very characteristic manner. He spoke as
though I must agree entirely with his point of view, yet
with a boastfulness and exaggeration that sought to beat
down beforehand any opposition that I might be tempted
to put up. He especially enjoyed saying things that would,
he supposed, shock my liberal conscience. Yet, like almost
everyone of his race, he was frank and truthful and said
without reticence what he thought of the weaknesses of
the regime.

His *bête noire* was the landowners, whom he accused of
being *cerrado* or stingy. They refused to raise wages, they
kept alive the black market and cared nothing if the regime failed. Even an American loan wouldn't make them
disclose their hidden supplies. Here of course he was vent-
ing the Falangist opinion. But it is also the opinion of
everyone else and if the higher ranks of the Falange were
not so corrupt and their system of control through the syndicates so rotten, they would be the strongest force in the
country.

When we left, Don Carlos, Doña María Luisa and their
whole family accompanied us back to our hotel with true
Spanish courtesy. Twenty years ago, they would have insisted on seeing us off at the railway station on the following day.

Going to the bank next morning to cash a check, I stood
waiting, while the usual forms were being filled in, beside
a nun of the order of St. Philip Neri. She told me that she
visited the banks twice a week to collect money for the
orphans whom her convent feeds and educates; they gave
her 5 pesetas at every bank and for that kept her waiting

half an hour. "Beggars have to learn patience," she said. Her merry face and twinkling eyes pleased me so much that I offered her a coin, and she told me that I was doing something for my happiness in the future life.

"If I thought that," I said, "I would give you all I had."

"Some people do," she answered with a smile.

GRANADA

OUR next destination was Granada. Instead of taking the usual bus or train, we decided to travel by the more direct but slower route through Alhama. This meant starting off in the little train we had taken before to Torre del Mar. So after an early lunch, we found ourselves rattling along once more beside the sea that glittered in the sunlight like a net of fishes. Black boats of the fishermen, white lateen sails and, when one stood on the platform at the end of the carriage, the peculiar salty smell of this sea which is so different to that of the Atlantic with its tides and wrack.

After Vélez the train began to climb on a cogged rail. All afternoon it wound among red earthy hills covered with vineyards, then descended at a breakneck speed, then climbed again toward the *bocada* or pass. Night fell. When we reached the summit, which is also the terminus, it was quite dark and we packed into the small bus that was to take us twenty miles on to Alhama.

It was ten o'clock when we arrived and very cold. We found our way to the *posada,* a clean whitewashed building which had a fire of oak logs burning under a great hooded chimney and a row of copper pots on a shelf above. Muleteers were lying asleep on the floor, rolled in their blankets. A meal was served and a lieutenant of the Civil Guard sat down with us. He was a Navarrese, precise and natty, with

a sharp, schoolmaster's voice and long white well-mani-
cured fingers.

"The times are bad," he said. "We are living among people any one of whom may have murdered our father or our
brother, and yet we have to treat them as if they were our
friends."

"And they," I answered, "as if you were theirs."

We went out to get a drink. The air of the street was
bitterly cold and the stars overhead shook and glittered.
From some way off came the sound of rushing water.

In the café sat the usual crowd of bored yokels; they
stared at us in their blank Iberian way while we sipped our
cognac; then we went home to bed.

At dawn we dragged ourselves up. A pale rosy light was
showing over the mountains and, going out to get some
coffee, we saw the long summit of the Sierra de Tejada,
apparently just above the town, covered with a deep blanket of snow. Below the square lay a deep gorge, at the bottom of which we could see and hear the river.

The castle of Alhama was once the key to Granada. Its
capture in 1482 from the Moors was a famous feat, celebrated in a ballad which Byron has translated. It still
stands, a square building with high, red, turreted walls;
today it is used as a granary.

As we drank our coffee, the market was opening. Groups
of dark-clothed countrymen stood about in caps and berets
and women wearing black handkerchiefs on their heads.
Although we had only come a few miles from the coast, we
were in a new world, austere, harsh, and puritanical. Even
the language was different. For girl they said *mozuela*

(maid) instead of *chica* and the accent struck an answering chord in me, for it was that in which I had first learned Spanish.

At eight the bus appeared and we set off. Bare, bone-colored hills, tinged with rose—thin young corn in places —no leaves or flowers. In the valleys a few poplar trees; every village smoking like a bonfire as the women lit their hearths with lavender or gorse. All the time we were descending. Soon we came to orchards bright with peach and apricot blossom, passed a cave village, passed low hills that looked like trains of pack animals, then another village destroyed by earthquake. Suddenly a great sight. Hanging in the air as if it were a cloud stood the Sierra Nevada, and below its smooth slopes of snow lay the green and brown plain of the Vega. Between them we could see Granada.

It was fifteen years since I had been in this town and more since I had lived here. I expected to find many changes. But in external appearances there were few. A new modernistic building put up here, a shop gone there and of course the usual decrease in the number of cafés and increase in the number of banks. But the change of atmosphere was striking. Granada had always been a sober town, austere and conventional as a provincial capital in Castile, though tempered by a certain Andalusian refinement, but now it seemed to me that it was more than austere—it was sad. The faces of the passers-by were long and gloomy, the shops were empty and the popular quarters had lost their animation. The Plaza Bibarrambla, once so gay and lively with its stalls of sweets, roasted chestnuts, and flour fritters, was dead and lifeless.

Yet the signs of great poverty, which had made such a painful impression in Cordova and Málaga, were lacking. People seemed to eat, even if they did not eat much; the irrigated Vega gave regular employment. But the result was not contentment. There was a suppressed anger and tension I had not seen anywhere else on my journey: the working men held their heads high and spoke with unconcealed bitterness, while even the beggars were disdainful, asked as if from right and pocketed the alms they got without thanks. I was told that the *fiestas,* once the delight of the city, had fallen off and that Corpus, with its famous processions, was observed without enthusiasm. And the police were everywhere.

The confectioners had been forbidden to make pastries and so were in a bad humor.

"There's no understanding our shortages," said one of them. "Last year there was a terrific crop of olives, yet this year oil is short. Two years ago there was a phenomenal wheat crop, yet the ration remained as before. The fact is that these gentry take our food and sell it abroad. This is a country of *pillos, muchos pillos,* rogues, many rogues. *Si, señor.*"

To change the subject I praised the large new blocks of flats at controlled rents that had been put up on the edge of the city.

"But their rents are a thousand pesetas a month. Who can afford that? *No, señor.* These flats are for the police and the black marketeers."

And two middle-class people who had come in to buy chocolate nodded their heads in approval.

Walking down the Gran Vía, we came to a new building of palatial size. It was a branch of the Banco de España. These new banks, put up on the proceeds of inflation, are to the present regime what the great cathedrals were to the Middle Ages. They symbolize the ruling passion. Close by stands the ugly Church of the Sacred Heart. As we passed it, a noisy crowd of several hundred young men was pouring out of it; they had been taking an Easter course of the Exercises of St. Ignatius. There is a curious connection between sweets and piety in Spain and every confectioner's shop has a notice enjoining young and old, masters and servants, to take them. Then in the church porch, beside the usual list of films that may safely and without risk to morals be seen, we observed a notice of the services to be held in honor of *Nuestro Señor de la Misericordia*, Our Lord of Pity, which are organized by a confraternity known as the Confraternity of Silence. I could not help thinking that the name of this confraternity had been well chosen, for when in 1936 *Acción Católica* was hunting down and killing the Liberals and Freemasons, the voice of pity was not heard. One is told—and not only by people on the Left —that during the first months of the Civil War between twenty and thirty thousand persons were shot in this town in cold blood. What reliance can be placed on such figures I do not know, but it seems to be the general opinion that in Granada the number of executions was higher in proportion to the population than anywhere else. It is significant that the patroness of the city, *Nuestra Señora de las Angustias,* Our Lady of Agonies, is represented by the figure of a weeping woman holding the head of the dead

Christ on her lap. In this city of blood and massacre she might stand for any woman of the working classes.

On the morning following our arrival we set off for a walk in the old Moorish quarter known as the Albaicín. Steep cobbled lanes, white houses rising above one another, terraced gardens. A stream of women and children moving up and down, but few men. A feeling of tension. After we had climbed a certain distance, we caught on our right the sound of dogs barking and the harsh jangling of a guitar; they came from the gypsy quarter with its whitewashed caves and grey-green cactus. Then we reached a little square with a crenellated gate and trees and in a few minutes were out above the houses on the open hillside.

How touching, in some way I cannot describe, are these *terrains vagues* of old cities, where the last houses meet and mingle with the countryside! Here was a wall of dried mud, an agave plant, and a leafless fig tree which, clumsy and babyish, groped in the air with its blunt fingers. An old woman carried a pitcher, a man was relieving himself, while far below lay the flat green plain, stretching away to its rim of mountains. From it there rose the crowing of cocks—faint, shrill and charged with distance and memory—into a grey sky that spread over everything.

Yes, that was the Albaicín as it used to be—yet why did it seem so changed, so different? As I sat listening to the cockcrows, the answer came to me. This was a city that had killed its poet. And all at once the idea entered my mind that I would visit, if I could find it, García Lorca's grave and lay a wreath of flowers upon it.

Next morning we set out to climb the hill of the Alhambra. The sun was shining and a dry wind raised the dust in eddies. As we passed the English pension, the intense pale blue of the sky, seen against the brown tops of the elm wood, gave me a thrill of excitement. This blue of Granada skies is to other blues what the color of fresh blood is to other reds and if one calls Spain, as well one may, the country of bloodshed, its pure sky-blue, like that of the Virgin's dress in a Fra Angelico picture, seems to be pitying that bloodshed.

We took the road that runs past the cypress avenue of the Generalife. Up this road, morning after morning, the lorries packed with prisoners had passed. The foreign visitors in the Washington Irving Hotel had listened to them changing gear and pulled the blankets over their heads when the shots rang out. After that the nightingales, noisy as frogs, had resumed their chug-chugging.

Crowning the hill in front of us stood the high white walls of the cemetery, where for generations all the *hijos de Granada* have been buried. As we came up to it we could see that a new enclosure, several acres in extent, had been added. We entered and began to wander among the graves. Soon, in the newest and poorest part, where the sun glared down and the wind blew the loose earth into eddies, we came on a man driving a small donkey.

"We are looking for a grave," I began, and explained the circumstances.

"Well," he said, "you will have to inquire at the office. The names of all those who were shot at the cemetery are recorded there."

"Really," I exclaimed, for I was surprised that they had taken the trouble to do this.

"Oh yes," he said. "Those who were shot here were shot by order of the military authorities and so all the formalities were observed. By every grave a label was put up with the name of its owner upon it and when three or four were buried together in the same grave, well, three or four names were written down."

"Were you here then?"

"Not me. I spent the war fighting on the Red side. When it finished and I'd done my term in the labor camps, I got this job."

Leaving his donkey, which was carrying a pannier of earth, he accompanied us back to the office. There a little old man, shabby and frail, came scraping up to us. On his nose, which was very thin, he wore a pair of steel-rimmed spectacles and on his head an official peaked cap which was too large for him. He listened to my inquiries with an air of reserve and obsequiousness, but the whole cast of his face expressed fear and sadness. At any moment, it seemed, these might descend in a landslide and bury him.

Whom did I say I was looking for? Federico García Lorca? Ah yes, he remembered the name, for we were not the first persons to have inquired about him. Only last year some foreigners—Argentines, he thought—had driven up to the gate with a wreath of flowers. But he had been unable to satisfy them. Señor García Lorca's remains had been dug up after the regulation five years in the earth because no one had paid the requisite fee for their removal

to a permanent resting place. They were now in the bone
pit.

"Could we see it?"

"Certainly. There is no objection."

And he handed to the man who accompanied us a large
key. Then, with the same sad, deferential manner with
which he had addressed us, he turned to bow to a funeral
party which had just arrived.

Jangling the key and talking breezily of the secrets of his
trade—how long, for example, it took corpses to decay in
the local earth—the gravedigger led the way across the
dusty, sun-drenched hillside, pitted with humble graves.
Then he stopped before a small enclosure surrounded by a
high wall.

"Here we are," he said, unlocking a door. "This is the
ossuary."

A curious sweetish smell met us as we entered and a disagreeable, uneasy feeling of isolation and silence. Like the
silence at a dinner party when someone has committed a
grave *faux pas*. Pulling ourselves together, we saw that we
were in a sort of open court scattered with torn and black-
ened fragments of clothing. It was as though a rag fair had
been held here a dozen years ago or a collection of gypsy
caravans made it their camping ground. But, quickly, our
eyes were drawn from these sordid remains to a pit which
lay in the center of the enclosure. It was some thirty feet
square, to all appearance deep, and filled to within a half a
dozen feet of the surface with skulls and bones. Among
these lay a few parched and shrunken bodies, lying in dis-

traught postures as though they had come flying down through·the air, and wrapped in moldering cerements.

"Here you have what was once the flower of Granada," said the man. "Look well and you'll see the bullet holes."

And in fact nearly every skull was shattered.

But what was that? Stretched across the rubble of bones, in an attitude of rigid attention, was a complete and well-preserved corpse, dressed in a green and black braided uniform. Its face, a little greenish too with dark markings, as though the flesh were trying to take on the color of the uniform, had the severe, self-concentrated look of a man who is engaged on some important task.

"Ah, that one!" exclaimed the gravedigger. "He's a fine bird. A colonel, if you please, of the Civil Guard. He's been lying for fifty years or so in one of the upper niches and that's why he's so well mummified. Even his complexion is as fresh as though he had just been laid out. We took him up the other day because his family have stopped paying the rent, and here he is."

A colonel of the police guarding the bones of the Reds whom his successors had shot! Could Goya have thought of a better subject?

"And how many would you say are buried in this pit?" I asked.

"Well, the list of those officially shot shows some eight thousand names. All but a few of them are here. Then there's a thousand or so more who had the originality to die natural deaths. *Vamos,* say nine or ten thousand. And all good friends, good company."

"Why do you say that?"

"Well, why not? They're all there together."

He laughed as he locked the door and, passing once more the donkey, still patiently waiting with its load of soil, we went back to the cemetery entrance.

"Can you point out to me," I asked, "where the executions took place?"

"I'll take you there," he said, pocketing my tip. "Then you won't lose yourselves."

"But what if that gets you into trouble?"

"No, why should it? They were officially shot, weren't they? By order of the military authorities. *Puñeta,* a great act of justice!"

And he led us out through the iron gates to the wall that bounds the lower side of the cemetery. The bullet marks were still there, and a few dried stains of blood. They had been bundled out of the lorries and machine-gunned in groups with the rope manacles still on them. Only the city councillors had been granted the privilege of lighting cigarettes and so showing the traditional contempt and defiance. There they had stood, looking at a red plowed field planted with olive trees and sloping up to the gradually brightening sky. After that—nothing.

We set off back to the town. Just beyond the Washington Irving Hotel, at the entrance to the wooded region of the Alhambra, lies the drive to the Carmen de los Mártires. Here St. John of the Cross had written his mystical works and M. Meersmans, a Belgian mine owner and prospector, had entertained his friends with bad dinners served on gold plate. A new, monstrous building had now shoved itself up, inscribed with the initials of the *F.E.T. de la Jons,* otherwise known as the Falange. Painted on the wall beside it was their symbol, a hand clutching a dagger dyed in red.

The more I thought over the results of this expedition, the less satisfied I was with them. The old man at the office had been elusive. The gravedigger's emphasis on official executions seemed to suggest that there had been others which could not be so classified. I decided to return to the cemetery that afternoon and to demand to see the list of those executed. If Lorca was really buried there, surely his name would be on it?

At four o'clock therefore we were back again. This time we made our way into that part of the cemetery where the middle classes are buried, either in niches round the patio walls or in more expensive marble tombs under the cypress trees. Here we started a conversation with two gravediggers, one of whom, the older and more talkative, had been present when the military rising began, and asked them to show us where those executed in 1936 had been reburied.

"You've come straight to the spot," replied the elder. "The most celebrated ones are all here."

And he led us to the grave of Montesinos, the Socialist mayor who had been Lorca's brother-in-law, and then to those of the city councillors and their officials, all of whom, with two exceptions, had been put to death. Next came the graves of various doctors, including that of a famous specialist in children's diseases. I knew his story: a much loved man, he had been shot, not on political grounds, but as a Freemason. Every group that supported the rising had had the right to proscribe its particular enemies and the

Church—or, to be more exact, Catholic Action—had put on its list the Masons and the Protestants.

Our guides, who took a professional interest in showing us the sights, now led us to a different part of the cemetery, where, among other things, we saw the corner where the postmen were interred; they had been shot, it appeared, because their jobs were wanted by other people. After this came what was evidently regarded as the highlight. In the civil section, where non-Catholics and prisoners who refused confession were buried, stood the tomb of the Protestant pastor, whose crime was that he had kept a free school for poor children in the Cuesta Gomeres. Poor man, he had been well liked by the foreign residents, including those who were Catholics, but even a British consul's friendship could not save him.

I observed that these tombstones all had the same formula for the epitaph, saying *ceased to exist* instead of *died* and at the end *Your mother (sister, daughters) will not forget you.* It would no doubt have been unwise to mention the unforgetfulness of brothers, sons, or fathers.

"All this is very interesting," I said at length, "but the person I am looking for is not 'here. Perhaps you can tell me where he is buried. He is called Federico García Lorca."

"That is a famous name," said the elder of the grave-diggers. "There is much talk about him."

"He is famous all the world over," I replied. "His poems are read from Buenos Aires to New York and London. Some of them have been translated into English."

"There you are," exclaimed the gravedigger to his companion. "These foreigners know more about us than we know about ourselves. I tell you, there's as much knowledge in one of their little fingers as there is in the whole of our bodies. Compared to them, we're nothing."

"That's it," agreed his friend solemnly. "Just savages."

"You don't understand me," I said. "This man whose grave I am looking for was a friend of mine. When many years ago I lived in Granada, I used to know him."

"Ah, that makes a difference. Still I must tell you that you've come to the wrong place. He is not here."

"I have been told that he was. Anyhow I want to see the lists."

"They are at the office. But I warn you that his name is not on them. I have been through them all many times."

"What are they like?"

"Well, there is just a list of names with a number after each. When the name was not known, as often happened, there was written *varón* or *hembra,* man or woman."

"Perhaps he was one of those unknowns."

"No, he was not. I tell you he is buried somewhere else —at Víznar."

"Víznar?"

"Yes, in the trenches in the *barranco.* They shot him there."

"How do you know?"

"How is anything known? These things come out." And he refused to say any more about it.

In the office I found the old caretaker alone, entering something with a scratchy pen in a ledger. I told him that I was not satisfied that García Lorca's remains were in the bone pit and asked to see the books in which the names of those shot had been recorded.

"I cannot show them without permission," he said, glancing up at me sharply. "You must go to the military authorities."

"At least tell me if my friend's name is on the lists."

He looked at me through his glasses in his half-frightened, half-appealing way.

"No, señor, it is not. The person you are inquiring about was not buried here."

"Then he was buried somewhere else?"

"Evidently."

"At Víznar?"

His eye met mine for a moment in an uncertain glance. Then without a word he gave a slight inclination with that perpetually deferential body of his and turned away. I could see his thin bent back and the scruff of grey hair that ran down his neck under his dirty collar as he scratched with his pen on the pages of the ledger. We went out.

The next two days were spent in making further inquiries. I had once known many people in Granada and though some of these were dead or absent, there were others who were ready to tell me what they could. One family in particular, who had had every opportunity for knowing what was going on, were most helpful. On calling on them I found that the horrors that had occurred when the military rising broke out thirteen years ago were as present to their minds as though they had happened yesterday. They described the nightly roaring of the lorries up the road to the cemetery, then the rattle of the volleys!

Every morning the wives and mothers of the people who had been arrested would climb the hill to search for the bodies of their menfolk. There they lay in heaps as they had fallen, till later in the day squads of Falangists would set about burying them. Since the labor of interring so many bodies was considerable, they were bundled into shallow cavities from which their feet and hands often stuck out. An English friend of mine who, at some risk to himself, visited the place a number of times, told me that he saw the bodies of boys and girls still in their teens. "But were they political?" Who could say? In the hysterical atmosphere of those days, anyone even remotely connected with the Left might find himself arrested and then, unless some person with influence put in a word for him, he would automatically be shot because the prisons had to be emptied to make room for fresh arrivals. The Spaniards' innate love of destruction, their obsession with death, their tendency to fanaticism found full vent in these orgiastic scenes because there was no civil or religious authority, no moral force or inhibition, that could restrain them. Were not the bishops, who alone could have put on the brake, as deeply committed as anyone else? The only pronouncement they made was no one should be killed without the opportunity for confession.

How catching the hysteria was may be seen from the fact that an ordinary English girl, whose parents were living in Granada, donned the uniform of the Falange, stuck a revolver in her belt and boasted that, like other Spanish *señoritas,* she had taken part in executions and shot men with her own hand. Later, when the European war broke

out, she returned to England and joined an ambulance
unit.

Whenever I inquired about García Lorca I heard, if any
place was mentioned at all, the word Víznar. Víznar is a
small village lying a few miles away in the hills and its
barranco or ravine was one of the Falangist burial grounds.
Such secret caches lie all over the country. But no one that
I met had visited the site and the story of Lorca's death
there was just hearsay. Further acquaintance, however,
with the gravediggers showed me that they belonged to a
sort of freemasonry concerned with the things of the dead
and that they had access to information that was not available to other people. Also they were without prejudices:
their interest in these matters was professional. This inclined me to believe that, when they said that García Lorca
was buried at Víznar, they had good reasons for thinking
so.

There was however a story current all over Spain about
his death that seemed at first sight to point to a different
conclusion. To explain this, I must recapitulate a little.
Lorca arrived in Granada a day or two before the military
rising broke out and, on the first news of this, took refuge
in the house of a friend and fellow poet, Luis Rosales, close
to the Cathedral. The fact that Rosales' brother, who also
lived there, was a leading Falangist appeared to offer complete protection, yet a couple of days later, during the
temporary absence of his hosts, a car manned by gunmen
drew up at the door and carried him away. None of his
friends ever saw him again.

For twelve years the Spanish censorship kept his name

and his books under an almost complete ban. Then in December 1948 José María Pemán, the leading publicist and author laureate of the regime, wrote an article in *A.B.C.* castigating his murder by unknown persons as a crime against the nation. The reason for this change in the official attitude seems to have been that Lorca's many admirers in the Argentine had created a prejudice against the Franco regime which was affecting the commercial negotiations then going on with that country. The blame had therefore to be shifted from the leaders of the military rising to certain irresponsible and criminal persons. But what persons? Only two authorized parties or groups of opinion existed in Spain—the Falange and the Clericals. They were on bad terms and it at once became the business of each to fix the blame on the other.

The first open blow in this controversy had already been struck by the Falangist ex-minister, Serrano Suñer. In December 1947 he gave an interview to a Mexican journalist, Alfonso Junco, in which he asserted that the man who had given the order to kill Lorca was the Catholic Conservative deputy to the Cortes, Ramón Ruiz Alonso. Such an accusation could not of course be published in the Spanish press, but it conveyed accurately enough what the Falangists were saying. They were organizing a whispering campaign to claim the poet for their friend and lay the blame for his death on the Clericals.

The story, as it is usually told, is as follows. A day or two after the beginning of the rising a rumor reached Granada that the playwright Benavente, who is still alive and well and writing as much as ever, had been shot in Madrid by the Reds. The Catholic deputy, Ruiz Alonso, was sitting in a café with his friends. "Well, if they have killed Benavente," he exclaimed, "we have García Lorca. Why doesn't someone go out and fix him?" And so, like Fitz Urse obeying Henry II's command to kill Becket, a couple of men got up and went out.

Now there is nothing inherently improbable in such a story; indeed, if there were not some truth in it, it would hardly be repeated so openly. García Lorca had scandalized the narrow-minded and provincial citizens of his town in the same way that Picasso scandalizes many people today. But there is more to be said about the motives for his assassination than that. Lorca was not only a poet; he was also the brother-in-law of the Socialist mayor of Granada, Montesinos, and the intimate friend and collaborator of Fernando de los Ríos, the leading Socialist intellectual in the city and the man most hated by every section of the Nationalists. Thousands were shot for less reason than this and, though Lorca had influential friends on the Right, he must have had even more enemies, not only among the Conservatives but in the ranks of the Falange. And who, one may ask, would have dared to take him from the house of a Falangist such as Rosales, unless he had the connivance and protection of other Falangists?

To understand the matter better, we have to throw our minds back to the confusion and horror of those weeks. The Falange was a loose, amorphous body organized like the Anarchists in small secret cells. The youth organization of the Catholic party had just joined it as a body and merged into it. Little terrorist groups drew up lists of peo-

ple to be shot, and no one questioned their actions so long
as they confined themselves to people who were not affili-
ated to the Right. So far as I was able to discover, all the
Black Squads which carried out the shootings wore Falangist markings. Thus, whoever bears the prime responsibility for García Lorca's death—and this is not a matter
which can be solved today—there seems no reason why it
should not have taken place at a Falangist center such as
Víznar. The only point to be decided was—had it?

As it happened, I was able to obtain a strong corrobora-
tion of the statement of the gravediggers. A friend put me
in touch with a person who claimed to have spoken to a
man who had been present. Lorca, this person said, had
been driven straight from Rosales' house to the Falangist
depot near Víznar. Then at dawn he had been taken to the
barranco or ravine close by and shot.

"Not everyone," said this man, "would tell you this, but
I am a person who has never meddled in politics or criti-
cized the regime, so I see no harm in repeating what I
know. Among ourselves we don't talk of these things, but
we haven't forgotten them. They lie at the bottom of our
minds and many people who have done things they had
better not have done are racked by fear and contrition.
Those most deeply implicated find themselves cold-
shouldered or have to put up with hints and pointed allusions, and some have fallen ill or gone mad through brooding on it. And now it seems that heaven is punishing Spain
for the evil her sons have committed. On both sides, of
course, on both sides—not only on ours."

The next step clearly was to go out to Víznar and see

whatever was to be seen there. Before doing this, however, we decided to drive to Fuente Vaqueros, the village where Lorca had been born and brought up. It lay some dozen miles away on the *vega* or irrigated plain, on the edge of an estate which had once been Godoy's and was now the Duke of Wellington's.

It was a beautiful drive. Clear, swift-running irrigation channels, islanded with watercress like a Downland stream; plantations of thin, mast-like poplars; barns for drying tobacco. The village, which was connected with Granada by a tram-line, was low, white and dusty; through the middle of it ran a broad thoroughfare, the plaza, planted with pollarded trees, at one end of which stood the usual group of unemployed laborers, staring in front of them with wooden expressions. Mules, oxcarts, pigs, goats, children— the whole place was one great farm, smelling of the soil and of its round of labors.

The house where Federico had lived was one of the largest in the village: a white, two-storied building with balconies, a roof of brown tiles and a concealed garden behind. Its unpretentious simplicity gave it a charm often lacking in more ambitious mansions. Next to it stood the church, long, low, color-washed, with a miniature tower—the image of a toy church in a child's picture book. Unfortunately, like so many other Spanish churches, it had been defaced by the Falangist symbols and claptrap set up over the porch. After this there was nothing more to be seen, so when we had paid our respects to the poet's aunt and cousin, who lived close by, we set off on our return journey,

over roads deeply rutted by oxcarts, between flat fields and
the grey poles of poplar trees.

Federico lived at Fuente Vaqueros till 1912, when his
parents moved to a house on the outskirts of Granada. We
visited this house too. It was a *casa de campo* set among
small fields, orchards and irrigation channels; white and
grave and secret, like all the old houses in Granada, with
two cypresses and a vine arbor in front of the door. Since
his mother and sister left for America, it has lain empty.

We were now ready to visit the burial ground at Víznar.
As soon as we had finished lunch we took a taxi at the
Puerta Real. Since our expedition required speed and
secrecy—for a visit to one of these caches was a delicate
affair, possibly dangerous had we been Spaniards—it was
important that we should have a taxi driver who would not
show too much curiosity in our movements. But to our dismay we found that the man we had chosen was not only
alert and intelligent, but a strong supporter of the regime:
he had been a driver to some important general during the
war and, though not a Falangist, spoke with high respect of
Franco. We should have to find some way of eluding his
vigilance.

The car left the main road and began to climb in sharp
twists and curves between corn terraces and olive trees.
Soon we reached the village, or hamlet rather, with its tall
white houses crowding round the church and a few large
plane trees.

"Where shall I stop?" asked the chauffeur.

"Here in the square," I answered. "I want to visit the
cemetery, where a friend of mine is buried."

Silent with astonishment the chauffeur got out and sent someone to fetch the woman who kept the key.

"I'll come with you," he said. But when he found that the cemetery lay some way off the road, he turned back reluctantly to guard his car.

We followed a narrow path along the edge of one of the *bancales* or stone-walled terraces. Drooping, feminine olive trees, corn and beans in flower and below us on the left the green flat plain, with Fuente Vaqueros in the distance. Here and there the frail tint of apricot blossom or a red-budded pomegranate tree.

The old woman who accompanied us prattled away without ceasing. Her mother, she told us, had always had a great devotion to the dead. Night and day she had kept a lamp burning for them in the cemetery and even when it rained, and even when snow fell, she would go there to tend it. "*Ay, Dios mío*," she used to say, "if it is wet and cold for us, isn't it colder and wetter still for them? There they lie, *los pobrecillos*, out in that place with nothing to comfort them." Then when she was dying, when she was about to set out on her last journey and join them, she had said to her daughter, "*Ay, hija mía*, how can I bear to die? For when I am gone, who will tend the lamp in the cemetery, who will look after the poor dead?" And so she, her daughter, had answered, "I will tend the lamp and look after the dead, please God, as long as I live." And her mother, hearing that, had died in peace.

She informed us that though she had worked at the factory at a wage of 1 peseta a day, she had never failed to find time to visit the cemetery and pray there. To her it was more than the church, more than the saints. She felt such pity for those poor dead, lying there so far from the village and its animation. Even when there was no oil to keep the lamp burning, she managed to find it. And all the time, as she walked, she kept sighing and turning her beads and muttering snatches of prayer, among which one caught a great many *ay ay*s and *madre mía*s and *pobrecillo*s.

Soon we saw the cemetery below us, a little high-walled enclosure like a cattle pen. Inside was a commotion of mounds and hollows, with here and there a few cheap wooden crosses and artificial wreaths, mostly broken and dilapidated: the rubbish heap of a country where the only things ever thrown away as useless are dead bodies.

The woman apologized: this was a poor village—the rich were taken for burial to Granada. And at once she began to pray, interjecting her mumblings with exclamations of how cold it was here on winter evenings and yet what a small sacrifice this was to make to the Lord.

The time had come for us to say what we wanted.

"Listen," I said. "We have come here in search of the grave of a man who was shot as a Red during the first days of the war. Can you help us?"

She did not answer, so I repeated my request.

"There are three or four buried here," she muttered and led the way to the place. Then, as we stood reading the names on the crosses, the impulse to talk became too great for her and she told us their story.

One day some civil guards had brought these men here in manacles and had shot them against the wall. But as soon as they had left, one of the men, who had only been wounded, had begun to creep away. Along the hill he had gone, under the olive trees, dragging himself on his hands and knees and leaving a trail of blood behind him on the ground. But someone had seen him and given word to the guards, and they had brought him back and shot him, this time dead. Ay, such a pity! The whole village had wept as though he were their own. Later they heard that a pardon had come for him. But of what use, *Dios mío,* were pardons to him now? Then, after many years, two women had come to visit his grave. Tall women, beautifully dressed, in black from head to foot, and they had wept a great deal. And after they had finished weeping, they had prayed and had asked her to pray too.

I now felt that the moment had come to put my cards on the table.

"My friend is not buried here," I said, "but in the trenches in the *barranco.* Do you know where that is?"

"In the *pozos* or pits, you mean. Ay, ay, who doesn't know? But since those days no one has dared to go there."

"Will you explain to me how I can find them?"

"They're quite close. I'll take you."

We were leaving the cemetery when a man appeared, wearing a brass-studded bandolier slung diagonally across his chest. He introduced himself as the *regidor* of the village municipality and asked, very politely, what our business was. I replied that I was looking for the grave of a friend who had been shot during the war. I wished, before returning to my country, to say a few prayers over it.

"Have you found it?" he asked.

"Not yet. It seems that he is buried in the *pozos.*"

The man did not speak for some moments. Then:

"If you wish to go there," he said, "that is your affair. But you must excuse me if I do not accompany you. The *consejo* has no jurisdiction in such matters."

"I shall only be there a few minutes," I said to reassure him.

"The fewer the better. *Vaya Usted con Dios.*"

We set off. After following the path for some time we came up onto the road beyond the village.

"Where does this road lead?" I asked.

"To the spring which is just beyond the *barranco*," replied the woman. "There it stops. That is why it is called the Camino de la Fuente. In the days before the war it used to be the village *paseo*: people walked along it on Sunday evenings and took the air. They drank a little water from the spring, for this water is famous all round these parts and very fattening, and the children played here. But now no one goes along it—no one."

The last patch of cultivation was coming to an end and the road began to plunge into the mountains. On our left, just below it, stood a largish red house, ugly and new, built apparently as a summer villa. It was known, our guide told us, as La Colonia. Before the military rising it had been a sort of Brown House for the Falangists of Granada, where they had met and received training. They had also brought their girls here and danced. Then, when the rising had broken out, it had been put to different uses. Every night three or four lorries had roared up the road with their load of prisoners and had deposited them here. A Falangist priest was waiting to confess them and the parish priest was

fetched as well; poor man, he had to be present—that was
the regulation. Then they were taken down to the ravine to
be — you understand, some by the light of the lorries'
headlamps and some at dawn. Women too. The *Escuadra
Negra* (here the woman lowered her voice), the Black
Squad stuck at nothing.

"And who dug the graves?"

"In the basement of the house they kept prisoners for
work of that sort and later on, so it was said, they shot
them too. *Ay, Dios mio,* what terrible things were done!
To think that Christian men should do such terrible
things!"

From where we stood we could see the road twisting like
a snake in front of us. It ran into a ravine—the *barranco*—
came out of it and ended. All round us were bare shaly
slopes, dotted with occasional dry bushes. Below lay the
green *vega* and its villages, among them that where Federico had been born, and in front, rising sheer above us, a
mountain of harsh grey rock, its summit crowned with
stunted pines and pointed rock pinnacles. On one of these
had been placed an iron cross.

A few minutes more and we had reached the bridge over
the ravine. As we drew near it, the woman, who had ceased
her chatter, began to mumble prayers and tell her beads
with increasing energy. A little path led up the side of the
dry watercourse and there, fifty yards on, was the place. It
was a gentle slope of blue clay, scattered with rushes and
thin sedge grasses, a deposit from the freshets that ran
when the *barranco* was in spate. The entire area was pitted
with low hollows and mounds, at the head of each of which

had been placed a small stone. I began to count them, but gave it up when I saw that the number ran into hundreds.

"They buried them here," said the woman, "in shallow pits and then pushed earth over them. What a thing to do! Weren't they all sons of God and Christians who crossed themselves as we do?"

And she began to pray aloud in a low tone, "Holy and Immaculate Virgin, be with us now and in the hour of our death. . . . Be with us now and in the hour of our death."

As I stood there on the pitted clay, I heard a sound and saw that our car had followed us and was drawn up below. The chauffeur had got out and, to the evident alarm of the woman, was climbing the path toward us. However, when he saw us standing motionless with bared heads, he stopped and removed his hat too.

I waited, trying to fix the scene in my mind. In front rose the red, shaly side of the *barranco*—just one little sample of the interminable, barren mountain slopes of this country; on the right lay the green *vega*, with the Sierra de Elvira rising like a volcanic island out of it. Above, the mountain. Such had been the poet's last view, as the dawn rose in brightening circles in the sky and the cockcrows floated up from the plain like their own echoes. I picked a blue grape hyacinth, the only flower growing there among the rushes, and came away.

> *Ay amor*
> *que se fué y no vino!*
> . . . .
> *Ay amor*
> *que se fué por el aire!*

We drove for some distance without speaking. Then I began to explain to the chauffeur why I had come here—to visit the grave of a great poet whom I had once known.

"Yes," he said, "there has been a lot of talk about this man. The truth is that many terrible things were done during the war by both sides. I fought for Franco and I have always been loyal to him, but there is no use in disguising the fact that we lost the use of our reasons. The only difference between us was that the Reds showed more savagery and the Nationalists more self-respect. We may have shot more than they did, but at least we did not rape women or torture. We killed, *y ya está*—and that was that."

And he went on to tell me of how, on entering an Andalusian village with the troops, they had found some men who had been tied alive to posts and set fire to.

"Yes," he continued, "between us all we have brought disgrace on Spain. Once it was a happy country; now it is a miserable one, racked from end to end with hatred. One can scarcely find a family that has not had some of its members led out to death like animals. The only thing the war has done for us has been to brutalize us."

I felt that he was speaking the thoughts of every decent person in the country, whatever his political persuasion. But when I suggested that they might at least take these bodies to the cemetery and give them Christian burial—

"No," he replied, "let them stay where they are. There are bodies buried like this in every *barranco* in Spain."

Was it certain that we had visited García Lorca's last resting place? I felt no absolute conviction. To resolve my doubts, I went to see a friend of the poet's who had Falangist affiliations. From him I got a vague and confused story: the real culprits were the Clericals; the place of burial was thought to be La Conijera, a rifle range about a mile from the center of the city. If I wished for further information, I should call on a person whose name he gave me at the Falangist headquarters. But I could not do this without risking an inquiry into my activities which might compromise the people who had talked to me. In Granada the Falange was still powerful.

I had however one last source of information open to me. I had been given the name of a well-known person in the city who, I was assured, could tell me the whole story. That evening I contrived to meet him. I was quite right, he said. García Lorca had been shot at the *barranco* at Víznar after being made to dig his own grave. There could be no possible doubt about it, for he had spoken to a person who had been present and who had recognized him. And he added other details. His sad and serious manner convinced me that he was speaking the truth and, as he was not a Clerical, there could be no question of his being actuated by political bias. I left Granada the next morning feeling that, though absolute certainty was impossible, my search for the poet's tomb had not been thrown away.

CORDOVA *and* THE SIERRA MORENA

Wε rose at dawn. The houses were the color of women's bodies, the air still. Through the bare network of the plane tree we could see far above us the snow banks of the Sierra Nevada, like a great double bed which no one had slept in. We watched them turn to a chilly rose, drank a coffee and cognac, and got into the bus.

The journey began. Pinos Puente, Alcalá, Priego, Baena, Castro del Río, Espejo, Fernan Nuñez, Cordova. Nine hours in a bus without a silencer, with broken windows, over mountain roads full of potholes. I had a feverish cold coming on and saw the things that went by in a sort of dream. I only remember that we passed peasants seated sideways on mules and carrying umbrellas, passed men wearing striped ponchos and driving black goats, passed white poverty-stricken *pueblos* packed round their ruined castles, passed olives, rocks, cornfields, rocks, olives, descended into dry riverbeds choked with tamarisk and oleander, ascended past little farms where the peach and apricot were in flower. After Espejo, where the Duchess of Osuna's castle was occupied, we crossed the hollow plain of Munda where Julius Caesar destroyed the army which the Spanish landlords had raised for the younger Pompey, but by this time I was too tired to take an interest in anything but the prospect of supper and bed.

We went to a different hotel, a larger, more expensive place which had recently been done up. Our room had a private bathroom with boiling water in the taps, a bidet called *La Santísima Trinidad,* and a lavatory with an American noiseless plug that, just to show that this was Spain, gave a low bubbling whisper. What a change from the fury and the mire of Andalusian W.C.s! They are the Achilles heel of Southern hotels. Either the whole place is choked and unapproachable, or the cistern echoes like a triumphant cockcrow when one pulls it and the water drips in large cold blobs on one's head. I once made a collection of the names of Spanish lavatory fittings and found that in the dry regions, where no water ever came when one pulled the cord, the commonest appellation was *Niagara.* A symbol, one might once have said, of the Spanish political scene. Yet it is precisely in the hotels and *fondas* that have these catastrophic lavatories that the food is best and the general atmosphere most sympathetic.

Ting tong, tingety tong, tingety tong. I am awakened by the bell of San Hipólito ringing in a low minaret just outside the window. It is rung by two little boys who stand in the bell tower beside it and push it with their hands. Andalusia does not know the bell rope, or rather regards it as a luxury reserved for cathedrals. All the Cordovan churches produce the same harsh cacophonous tintinnabulations excepting only the Church of the Sacred Heart which, being Jesuit, gives out a correct and punctual sound like a dinner bell. Then as I lie in bed, for I have a slight temperature, my wife brings me a packet of letters from the post office and it is strange to remember that there is a country called England with people in it whom long ago I used to see and talk to. Here, but for three or four friends, I could live *ad aeternitatem*, speaking my bad Spanish and sunk in the pleasure of contemplating the scenes around me. Such is the efficacy of the Southern sun and light and of the easy ways of eating, drinking, idling, and conversing which these old Mediterranean civilizations have evolved! England is a fine country for many things, but, unless they go abroad, its inhabitants cannot know the true meaning of *la douceur de la vie*.

I spent the day reading a little booklet which someone I scarcely knew had pushed into my hands at Granada. It was a collection of letters, clandestinely published a year ago, by a man called Manuel Hedilla, with the answers to them by Serrano Suñer and other political personages. Hedilla was the successor to José Antonio in the leadership of the Falange, but when in 1937 this party was compulsorily united to the Traditionalists, he was pushed out. His friends prevented him from being taken for a ride, but they could not stop his serving a sentence of ten years' imprisonment, without any charge having been preferred against him.

Hedilla's letters give an interesting picture of how revolutionary leaders feel when the tide turns against them. He complained bitterly that he had been starved and ruined in health, while his family had been reduced to poverty because he was unable to support them. Such cruelty revolted him, yet not for one instant did it pass through his head that more than a million Spaniards had suffered worse treatment than this, and that he had been and still was one of the chief supporters of these things. What seemed cruel when applied to himself was proper and right when applied to his political opponents. Such egoism—it is one of the marks of our charming times—is surely revolting.

Another interesting thing in this book was the complete frankness with which Hedilla recognized the fact that in political trials the judges received previous instructions from above. As in Communist countries, no case was judged on its merits. Here for once his own sufferings seem to have opened his eyes, for his letter to Franco on the injustice of the regime is as outspoken as anything that has been written from the anti-Fascist side. Certainly the Falangists are as disillusioned as anyone else.

March 30

GOING out for the first time since our arrival, I find the poplars and the plane trees in leaf. It is spring. The sky is blue with a faint tinge of white cloud dissolving in it, the sun is hot and the streets bathed in warmth and color. The city has opened out like a flower in the sunlight. We went for a stroll in the northeastern quarter of the city where the working classes live. Here too every house has its interior court or patio, and I was struck by the fact that these patios of the popular districts, with their flower pots and lemon trees and thick coats of whitewash, are more beautiful than those of the baroque palaces with their *azulejo* wainscots and marble columns.

Cordova certainly makes the impression of being a great city. Its walls give out a feeling of history and of the suc-

cession of civilizations. It spreads far over the plain in spite
of its narrow carriageless streets because every house, even
the poorest, has to have its interior court. There is hardly
a corner in it from which one cannot see some church
tower of worn yellow stone, carved in baroque scrolls or
inlaid with Mozarabic lattice work, rising from a nave
that, on the outside at least, is medieval. Then, sooner or
later, stretched across the top of the street, one catches sight
of the long horizontal line of the Sierra Morena, lowest of
all the great ranges, yet imposing by the sense it gives of
being a wall or curtain.

Bearing off to the right we came to a long thorough-
fare, lined with flowering orange trees, that sweetened the
air with their scent. At the bottom lay the square of the
Potro with its obelisk to the Archangel Michael, its *posada*
where Cervantes may have stayed and its exquisite fountain. Beyond it the river, which had more water in its
channel than when we had seen it last. A few tub-shaped
boats, belonging to fishermen, were being rowed up it,
and across it—on the further shore—we could see the well-
remembered line of straggling poplar trees, the dejected
village, tethered horses, and all the lineaments of a scene
that appeared to come straight from the pages of Borrow.

On our way back to the hotel a group of young friars
passed us, striding along with their characteristic loose
gait like so many black, flopping birds. It is remarkable
how many new recruits the Church has obtained, seeing
what a dangerous profession it offers them. In the Cathedral
a marble plaque gives the names of eighty-one priests of
the diocese who were murdered during the first weeks of

the war. A large number, when one remembers that only a part of the diocese was occupied by the Reds.

In one of the narrow streets by the market place a man came up to us and asked in a shamefaced way if he could show us the sights of the city. He was dressed in old frayed clothes, but belonged to the middle classes. I asked him what he worked at. He told me that he was a *cesante,* that is an unemployed government clerk, and that he had a wife and four children to support. How do such people live? This middle-class poverty touches me even more than that of the working classes because, with its loss of status, it gives rise to greater suffering. One cannot move in this town, or indeed anywhere in Spain, without meeting the furtive eyes of some famished father of a family, who is too proud or too clumsy to beg. As a contrast one may see in the smartest men's hat shop in the city a resplendent gold crown or tiara which has been made for the *Virgen de la Soledad.* There it lies among the natty felt hats, and a knot of people is always gathered on the pavement in front to look at it. In medieval times such spectacles consoled the poor for their poverty, but today they have, I feel sure, the opposite effect. What the Church needs at present is the spirit of San Juan de Dios and St. Francis, but, so far as my observation goes, only the nuns of the charitable orders and one or two bishops have realized this.

Our object in returning to Cordova was to visit certain places connected with the poet Góngora which we had not been able to see before. For this purpose we went to call on Don José Rey, the official chronicler of the city and part-time teacher at the Escuela Normal. He was a tall, stout, well-dressed man, the type of successful lycée schoolmaster, a little pompous and self-satisfied in his manner but with a pleasant sense of humor. When I told him that I had a house near Málaga, he said that he knew it must have the best climate in Spain because once, when he was visiting the town in winter, he found eight bishops staying there. He was very anxious that I should call on a certain canon of the Cathedral of Cuidad Real, where I had said we were going, because he spoke the most beautiful Castilian he had ever heard. His idiom, he said, was so rich that often he used four adjectives to qualify a noun. How typical of a Cordovese (Cordova was the birthplace of Seneca) to admire eloquence!

He took us to see Góngora's house—a modest two-storied building with an arcaded patio—in the Calle Tomás Conde, off the Plaza Maimonides. Góngora's poetry, he said, was full of local allusions: when, for example, in his early and delightful *romance, Hermana Marica,* he mentioned a *panadería* or bakery where he had played as a child, he was speaking of a place that really existed a few doors from his own house.

Don José then took us to his office at the town hall to show us a large scale map of the surroundings of the city, by which we might find our way to the Huerta de Don Marcos. This is the country house to which Góngora retired in 1612 to write what is without doubt the greatest long poem in the language. *Soledades,* as it is called, introduced a new era in poetry by its combination of brilliant and daring imagery with that sense for the aural values of words which one associates with Vergil and Milton, but its diction is precious and obscure and for that reason it was condemned by the taste of the eighteenth and nineteenth centuries. Clearly one could scarcely have a more interesting literary site than the house to which this great poet deliberately retired to compose his masterpiece, yet till I met Don José Rey I had been unable to discover a single person in Cordova who had heard of it. I suspect that at bottom no Spaniard really believes that there are such people as great men, or, if he does believe it, he resents it. If he cared to take the trouble, he thinks, he could do as well or better himself.

Since my cold was still heavy, we took a taxi for a couple of miles along the main road to the sierra. On our way we passed a settlement of several hundred miserable shacks built of corrugated iron and branches. The new housing estate of the working classes! I asked the chauffeur if any houses with cheap rentals had been put up since the war. "Thousands," he replied, and when I asked where they were, he said, "Everywhere." It turned out, however, that these only existed on paper: the Bishop of Cordova was planning to build a model workmen's estate of eight hundred houses, but work on them had not yet started. So housing has become a Church affair in Cordova too and the money is collected not from taxation but by charitable subscriptions!

After crossing a ravine we dismissed the taxi and started walking up a small path. We were in a valley of thin grass and rocks, with stunted olive trees and ilexes dotted about and a rushy stream at the bottom. Women were washing clothes and spreading them out to dry on the stones and a ragged child was herding cattle. After some ten minutes the valley opened out and we saw in front of us a whitewashed farmhouse with an old dilapidated building at its door. Behind, the viaduct of the Sierra Morena railway spanned the valley with an iron bridge. The ground about us was scattered with flowers—star of Bethlehem, dwarf iris, periwinkles—and yellow swallowtail butterflies fluttered about. Under an olive tree I picked a specimen of that rare plant, the military orchis, which I knew from the plate in Bentham's *Flora* but had never found before.

The Huerta de Don Marcos is today a small, poorly kept farm, with an *alberca* or tank fed by a spring and below it a scrap of derelict garden planted with orange trees. The farmer was out, but his wife showed us the place. Her amazement on learning that a famous man had once lived in her humble dwelling reminded me of that of Molière's *bourgeois gentilhomme* on being told that he spoke in prose: she begged me to write down all the particulars, so that she could show them to her husband. The stone house where Góngora had lived had been in good condition twenty years ago, but was now falling into ruin. The bridge-like entrance leading direct to the upper floor had half collapsed, though the ogival door on the other side was still in good condition. At present the building served as a hen house, but the landlord had announced that he meant to pull it down and use the stones to put up a pigsty.

O Cordova, Cordova, city of the Senecas and the caliphs and still rich in oil and corn and money, is this how you treat the house of your illustrious poet? I believe that we are the only people to have visited this place knowing its history since Góngora's biographer, Don Miguel Artigas, rediscovered its existence in the 1920's and a group of young writers posed for their photographs here. Yet no name is held in higher esteem among lovers of Spanish literature today.

We stood looking out on the valley with its rocks and olives and ilex trees. No other house was in sight, though in the seventeenth century a mill stood below on the stream. A Spanish Arcadian setting, which made one understand why Góngora had called his poem *Soledades* and how the whole enterprise—for the poet was a lover of towns and gaiety—bore an analogy to the hermitages of the sierra and the habit worldly people had of making retreats there. Góngora, with his aspirations for a purer poetry, was the first of those famous hermits who have segregated themselves for the sake of literature.

The farmer's wife was full of complaints of the difficulty of life. Their landlord, though he lived in Cordova, had not visited the place for ten years, yet he refused to spend a penny in repairs and had several times raised the rent. He lived above his means and had no profession.

"Times such as these," she said, "have never been known before. Today the people who work are ground to dust."

As we climbed the slope, we saw a decent-looking young couple squatting in a scooped-out rock shelter that gave only a few feet of protection from the weather.

"Where else can we go?" the man said. "I work in Cordova and there are no rooms available. All over the country people are living like this."

Just across the brow of the hill was a large new building,

comfortably appointed, with the air of a palace hotel. It was evidently just finished. I inquired of a woman who was living outside its gate what it was. "The friars live there," she answered, but when I asked what friars, she did not know. And no one knew, for no one had spoken to them.

We came up with an elderly man who was walking along, bent low under a sack of charcoal. He looked thin and haggard; his trousers had long tears in them and his rope shoes barely kept on his feet. He told us that he made a small living for his family by carrying charcoal down from the sierra and selling it. Once he had had mules and had been in the charcoal business, but the Falange had taken his mules and his house and everything.

"I suppose then that you fought on the other side."

"No. I was in hospital when the war started, so I never had the chance. But I was a working man and for them that was enough."

He spoke with admiration of the humanity and fairness of the English, for his father had been the foreman to an English mining engineer and he had heard much about them. "If it were possible to emigrate to England or America," he added, "not a single working man would remain in Spain."

One simply cannot escape from this horrifying poverty. When we sat down to drink a lemonade in a small café by the station, a number of wretched children walked past us; some were covered with sores, another had only one eye, another an enormous growth behind her ear, another was crippled. Such is the young generation of Spaniards which the Franco regime is bringing into the world! Yet the papers are full of photographs of a train full of Austrian working-class children who are being received and fêted all over the place. What can the Spanish poor think who read that? As in Mussolini's Italy, everything in this country is done for show and advertisement.

Take for example the tuberculosis hospitals which are being put up in many provinces. The local papers today contain an announcement of a 600,000 pesetas fund which is being raised to build one in the sierra. One may recognize the good intentions shown by such schemes, even when many of their promoters merely see in them new opportunities for graft, yet ask what is their use when, owing to the lack of sufficient nourishment, every working-class and lower middle-class street in the province is a tuberculosis factory.

As we were to leave Cordova the next day, we walked down for the last time to look at the river. Taking a new route, we came on it suddenly at the end of a narrow street. It was six o'clock; the further shore was flooded by light from the sun, glowing with pale golds and clamant greens that were higher in key than are usually to be seen in a landscape. The water was a dim glassy blue, the line of houses low and white, while in the background the wave-like downs of the *campiña* took on a rich crystalline translucence. No wonder that the emir Abd-er-Rahman I felt himself at home here, for we seemed to be standing in an Eastern city on the banks of the Euphrates.

April 1

We had wished to travel through the Sierra Morena to Mérida in Estremadura. There is a railway line serving a number of small mining towns, but the only train left Cordova just before dark and ran all night As we wanted to see the country and also to sleep, this route was useless. On my asking the woman at the tourist office why Spaniards preferred to travel by night, she replied, "Because they thus save the expense of a night in a hotel and do not mind missing a night's sleep." That is the Spaniard all over. He is a man without conflicts. He believes he is always in the right whatever he does and this conviction gives him more vitality and allows him to do with less sleep, since it is in sleep that psychic conflicts are resolved.

We decided therefore to change our plans: to go in two stages to Ciudad Real in La Mancha, see whatever was to be seen there and then turn westward to Mérida. This would mean having less time to spend in Estremadura, but we already knew that country fairly well, whereas we had never set foot in La Mancha. Our first stage would consist in a motorbus drive through the Sierra Morena to Pozoblanco.

We started early and soon began to climb. The hillslopes were thickly wooded with ilexes, cork oaks and Turkey oaks, the latter in the wealth of their pale golden blossom. Under them grew the mauve and the white cistus, two kinds of lavender and whitish lupins, together with evergreen shrubs such as lentisk, arbutus and myrtle. All the

175

usual flora of the maquis. After ascending for a thousand feet or so we reached the Cerro Muriano, a small plain famous for its paleolithic implements and for having been the scene of various battles in Arab times. There was also a characteristic skirmish here during the Civil War, which has been vividly described by Dr. Borkenau in his book *The Spanish Cockpit*. After passing it, the labyrinthine nature of this sierra, which is not a mountain range but the edge of the Castilian tableland, flexed and fractured in a number of parallel lines, began to reveal itself. We plunged into a deep valley planted with olive trees, which with its spurs and tributary water channels took us over an hour to cross. These olive trees, by the way, are of recent growth and, since there are no villages near, the pickers—men, women, and children—come in their thousands from all the districts round and camp in the open for a month.

Another col and we were in a wilder country of ilexes and *jarales*, as heaths covered with gum cistus are called. In the *monte bajo* to left and to right there are wolves, wild boar and red deer, as well as bandits. One may read in Cicero's correspondence of the bandits who hung out here in Roman times and no doubt these hills were never free of them till the Civil Guard rounded up the last in the 1880's. Now, as a result of the Civil War, they are back again, though posts of soldiers keep the road open for the twice-weekly bus. We drove past some ruined houses which mark the old trench lines and then, after three and a half hours of driving, came out on the open *meseta* or tableland. In front of us lay Pozoblanco.

It was an ugly place. Its glaring red tiles contrasted with its whitewashed granite building stone gave it a crude, unfriendly appearance. The plain around it, intersected by loose stone walls, was treeless, like the country about Aberdeen. However, the small *fonda* was clean and pleasant and we sat down to an adequate meal.

After coffee we went out to explore the neighborhood. Soon we came to a large open space at the edge of the town. Threshing floors, a fountain and washing place, donkeys grazing, women carrying pitchers on their heads. Not a tree anywhere and all round us the great bleak plain, rising here and there into rock-crowned eminences.

The road we took led across the *dehesa,* or town common land, and on it there were many yokes of mules and horses plowing. After a little we came to two men sitting by the side of the road. We saluted them and a conversation of the usual sort began.

"When the war ended," said the elder, "we thought we could live as well under Franco as under anyone else. All we wanted was to work and eat. But on the wages we get, how can we eat? The day laborer's wage is 14 pesetas and when the rent is paid we have only enough left to buy our rations. And what are they? A hundred grams of bread a day and a liter of oil a month. Yet Spain is *la madre del aceite,* the mother of olive oil."

"The only hope," said the young man, "lies in emigration. But that is almost impossible. I would like to go to France, but the frontier is too well guarded. A few weeks ago they caught some young men from this town trying to cross it. Well, you know what that means! Beatings and more beatings and more beatings. And then a prison sentence that takes ten years out of your life."

"If only," chimed in the elder, "we could get back to the times of Primo de Rivera! Never have we lived so well as we did under him. He built roads, railways, irrigation works and saw that the working man got good wages. That was why they sent him off to die brokenhearted. No, Spain has never before had such a great man as him."

"You English are to blame," said the young man. "You defeated Fascism in Germany but you left it in power here. You had only to flick your fingers and Franco would have gone and the Republic come back. But for your own reasons you preferred not to flick them. Now our only hope lies in Russia."

"Do you see those boys hoeing in the furrows?" said the elder. "I'll bet you'll never guess what they are doing. They are collecting grass roots. They carry them off in sacks and wash the earth out of them and feed them to the mules and asses. That's all the fodder they get now—the roots of couch grass!"

"Beyond that hill," said the young man, "the whole country for leagues around is covered with evergreen oaks. We used to go there when we were short of food and pick the acorns to make them into *gachas* (porridge) or else bread. But if anyone goes there today the Civil Guard beats him and drives him off. The acorns are kept for the pigs."

"For example, do you know what we have eaten today? A few scraps of bread with some bad oranges. Tonight we shall go home and the wife will have a little flour and beans cooked in water to give us. No oil, as our ration is finished. But the cruel thing is that this hunger is destroying family life. The children cry, their mother beats them and everyone scolds everyone else. There used to be a great deal of love and affection in our families, but there is little now. We are becoming brutalized."

"That's what they want," said the young man. "They want to destroy our human nature. They want to turn us into animals. That's their program. And meanwhile the rich, who own all the land except this *dehesa,* do nothing but eat and drink, drive about in cars, and seduce our women. Those are the people you English keep in power over us."

They were an unusually alert and intelligent couple. The young man had got the rudiments of an education while attached to a Republican division during the war; there too he had learned to hope, and now his hopes had been disappointed. As I did not know how to answer him, I inquired about the *dehesa.* Every townsman, they said, had the right to a strip of land on it, but he could work it only if he possessed a *yunta,* or yoke of horses or mules, and some seed corn. The price of such a *yunta* was £ 300.

We continued our walk to the summit of the rise. Granite boulders, thin sandy soil, and a few ilexes. Below lay the broad stony plain of Pedroches and beyond it a rim of mountains, rising steeply like islands out of it. No flowers except for a minute geranium and a chickweed.

On our way back we met a road mender, who told us that his daily wage, paid by the State, was 11 pesetas.

"How on earth do you live on that?" I asked.

"One can't call it living," he replied, "but we get along somehow because we keep a few goats and chickens. Also we pay no rent."

Although Pozoblanco belongs to the province of Cordova, it cannot be said to lie in Andalusia. That low step up from the Guadalquivir valley to the *meseta* lands one in an altogether different geographic and ethnic region. Take architecture. The houses with their deep windows and granite lintels look cold and severe, and the streets new and plain. The absence of weathering robs them of their age. On passing through the main door one comes as a rule to a large vaulted room, low-roofed like a *bodega* or cellar, with other smaller rooms of the same kind opening off it. No patio. In the café, for example, where several vaulted rooms have been run together, one has the impression of sitting in a crypt.

The people, too, are quite different to the Andalusians. They are hard and dour, with a look of purpose and determination which one certainly does not see south of the Sierra Morena. The prevailing type, to which everyone tends, is the *yuntero,* or owner of a team of mules. Big, stolid men dressed in blue or black blouses that are buttoned tight at the neck and then hang loose to display a corduroy waistcoat and cotton trousers; on their heads a black cloth cap or beret. A real peasant type, hard working and relatively prosperous. In Andalusia, on the other hand, the peasant does not exist. The land there produces a lighter, more mobile sort of man, who, as soon as he has a little money, shines his shoes and dresses up as a *señorito.*

At heart all Andalusians are town dwellers, quick, emotional, talkative and artistic.

The war history of Pozoblanco is as follows. At first the Civil Guard seized the town without fighting. Then, a month later, the Red militia captured it and massacred its defendants to the number of 150. Although seven months later the Nationalists advanced from Cordova to its outskirts, they were driven back and did not succeed in taking it till the end of the war. During their occupation the Reds killed 500 of its 15,000 or so inhabitants (or according to another informant 300)—in other words all its white-collar citizens who had not managed to escape. Most of these were shot in the prison ship at Valencia during the last Communist-controlled stages of the war.

The confectioner of La Primitiva—this was the appropriate name of his dingy little shop—gave me a graphic account of his escape through the sierra, but did not seem to bear any grudge for the danger he had run. Generally speaking the small shopkeeper class is so hostile to the regime that it is inclined to look leniently on the past deeds of the Reds. I asked him if they had been much troubled by the brigands. A short time ago, he said, they had terrorized the district, killing and robbing with impunity, but now they rarely left the sierra. Last month the police had shot three or four and hung them on a gibbet as a warning. They were young men in their teens, who had taken to this life because they did not want to work. In winter the wolves and wild boar came down from the hills and visited the farms. As no one shot them, they had multiplied greatly.

I asked him how he did for food. There was plenty of food in the district, he said, but wages were too low. Everyone except the wage earners got enough to eat.

"But mind you," he went on, "I would strongly advise any nation that is inclined to a civil war to put up with anything rather than begin one. In such wars no one wins. We are far worse off today than we were even in the time of the Republic, and heaven knows when we shall be as well off again. Then all these executions and reprisals destroy a nation. The hatred set up by them will last a century."

I have made friends with the innkeeper and his brother. They are two sensible, well-informed men who listen to the B.B.C. Spanish program every day. In the war they supported the Nationalists—a natural attitude in a district where all the Republicans were working-class and Socialists —but, although they profess admiration for Franco, they do not conceal their belief that all the men round him are robbers. (This opinion is almost universal.) I asked them if they thought it would be a good thing if the Americans offered Spain a loan.

"If they give it," they replied, "let them control very strictly the way in which it is spent. Otherwise every penny of it will go into the pockets of this gentry."

I told him that this was what the foreign consuls thought too.

"And how do people abroad think that we live?" the innkeeper asked.

"They think," I said, "that you live under a severe dictatorship, but have no idea of the extent of the hunger and poverty."

"The dictatorship used to be more severe," he replied, "but lately it has grown less so. Its defect now is that it is too weak. The government does nothing to seek out and punish the black marketeers or to compel the landowners to provide work. The rich, in fact, do exactly as they please: for them the laws don't exist. Now I should like to see a strong compulsion put on the landowners to abandon casual labor and to keep a permanent labor force, paid all the year round."

"But how could that be done on the olive estates?" I asked.

"Why, as it is done in other countries—by cultivating them better. At present they don't prune the trees or sow the land round them. Our landowners aren't interested in a large production. All they think of is how to save themselves trouble and keep their labor costs down. Since Primo de Rivera's time we have had no good government."

I found myself agreeing with these men. The moment the doors of an ideology are unlocked in Spain, the old utopist spirit bursts out and miracles are just round the corner. Besides, in a country where injustice is mixed in the air, the real force in all political movements is given by envy and hatred, which grow with what they feed on and soon assume enormous proportions. Democracy with its Queensbury rules becomes unworkable, because the moment politics cease to be a mere game, the issues become too serious. For this reason I would think well of any government which, while leaving the social pattern much as it is, made a real and sustained effort to increase production. This would at least distract the attention of Spaniards from their usual futile struggles and put into their minds the idea, so new to them, that prosperity is the result of work and intelligent organization. Yet I fear that such a plan has something utopist about it too, for where could one find a force strong enough to compel the landowners to alter their present methods of cultivation? The land is difficult to legislate for, and those who own it are past masters in passive resistance.

On the following morning we took the train for Puerto-llano, at the entrance to La Mancha. For the first hour or two we traveled through a monotonous forest of evergreen oaks, whose acorns in autumn serve to fatten herds of black swine, but now we saw no sign of life but chattering magpies. At Conquista, where the railway has been electrified, the country becomes shaggy and mountainous. A French mining company has planted the hills with pines and eucalyptus trees and under them grows a vigorous flora of maquis plants, among which we saw bushes of handsome pink and white heather (*Erica ciliaris*) that reached to ten feet high. These plantations show what could be done in the way of afforestation, if only the State cared about such matters. Then a tunnel, and we emerged high on the mountain side above a bare, yellow valley. It was some five miles wide and came sweeping down between its banks of purple hills as if a broom had made it. This is the valley of Alcudía, used as a winter pasturage for close on half a million sheep. Its flat, featureless surface, without a house or tree to break its monotony, was covered with dry grass.

But when we crossed it, we found it was watered by a stream, with clear water, tamarisks and feeding storks.

Puertollano stands in a gap between two hills, guarding the entrance to the plain of La Mancha. It is a coal mining town, ugly and sordid as such places always are. One building though is impressive—the church, standing up like an elephant above the cluster of low-roofed houses. Even when we came up to it, it seemed enormous, with its high almost windowless granite walls and its bell-topped tower. Though put up in the Renaissance style, its general design, as we realized later, follows that of the fortified medieval churches of the Knights of Calatrava. Puertollano was one of their southern outposts.

Going in, we found ourselves in an aisleless nave, widely vaulted and high. The interior had been completely renovated, the joints of the stones being marked by hard black lines and the granite pillars polished. This is a favorite trick of the French restorers of the Beaux Arts school and it has the effect of arresting and bogging down the free movement of the eye as it travels round the hollow interior. The great Romanesque cathedrals of Aquitaine have mostly been ruined by this imitation of the public lavatory.

As we stood there, the parish priest came up to us. He was a tall, energetic man with a commanding manner—a not unworthy successor of the religious Knights of Calatrava. He told us that the Reds had burned all the *retablos* and pictures in the church and had tried to set fire to the building too, but its strength had resisted them. Only a corner of the roof had fallen in. He himself had spent two

years in prison with fifty-six other priests, fifty-two of whom
had been shot. During this time he had slept on the floor
in a very confined space, suffering cold and hunger; on
several occasions he had been led out to be shot, placed
against a wall and then brought in again. They did this in
the hopes of breaking their spirit.

On learning that we were English, he gave us a political
lecture. The Reds, he said, had found many admirers in
England, because we did not know the things they had
done: we had even ostracized the Franco regime. Yet Franco
had brought to Spain order and peace. He had been gener-
ous too: six hundred men of this town who had been condemned to death for their crimes had been permitted to
redeem themselves by work and were now employed as free
men in the mines. They earned enough to eat and dress
themselves. While the rest of the world was racked by dis-
orders and strikes, life in Spain proceeded in an orderly
way.

After this harangue, he showed us with great pride his
new altar. It was the latest thing in mechanical toys, full
of ingenious devices that worked when one pressed an electric button. Lights came on and went off, a door opened
and the *custodia* containing the sacrament rose slowly "like
a golden sun," as he expressed it, into a blue sky full of
angels. When I offered him a small donation for his restoration fund, he replied with a smile that was full of
diplomacy:

"No, it shall not be for the church, it shall be for the
poor."

It is not wise to argue with Spaniards over their own

affairs; otherwise I might have pointed out to this excellent priest that, if the military and the Falange had not risen in July 1936 and from the first day started killing in holocausts, none of these terrible things would have happened. However, had I said this, he might then have replied that the Asturian miners had risen in 1934 and that in 1931 there had been a great many church burnings. And so the story could be taken back to the Carlist Wars and the Constitution of Cadiz, one act of provocation leading inevitably to another. Some day perhaps Spaniards will realize that in the long run more is lost by the struggle than by a compromise, seeing that in their affairs the greater the victory today the greater will be the defeat tomorrow. No pendulum so monotonous as the Spanish one.

It was growing dark when we left the church, and the change of temperature had brought down into the streets a fog of coal smoke, which made one choke and splutter. How out of place this atmosphere of St. Helens seemed under Southern skies! The town was full of Moorish troops, who had been brought over to hunt the Reds in the neighboring hills; they came here to rest and enjoy the amenities, by which, as they do not drink, must be understood the brothels. The general poverty has made these more numerous in Spain than ever: they are the only luxury which has not gone up in price since the war.

Tired of walking about, we took our seats in the café: a long, low, once garishly decorated room, now however dark and squalid, with its mirrors and pin-ups of dancing girls and bullfighters spotted with fly droppings. Men with large leaden heads and blue unshaven faces sat spitting and clearing their throats or talking their raucous lingo, while outside in the street we could see the crowds passing slowly up and down as through the windows of an aquarium. We had plenty of time to watch them, as our train did not leave till ten o'clock.

LA MANCHA

CIUDAD REAL: we arrived at midnight. Guided by a porter, we found ourselves in a large, gloomy, run-down hotel, built thirty years ago for a prosperity that did not arrive and now decaying steadily. At present it is a sort of aviary for disgruntled commercial travelers unable on account of the general poverty to sell their goods, and their coughs, croaks, gargles and retchings resound lugubriously in the dirty corridors and stairways. To be permitted the entry to this place we had to fill in more forms than we had done anywhere else and the proprietor, a figure from a Balzac novel, with drooping Niagara moustaches, fluffy whiskers, and long greyish white curls that hung down from under a black skull cap, was politely insistent that every space should be scrupulously filled in. Next morning we discovered that the dining room and bedrooms were under separate ownership and management—evidence, it was clear, of some past economic cataclysm. In fact the hotel had never recovered from having been used as a military headquarters during the war.

We went out to look at the town. A dull, one-horse little place, in spite of its being a provincial capital: the only thing to draw the eye was a broad arcaded plaza, built in the sixteenth century but restored in 1860. The Cathedral, a granite edifice with tower-like buttresses and Gothic vaulting, hunched up like a high barn, had a family resemblance to the church of Puertollano, but was less imposing. Round its tower flew bevies of small brown hawks, with delicate fan-like tails and wings. They live on insects, which they catch, as swallows do, in the air, and at night they share the niches of the stonework with the pigeons. There is also a fifteenth-century church, quite attractive. But, alas, the glory of these churches, which is their baroque interiors, has gone, for they were all gutted during the Red occupation. The Cathedral lost a particularly fine *retablo*, carved, it is said, by Montañés.

We walked to the edge of the town. Until a few years ago the circuit of pisé walls built by Alfonso the Learned was still standing, but during the Civil War they were pulled down by the Republicans. Why? No one knew. Only one gateway—a fine example of the Mudejar style—is left. On the northern side of the town the buildings stopped abruptly and the *campo* began. Open fields of green corn, sloping down to the Guadiana and, beyond, the inevitable rim of the sharp, brightly colored mountains. It was a vista of air, space and light, with invisible larks singing. The sudden transition from the compactness of the streets to the immense spaces around was exhilarating.

This corner of Spain was given in 1090 by the Emir Motamid of Seville, famous as one of the best of the Spanish Arab poets, to Alfonso VI as the dowry of his daughter Zaida, who became, in Moslem style, Alfonso's second wife. Eighteen years later it was lost, after the battle of Uclés, to the Almoravide Sultan and when recovered later in the century, was handed over in fief to the newly founded Military Order of Calatrava, who erected their castles on it and defended it fiercely, though with varying success, against the attacks of the Moors. Then, in 1248, these were driven out from the greater part of Andalusia and the Knights of Calatrava settled down to enjoy their rich lands in peace. But there was danger of their growing too powerful and so, to keep them in check, Alfonso the Learned founded in 1252 the royal burgh of Villa Real, which later became promoted to the rank of Ciudad Real, or Royal City.

While we were inquiring about motorbuses across the plain to Daimiel, we made the acquaintance of an elderly man and invited him to a drink. He was a fine figure of a man, handsome and well spoken, with a bold twinkling eye and upright carriage; he belonged to the class of the genteel poor, who wear decent clothes and perhaps a nickel watch chain, even though they cannot afford to eat. He was an Andalusian, he said, and had only recently come to live here.

"But, to tell you the truth, I am not at home in this place. I like neither the country nor what it produces. Notice I say deliberately—*what it produces*. In Andalusia, for example, people are frank. They laugh and say what they think, however unconventional it may be. And they say it well, in good language. But in this town one must be careful never to say what one thinks; one must only say what one is supposed to think, which is usually very different. Begging your pardon if I offend, but this comes from their being all under the influence of the clergy. The clergy are the kings here and so the people have acquired the habit of saying one thing when they feel another. I find them dead—frozen."

He went on to tell us that his sons were in France—refugees He was now seventy-eight and—here his eyes moistened—he doubted if he would ever see them again. His only hope was that the monarchy might come in, for then the exiles would return.

"You ask how we live," he went on. "Well, badly, badly. There is a lot of poverty. But, mind you, you won't see it. When you meet a man walking down the street, how can you tell if he has eaten that day? People here are proud and hide their poverty. They spend their last penny on their clothes and walk about all day to keep the pangs of hunger down."

A gypsy woman came in to beg, and he began to tease her.

"You say you're a gypsy from La Mancha! I see little grace in that. Don't you know that real gypsies are all Andalusians? And if they are *castizo,* if they are of true gypsy stamp and breeding, why then they come from Granada. No, no, you're a fraud, you are, not a proper gypsy at all. Go away, I won't give you anything."

The woman laughed, but it was true what he said, that she lacked the blarney and gift of the gab of the Andalusian *gitana.*

We wished to visit the battlefield of Alarcos, where the Moors destroyed the army of Alfonso VIII of Castile in 1195, but for some time could not get a taxi. It was Sunday, when the townspeople visit their country estates, so that it was not till they returned toward sunset that we found one.

As we drove out across the empty plain the sky changed

to deep crimson as though a river of blood had been turned into it, and the low barren mountains we were approaching became as dark and mysterious as the shores of Styx. Soon we caught sight of the Guadiana, a broken string of silver surfaces, winding among the reeds and bushes in its valley. On our left was a rocky hill, dramatically pinned against the sky, on top of which stood a chapel dedicated to Our Lady of Alarcos, the patroness of the battlefield. Then we dipped and came suddenly to a bridge over the river. The car stopped, we smelled the fresh smell of poplar trees and heard the rushing of water.

The battle of Alarcos was the last great defeat suffered by the Christians. The Almohade Sultan, Abu Yusuf, had passed the Straits of Gibraltar with a vast army. "With his advance," the chronicler wrote, "the plains were robbed of their herbage, the mountain paths were trodden out by the hoofs of the horses and the rivers dried up with the multitudes who drank from them. The news of his coming flew as the bird flies and spread over the lands and resounded in every place, and it moved some men to joy and others to anger." Then Alfonso collected his forces and met Abu Yusuf by the bridge of Alarcos, but the defeat he suffered was so great that only three hundred of his horsemen escaped. The town of Alarcos was razed to the ground and the Moorish cavalry laid waste the Christian lands as far as the gates of Toledo and Avila.

As we stood leaning over the parapet, night collected round us. Splash of water falling from the weir, din of frogs from the marshy edges, hoot of a solitary owl, or shriek of a bat. The stars came out one by one like the first arrivals at a

party and then shone all together fiercely in their battalions. The known world had receded, night and the forces
of night had entered on their own. So strong was the impression, we could almost believe that the clash and tumult
of their ancient battlefield still lingered round us, just out
of sight and hearing.

After a little we lit cigarettes and began to talk. The
chauffeur told us that beyond this point there were nothing
but dry hills, scattered with scrub and cork oak, for a hundred kilometers. That is to say, to the beginnings of
Estremadura. These hills abounded in boar, wolves and
red deer and also sheltered the *partidas* or brigands. They
were using Moorish troops to round them up, but the
process was slow.

I drew him onto political subjects. Land was fairly well
divided, he said, though there were also large estates. For
that reason there was less poverty than in other districts.
Still there were always the two parties—the party of those
who eat and the party of those who don't eat.

"The whole of Spanish politics," he said, "can be explained in that way. This is a country of cannibals, in
which one half of the population eats the other half. As I
am an eater, or at least a nibbler, I belong to the Right."

I inquired what he had done during the war. He said he
had been a lorry driver. Before that he had been a member
of a Catholic trade union, but since "the others"—by which
he meant the Republicans—had ruled here, he had been
obliged to work for them.

"And how did they treat you?" I asked.

"I myself have nothing to complain of, but with the

Church they were terrible. Our churches had famous altars
and images, some of them by Juan de Mena. But they were
ignorant people, full of fanaticism, and they destroyed
them all."

Here I remembered that the priest at Puertollano had
told me that the Red soldiers had burned fourteenth-cen-
tury Mudejar chasubles "just to cook their dinners."

"And did they kill many people?"

"Well, here on this very spot where we are standing I
once saw fifty bodies. Then at a village near by there is a
deep well. They threw people down it, men and women,
some of them still alive. They did the same at another place
where there is a natural chasm."

I remembered how in the first Carlist war a certain priest
had thrown Liberals alive into a chasm in the Maestrazgo.

"And who did these things?"

"Mostly the Anarcho-Syndicalists of the C.N.T. They
were young men from the mountain villages who, when the
war broke out, came trooping into the town in search of
loot. At home they lived by poaching game, for their villages grow next to nothing and haven't even a road to
them; not one of them could read or write and for people
like that it was the same thing to kill a man as not to kill
him. Then later a Communist *cheka* was set up, headed by
an Italian, and it was responsible for some of the worst
killings."

The man spoke without hatred, avoiding the deprecia-
tive term *Reds*, partly no doubt because he had known
them personally but also because they had in their turn
met their fate. He seemed to have a certain regard for the

Socialists, in spite of the fact that it was they who had killed
the Catholic doctors. But he talked with circumspection.
An intelligent man, who had seen many changes, he had no
doubt formed the habit of not expressing opinions. The
only comment he made on contemporary affairs was his
statement that the irrigation dams, which had been started
by the Republic, were progressing slowly on account of the
shortage of cement.

Daimiel is a town of some size, separated from Ciudad
Real by fifteen miles of well-cultivated plain, yet only one
small bus makes the journey daily. Naturally it is extremely
crowded. On the morning on which we took it, there were
two people standing for every one who had a seat, and the
atmosphere was suffocating.

Daimiel turned out to be white, dusty, and undistin-
guished. It has dull little streets, a dull little square, and an
air of profound boredom. Spaniards express the fact that
they are bored, not by opening their mouths in a yawn, but
by closing them firmly and allowing their faces to sag and
collapse, and the streets and cafés of Daimiel were full of
these collapsed and expressionless faces. The hotel where
we had lunch was, like at Ciudad Real, a large roomy place,
built in Primo de Rivera's time for a prosperity that faded
quickly, and the lunch they gave us was the usual Manchegan repast of mutton cutlets and fried potatoes. After we
had finished it, we went out to have a coffee and see the
town. The day was hot—the papers spoke of a heat wave—
and the light reflected from the white walls was blinding.
We walked mutely round the arcaded square and peered at
some of the older houses, with their interior patios sup-

ported on wooden columns. Then we came to a church—a
handsome late Gothic building with a fine span of arch
thrown over its broad nave. But how bare it looked, with
its gilt *retablos* and rich side chapels torn down! This
senseless destruction appears to have taken place wherever
the Republicans were in occupation. When it was not done
deliberately, it took place because the churches were used
as stores and garages, and the soldiers stripped the woodwork for fuel.

Too much has been written of the care shown for works
of art by the Republicans. The spoliation of half the
churches in Spain, of which we were here seeing a small
sample, represents an enormous artistic impoverishment
for the country. In recent times we have learned to value
popular and local art and to regret the tendency to canon-
ize only what is collected into large galleries and museums,
yet here and through a vast area of country every town and
village has been deprived of its particular historical treas-
ures. This is the more grave because the things that we
make today are ugly and spiritless. Much of the destruction caused in war is unavoidable, but when one side
wantonly destroys the great works put up by other men in
the past, they should remember that they are attacking the
spirit of humanity and by this proclaiming their own un-
fitness to win. In writing this I am not forgetting the vast
and often unnecessary destruction wrought by the British
air force in Italy and Germany.

Making our way into another church, we found the
pasos, or floats holding images, pulled out into the nave in
preparation for the Easter processions. Some little boys had

got in by a side door and were staring curiously at them, as
at life-size dolls. One particularly large *paso*, supported on
cart wheels, showed the scene of Christ being whipped by
Roman soldiers: blood ran in streams down his back and
his shoulders were drawn together in agony. Another *paso*
held a glass-walled coffin, within which one saw his lacer-
ated body and pale, extenuated face, frozen in death. How
strange that this gloating attitude to the physical details of
the Passion should take place in a land where beatings of
prisoners and judicial murders have gone on and still go on
regularly, on a scale not seen anywhere else in the West!
Does no Spaniard see the connection?

Till evening comes on with its cool air and its miraculous light, the only restful place in Daimiel is the interior
of a church. There one can escape from the heat and the
glare, the flies and the boredom and steep one's senses in
the half darkness, through which—till the war destroyed
them—long mote-eddying beams fell slantingly on sump-
tuous gold work and twisting tracery. By such impressions,
no doubt, the mind is enabled to take flight from the
tedium and monotony into a state of interior solitude and
contemplation. Religion in Castile is the product of little
stagnant towns set in great sun-drenched plateaus.

We should have liked to continue our journey eastward
to Argamasilla and Toboso and the Campo de Montiel—
the country made famous by the exploits of Don Quijote
de la Mancha. However our time was short and the means
of communication bad. We decided therefore to take a taxi
to the place where the Guadiana issues from the ground
after a subterranean passage of some twenty miles. This

river has always fascinated me. Its long solitary course, avoiding during almost the whole of the way inhabited places, its frequent alterations of size and current, its use-lessness—for except between Mérida and Badajoz it pro-duces no fertility—its majestic entry into the sea by a broad estuary, give it a place in my mind that no other European river holds. Its name too: in names there can lie so much mystery and beauty. We would go therefore to visit the spot where it recovers from the first of its periodic crises, welling up from the ground in a succession of pools which are known as its *Ojos* or Eyes.

The chauffeur brought a friend with him and as we drove along they explained the geography of the country. The whole of this great plain, the Campo de Calatrava, floats, as it were, on a water-bearing stratum which lies some twenty or thirty feet beneath the surface. We had noticed on our drive from Ciudad Real to Daimiel a multi-tude of stone wellheads, standing at a distance of three or four hundred yards from one another; the water from these is pumped up, it seems, either by *norias* worked by mules or donkeys, or else by motor engines, and allowed to run out over the fields. Hence the fertility, shown by the healthy look of the crops and by the plantations of olives and fruit trees. The chauffeur told us that there were fifteen thousand of these *pozos* or wells round Daimiel, as well as a central pumping station that irrigated several thousand acres. Yet till sixty or seventy years ago none of this land was cultivated.

We came to the Ojos suddenly. Topping a low rise, we saw a gentle hollow before us, filled with a bed of reeds and bulrushes; in the middle of these we could just catch sight of some pools of blue water. We got out of the car and walked down to the edge. On either side stood a couple of white farmhouses, built each of them on a low knoll, and a clump of poplar trees. In front, the brown, reedy valley stretched away between fields of green corn till the view was closed by the lilac skyline of the Sierra de Toledo. Although the sense of the *genius loci* was strong, it was a place almost too simple and idyllic to be mysterious.

Pushing aside the bulrushes, we advanced through the mud to get a sight of the pools; they were calm and clear like the eyes they were called after and joined to one another by narrow water channels. A detour round the edge took us to a place below the pools where the young river was beginning to gather strength. A couple of miles further down it was swift enough to turn its first mill. Then it entered a marsh and when it came out, reinforced by a tributary from the north, it was already a great river.

"Not far above the Ojos," said the chauffeur, "there is a place where one can hear it running underground. Would you like me to take you there?"

But the sun was getting low in the sky and we left it.

As we drove back to Daimiel the chauffeur talked to us of the Don Quixote country. He told us that the famous knight was there regarded as a real person and that in the town hall of Toboso were shown the embroidered skirt of Dulcinea, her spinning wheel and one of her tresses. I have much of the easy credulity of the relic worshipper myself and find these *dulces prendas* of the peerless lady at least as worthy of devotion as the drops of the Virgin's milk pre-

served in the Camara Santa at Oviedo or, to quote a few
even rarer examples, the flask containing the breath of the
donkey from the stable at Bethlehem, the shadow of the
stick of St. James, the doublet of the Trinity, or the feather
snatched from the right wing of the Holy Ghost—all of
which, according to the Spanish humanist Juan de Valdés,
were once displayed for the veneration of the faithful in a
convent at Rome.

The chauffeur was proud of his town and pointed out
how well the land was cultivated. They were beginning to
plow with tractors. There was a soap factory owned by a
Frenchman and other Frenchmen were buying up land and
investing capital. But there were not enough small farms.
An attempt had recently been made to break up two large
estates into lots for landless men, but it had met with strong
opposition. The landlords had protested that this was
Communism, and word had come from Madrid that the
project must be dropped.

We had arranged to take the car on in a southerly direction to Almagro and there pick up the night train for
Ciudad Real. A stop for a drink and we were off. As we
drove out of Daimiel, the sun was setting on a flat and
treeless plain and the air was as clear and transparent as
the water of a well. A few small *cortijos* or farms, gleaming
like white gulls in the horizontal light, stood out of the
floor-like expanse, each with a black poplar tree planted
for shade by the entrance. One of these farms had in front
of it a substantial mound which I took to be a prehistoric
barrow, but on inquiring of the chauffeur I was told that
it was an artificial tumulus, made for a rabbit burrow.

Then we came to some evergreen oaks, last survivors of an ancient forest; then to a village clustered round a medieval castle. Battered and derelict, it rose above it in a single massive tower. As we passed, the village girls were sitting outside their houses in their cotton dresses making lace, and we would hear the rattle of their spools above the noise of the car.

We entered Almagro as the sun set. The car drew up in the square, the prototype of that at Ciudad Real, but built on marble pillars instead of on iron ones and not spoiled by restoration. Under the arcades were shops, while the upper stories were of wood, painted a deep green, with an almost continuous series of windows like Regency verandas. The general effect was strikingly lovely.

Almagro was the principal seat of the Military Order of Calatrava and so is crowded with fine houses and churches. The parish church is a Renaissance building with a wide nave and a dome. Begun by the Jesuits in the sixteenth century, it was finished just as they were expelled, in 1766; beside it is their college, which they never occupied. Another church which we stumbled into in the growing darkness was of the fortress type of the church of Puertollano, with windows built high in the nave and massive walls. Both of these churches had of course been stripped by the Republicans, who had also killed the clergy and the monks of the Dominican college.

In the failing light we walked about the old town, the most delightful we had yet seen in La Mancha. Then we began to think of supper. The inn to which we made our way turned out to be a homely little place kept by a widow and her pretty and agreeable daughter. The meal was, alas, the usual Manchegan one of eggs, mutton chops, and fried potatoes, but the other diners were friendly and included one man who was an addict of the B.B.C. These people belong to a special type—mild, sensible, un-Iberian—which almost makes them qualify for being a political party.

When we had finished our dessert, one of the company, a lawyer, took us to see the palace of the Maestre of Calatrava, which is today used as a casino. It has a fine *artesonado* ceiling of dark cedar wood. On our way back he pointed out to us the palace of the Fuggers, the Augsburg bankers to whom Charles V leased the famous mercury mines of Almadén in return for a loan. Since Almadén lies in an inaccessible wilderness, they had their chief office here. Then we set off for the station. Night, silence, and a glittering dome of stars, reaching down to the horizon. Dogs barking far away in lonely farmhouses. On the platform, one passenger. The train came in slowly round a long curve and, rattling and jangling, as if every nut and screw in its frame was loose, carried us back to Ciudad Real.

Our visit to La Mancha was ended. Without much regret we boarded next day the thrice-weekly express that runs from Madrid to Lisbon. Our destination was Badajoz, on the Portuguese frontier.

For the first three hours the train threaded its way through the bare, dry sierras that separate La Mancha from Estremadura. From the carriage windows we looked out on a monotonous wall of slate or basalt mountains, hard in color as iron slag and marked with innumerable folds

and wrinkles. Below us, in one or another rough gorge or
deep-clawed valley, lay the bed of a torrent which, according to circumstances, now ran almost dry, now coiled itself
up in green snake-like pools, now spread out in sandy shal-
lows overhung with tamarisk. Occasionally we caught sight
of a tumble-down farm, surrounded by a few lean olive
trees and plots of wheat, and there was a time when I
would have been intrigued by the remoteness of such places
and would have imagined—it is certain, quite wrongly—
that some strange mode of life went on there.

We passed Almadén with its mercury mines, hidden
behind a hill, and after it the Castillo de Almorchón. Then
came a breath-taking sight. As we surmounted a low rise, a
great plain came suddenly into view below us, tawny yellow or glowing ocher in color and stretching away as far
as the eye could see. A long way off blue mountain islands
rose out of it—the crags of Guadalupe and Montánchez—
giving for a moment the impression that it was a reed-
choked inland lake. We were looking at the *Llanos,* or
Plain, of La Serena, the most easterly of the great sheep
pasturing districts of Estremadura.

As the train rattled along, we had time to take in the
character of this new region. Grey tufted grass, with clumps
of Spanish broom and asphodel; flocks of merino sheep,
guided by fierce-looking dogs and shepherds clad in sheep-
skins; round, thatched huts, like those of the Berbers of
North Africa; earthenware beehives that were mere clus-
ters of drain pipes, with stones laid on top of them. Yet
when we stopped at a small station, there was the invariable

group of middle-class people, with their creased trousers, polished shoes and spruce, natty hats, waiting to board the train. Even in the troglodyte villages of Almeria and Murcia one finds them got up in their conventional, towny uniform, like commercial travelers on their rounds. How the monotony of Spanish culture contrasts with the variety and wildness of the background against which it is lived!

At Villanueva the pasturage ended and vineyards and cornfields began. Then we came to Medellín. Here the Guadiana reappeared on the scene, broad as the Thames at Oxford, and flowing under a steep rock, crowned by a Moorish castle. This little town is the birthplace of Hernán Cortés, the conqueror of Mexico, and just outside it was fought one of the bloodiest battles of the Peninsular War. A French army under Marshal Victor annihilated a Spanish army under General Cuesta and, so an eyewitness relates, the flocks of vultures that settled on the battlefield became so gorged with corpses that for days after they could be knocked down with a stick. Ten thousand fell, and for many years their bones lay bleaching on the fields. Victor, a complete savage, shot his prisoners and sacked the town, deliberately pulling down Cortés' house.

Soon we were at Mérida, littered with its Roman ruins. The broken viaduct that sprawled across the goods yard above the standing trucks of coal had the hard, ugly look of modern factory buildings. A few miles further on we entered the great cultivated plain that extends across the frontier into Portugal. Alongside the railway ran a new, unfinished irrigation channel, commenced by the Republic:

it is an important work, which will bring large new areas into cultivation, and it was nearly completed. Yet we saw only a couple of dozen men at work on it; the credits, we were told, were exhausted. And now the sun was going down as we pulled into the station of Badajoz.

BADAJOZ

Badajoz! What queer, far-off, schoolboy memories that word calls up! The boring classroom and the smug tone of the history master's voice as he spoke of its sack by Wellington's troops—the pun in Thomas Hood's poem, printed in a little red school edition that cost sixpence—the look of the name itself, so absurd in its English pronunciation! Then a year or two later I read in Borrow's *Bible in Spain* of how he had crossed the wild heath of brushwood that surrounded the city, listened to the washerwomen singing their songs by the shallow river, and fallen in with the gypsies. This fixed it in its permanent lineaments. And now here, after all these years, it actually was! That white town clustering on its hill in the grey evening light was the famous fortress of the Guadiana.

We crossed the river by a low, many-arched bridge built, so the guide book informed us, by Herrera, the architect of the Escorial—and climbed by narrow streets to the hotel. It proved to be a well-run, up-to-date place with a lounge and cocktail bar—not in the least in the Borrow tradition. I was told that it exists chiefly to cater to motorists traveling between Spain and Lisbon. We engaged rooms and went out to get a drink.

Badajoz, as a glance told us, has preserved its Moorish plan. Its streets are steep and narrow and few of them can take wheeled traffic. Following one of them, we came out at what was evidently the center of the town—the Ca-

thedral Square. The crowds amazed us. Up and down the
street that traverses it, which, since it runs along the summit of a ridge, is relatively flat, moved a dense pack of
middle-class people, talking, laughing, gesticulating. It was
the hour of the evening *paseo*: the girls were in their best
frocks, the young men had oiled and smoothed their hair,
and so many rays and flashes of eyes and teeth passed between them that one would have said that this was some
special feast day. What a contrast this scene of life and
gaiety made to the deadness and glumness of La Mancha!

We had a drink at one of the large cafés that faced the
Cathedral and then joined in the two-way procession that
shuffled up and down the narrow street. At a certain point,
marked by a rise in the steepness, its character changed: the
middle-class promenaders turned back and a procession of
working-class people succeeded them. Following this, we
came to the market square, known as the Plaza Alta. This
is an oblong enclosure of high, white, arcaded houses, having that reserved and sphinx-like air of houses built in a
classical style, and dating, I imagine, from the early seventeenth century. At its further end it is continued by two
rows of lower but extremely massive houses, whose arcades
are supported either on short columns or on heavy piers
of masonry; these houses, I was told, go back to the thirteenth century. They are by far the most impressive thing
in Badajoz, and seen by lamplight, with their thick, white,
lime-encrusted walls and cave-like interiors and the towers
of the Arab castle rising spectrally behind them, they satisfy all one's unspoken desires for romance and mystery.
This is also the red light quarter of the town; returning to

it later that evening, when the hour of the *paseo* was over, we found that it had acquired a sinister and malign quality. The brothels, which occupy the Calle de la Encarnación (in English, Street of the Incarnation) had disgorged their occupants, and tawdrily dressed and undressed girls lolled in the archways and exchanged glances with prowling apache types and drunken soldiers. The police withdraw their post from the square at ten o'clock and the narrow lanes that lead off down the hill are unlit. It is not then a place to linger in.

Badajoz viewed by the morning light makes a less exciting impression. One sees then a dull little provincial town with a core of middle-class shopkeepers and officials, a few soldiers, smugglers, cattle merchants and horse-copers and a broad fringe of extreme poverty. The Cathedral, built in 1258, is a cramped, fortress-like affair, choked up inside by a box-like choir that almost completely fills it. It is so dark that the paintings it contains by Zurbarán and Luis de Morales are invisible.

This Morales, surnamed *el Divino*, seems to require a word, for he was a native of Badajoz and spent his life here. His dates are c. 1509–1584. He was one of the first of the Spanish mannerists and painted devotional pictures of the sort that were later to be so popular, of ecstatic saints and agonized Christs and Madonnas. In his own time he was not much appreciated, in spite of his being the painter of the ascetic and mystical movement that derives from San Pedro de Alcántara and Santa Teresa, because the taste for this kind of expressionistic painting came in later. But recently he has attracted some notice as a clumsy forerunner of El Greco. However no one but an art expert need visit Badajoz to see his work; he was an uneven painter and his best pictures are in Madrid.

From the Cathedral we climbed up past the Plaza Alta to the Moorish Castle. This is a fine, decaying ruin, crowned like an Edwardian lady with strange ramshackle objects which turn out to be storks' nests. One elegant octagonal tower dates from the time of Al-Motawakkil, the last king of Badajoz, who was dethroned in 1094 by the Almoravides. But not all the remains are Moorish. Alongside the castle are other buildings of a later date, as well as an open space where the inner city, with the palaces of the Dukes of la Feria, the Archbishop and the Knights of Calatrava, once stood. This space forms today a sort of park: children play here among the crumbling walls and trenches, and soldiers and workmen stare in their incurious, melancholy, Iberian way at the view. For a view there is: the battlements fall away sheer to the river and all around lies the great plain— green, treeless, dotted with white farms, but not a village to break the monotony. The reason for this is that, although today the plain is cultivated, a hundred years ago it was heath.

As we stood looking round us, an elderly man—fierce, grizzled and hoarse-voiced, and wearing a cap that fell low over his watery eyes and a black muffler—came up to us and offered to show us round. We accepted.

"Few tourists come here nowadays," he said, clearing his throat loudly. "Very few. The last I spoke to was a Jew from Tangiers. He told me, this Jew, that one of his ancestors, a famous man in his time, occupied a house in the

Plaza Alta in the fifteenth century. He had come from
Tangiers to see it and had brought with him the door key
which his family had carried away when they were obliged
to leave Spain five centuries ago. And what do you think—
it fitted."

I tried to look as if I believed this old chestnut, on which,
stretching out his stick toward the War Memorial to the
Foreign Legion beside which we were standing and clearing his throat once more, the man began, in the solemn
rhythmical tones of an official guide, to describe it.

"You see here a monument of remarkable—historic importance. To commence at the bottom, the base, which you
see here, is composed of limestone slabs cemented together.
It weighs, without the cement, seventeen—and a half tons.
This block, which lies upon it, is of red granite and comes
from a granite quarry. It weighs five—and a quarter tons.
Note that it is all of one piece and that the polishing was
done by—special machinery brought here for the purpose.
The shaft which stands upon it is of a different granite
brought expressly from another quarry. Its weight is seven
—and a third tons. Observe the gilt lettering of the inscription, which was executed by—a special process. The
ball. . . ."

"And so the English troops climbed up this way to the
citadel?" I asked.

"What English troops?"

"The troops of Wellington, when he captured the city
from the French in 1812."

But either the man did not like being interrupted or else
the subject was distasteful to him—what business had for-

eign soldiers doing in his city?—for the answer he gave was inaudible. Then I noticed that he was wearing a metal badge that had on it a cross, a chain and a sheaf of arrows.

"Is that a medal?" I asked.

"No," he replied, his eyes lighting up. "It is the badge of the Confraternity of Prisoners. I earned it because I was the first man to be thrown into prison by the Republicans when the Army rose on July 17, 1936. Had the relieving troops not arrived just when they did, I should have been shot. *Si, señor.* I before anyone. They would have paid me that honor."

"Were you a Falangist?" I asked.

"All my life I have been a Monarchist," he answered proudly. "A Monarchist from the feet upward. When I was in the Civil Guard I was one, and today I am more of that persuasion than ever. I wrote a letter to Franco to tell him so."

"And what did he say?"

"He did not answer."

"And so you want the King to come back?"

Suddenly all his bitterness poured out of him.

"Today even the dogs in the streets are wishing that, let alone his old followers. I tell you that things couldn't be worse here than they are. One can't live, one can't eat. Everyone is starving—everyone, that is, except the people who are plundering the country. Never, never, has Spain sunk so low before. And there's nothing to be done. So long as *ese hombre,* that man, is at the head of things, there's no hope. You're a foreigner—tell me, why don't the other nations do something to help us?"

And in his hoarse ex-policeman's voice he went on to explain that while he had to live on 10 pesetas a day, the price of potatoes, which were his chief food, had recently been raised by the Town Council above the market value to benefit their friends. We left him muttering and mumbling under his breath, while the storks and crows and hawks and pigeons, which nest in the ruins, flew in streaks and circles round us.

It is down by the river that the Eastern character of Badajoz strikes one most forcibly. No washerwomen sirens as in Borrow's time—few people sing in Spain today—but plenty carrying bundles and pitchers on their heads. One does not see this in Andalusia. Many of the poor went barefoot and there were more mules and donkeys than I have seen in any other Spanish city.

The eighteenth-century ramparts are still much as they were when the English redcoats swarmed over them. But another more recent assault interested us more. This was the occasion when, on August 14, 1936, the 16th Company of the 4th Bandera of the Tercio, or Foreign Legion, forced their way into the city by a narrow breach. A notice on the wall recalls their feat and *su desposorio con la muerte*, their "marriage with death." Out of one company only ten men were left; in all two thousand men of the Tercio were killed within an area of a few yards, and had the Republican municipality not a short time before removed the gateway to give more room for the traffic, the city, which was defended by a strong force of Carabineers and Assault Guards as well as by several regiments of conscripts, could never have been taken at all. As a grizzled sergeant said to me, "They would be fighting there still."

The massacre that followed became famous. All the prisoners who had used their arms—to the number of many thousands—were mown down by machine guns in the Cathedral Square and bullring. Shocking though this is, it seems to me more excusable than many other things that happened during the Civil War. The Foreign Legion had taken the ramparts by storm after terrible casualties; they were a corps trained in a neurotic cult of death, and in Africa, where they had been formed to fight against the savage Moors of the Riff, they were not in the habit of giving quarter. And then, during the first year of the Civil War, neither side gave quarter. The old, cruel habit of the first Carlist War reasserted itself and all prisoners were shot automatically. What I find more distasteful is that certain English journalists, who knew the truth, denied it. By their determination to prove that all the atrocities that took place were committed by one side, they helped to increase the bitterness and venom of the struggle.

I must now relate a small but characteristic incident that happened to us. On the previous evening, about an hour after our arrival, a slight, dapper young man, with a smile like that conjured up by the studio camera and a sad, hangdog look about the rest of his person, had come up to us in the hotel and—speaking, he said, as one writer and journalist to another—had offered his services. I asked him why he thought I was a journalist and he replied that his instinct had revealed it to him. I realized that he must have seen the form I had filled in on arrival and that he was therefore in all probability a police spy. Accordingly I answered that

I was here merely as a tourist on holiday and, since I happened to be studying the city plan given in Baedeker, asked him if he could tell me the name of the street that the hotel was in.

"The street?" he exclaimed vaguely. "The street? But I don't know the names of any streets here. I have only been in this town a few days. You see, I come from the Canary Islands."

"Ah really! Then you are a compatriot of that great novelist, Pérez Galdós."

"Yes," he said. "I am. It's such a pity he's dead, isn't it?"

"But surely," I replied, "not unnatural, seeing that he was born more than a hundred years ago."

"Really . . . a hundred years! Oh, I say!"

And his face went so completely blank that I thought he might vanish altogether. However, I was mistaken. In a moment he was back again and, pulling some newspaper cuttings out of his pocket and holding them up as a sort of talisman, he began to press on me his services as a guide to this town which he had just told me that he did not know. Such stupidity seemed to prove that he could be nothing else but a police agent—one of that super-idiotic tribe of whom Trotsky has drawn so brilliant a picture in the little book he wrote on his Spanish visit. I thanked my fellow-author and left.

Next day, as we were finishing lunch, he came briskly into the dining room and sat down without being invited at our table. Pulling out again the wad of newspaper cuttings and then a pad, he said that he wanted my name and some particulars about me "so that he could write an arti-

cle on my visit." Then, when I refused, he began a hard-
luck story. His wife was ill and staying at another hotel (as
though he were really staying in this one!); his last articles
had been badly paid; he could not raise enough to buy
their tickets back to Madrid. He needed altogether 150
pesetas—could I lend him the money?

So they underpay their police agents! I thought. The
poor devils probably have to work on a commission system.
It seemed to me such a pathetically Spanish arrangement
that I put my hand in my pocket and gave him a few shillings. He thanked me effusively and left.

Our visit to the battlefield of Alarcos had pleased us so
much that we thought we could not do better than spend
the afternoon inspecting the site of another and greater
battle, that of Zallaka or Sagrajas, where a Spanish army
suffered an even more catastrophic defeat. The story of this
battle is so extraordinary and so little known even to read-
ers of Spanish history that perhaps I may be allowed to give
it.

The date is 1084. Alfonso VI of Castile had just occupied
Toledo and was pressing harder every year on the Arab
kingdoms of the South. They had no prospect of resisting
him much longer, so, in despair, they decided to appeal for
aid to Yusuf ben Taxufin, the Almoravide Emir of Morocco, even though they knew that his coming to Spain
must mean their ruin.

These Almoravides were a curious people. Some forty
years before this time a camel-riding tribe of the Touaregs,
the veiled Bedouin who live in the Sahara, had been converted to Islam. Led by a certain *faqui* or prophet, they set

up a military order, known as the Almoravides from the *rabidas* or frontier castles they garrisoned, with vows that required them to wage perpetual war on unbelievers and to abjure both wine and music. Their progress was rapid: they conquered and converted the black races of the Niger and Senegal and occupied Morocco. Here they founded Marrakesh to be the capital of their empire and in 1084, in answer to the appeals of King Mutamid, the poet king of Seville, crossed the straits of Gibraltar to Algeciras.

The month of September of that year saw the African army assembled at Badajoz, where it was joined by contingents from the principal Arab states of Spain, led by the kings of Seville, Granada and Badajoz. Yusuf, the Almoravide Emir, was in command. He was an old man of seventy, dark, wizened, with a high-pitched voice and a thin goat's beard. He had been born a pagan and had spent his life among the sand *ergs* and *ashab* pastures of the Sahara, and his only food consisted of barley cakes and camels' flesh. He wore the Touareg veil that covers the face from the eyes downward and did nothing without consulting his holy men.

Meanwhile Alfonso had assembled his army, among which were French, Norman and Italian knights, and had marched to meet him. Prudently Yusuf waited till he was far from his base, and then sallied out. The two armies drew up some ten miles beyond the city, on either side of a stream called today the Guerrero, while messengers passed to and fro between them, fixing, as was the custom in those times, the day on which the combat should take place. For three days the armies waited, drinking the muddy water of the same stream, till at dawn on October 23 the Christians, anticipating the hour that had been agreed on, attacked.

On the first charge Yusuf's line was surprised and thrown into confusion. Alvar Fañez, late the Cid's lieutenant, routed the Andalusians, and Alfonso's center drove the Africans back. Then Yusuf sent his Touareg camel corps to raid the Christian camp. The smell of the camels terrified the horses and caused them to stampede, so that Alfonso, who had forced his way through to the African rear, halted and turned back. Then in massed formations the African infantry began to press in upon his flanks, while the rolling of the African drums—heard for the first time in Europe—made the air rock and reverberate. The Christian ranks began to break as Yusuf's guard of four thousand black Senegalese, armed with Indian swords and with shields of hippopotamus skin, drove forward in a compact mass, with drums beating and standards flying, against the Castilian knights. They forced their way to where the king stood and a black man drove his sword through his chain mail and wounded him in the thigh. By this time the whole Christian army was in flight and it was with difficulty that Alfonso's companions formed a guard round him and got him away; they had a headlong ride through the darkness to Coria, eighty miles distant, before they were safe.

That night Yusuf had the Christian bodies decapitated and with their heads built a high mound. At dawn the muezzins mounted upon it to call the sleeping army to prayer. Then the heads were put into carts and carried to the Moslem cities of Spain and Africa, as had been the

custom in Almanzor's day. But Yusuf recrossed the Straits
to Ceuta, where his son lay sick, and did not follow up his
victory. When four years later he returned, it was to sub-
due, not the Christian kingdoms, but the Arab ones.

The Battle of Zallaka was a blessing in disguise for
Spain. It led to no new Moorish advance, but it prevented
the Christians from overrunning and conquering the
Moslem states, as they would otherwise have done. Had
this happened, they would have been compelled to absorb
a vast hostile territory with a population many times greater
than their own and a culture that was incomparably higher.
They would thus have been Arabized, their vigorous if
primitive institutions would have decayed, and they would
have sunk to being an effete, slave-owning, semi-Oriental
oligarchy.

We started out in a taxi along the road to Cáceres while
the sun was still high in the sky. The country was monotonous. Rolling hills thinly scattered with ilex trees, open
spaces of green corn or stubble, then more ilexes. Every
tree had the same shape, every shape cast the same shadows,
every shadow revolved round its trunk in an identical
way. We were in a country of sun clocks, but why so much
chronometry when nothing but the shadows ever moved
and nothing recordable ever happened? Except for the occasional chatter of a magpie, there was complete silence.

The miles passed, the trees became continuous, the road
rougher. We crossed a valley bottom, passed a house,
climbed a ridge. There before us was the place. Or at least
there was the Guerrero, that insignificant stream, dawdling
along in its narrow earth-walled bed. Beyond it the country

was more open, and somewhere in that wide expanse the
Battle of Zallaka must have taken place. But had it? Nothing in this emptiness, airiness, silence recalled the trembling
rolling of the drums, the screaming of the horses, the panting of the men at arms, as they gripped their swords tighter
and the sweat ran down their cheeks. Nor did the site seem
to have any strategic or battle-provoking qualities. We
turned back without going further, and as we passed again
the metallic trees, each with its flat shadow lying monotonously before it, felt that nothing beyond the quivering
of the air in summer, the cracking of a seed pod, the dip-
ping flight of a magpie could ever have disturbed these
wastes.

At length we came out among cornfields and saw before
us the city on its hill, the plain beyond it and the river, lit
mildly by the sun's diagonal rays. The chauffeur pointed,
with the gesture of Ulysses sighting land; we were in the
world of human beings again. The relief felt was an entirely
Iberian sentiment. Spanish civilization is built upon a
dread of and antipathy to Nature. In the huddling together of their houses and streets, in the intensity of their
town life lies an anxiety to escape from the emptiness of
the surrounding spaces. Every little *pueblo* feels itself
beleaguered by the deadly boredom of the sun-drenched
sierras and plains and, since the centrifugal forces that are
so strong in Northern countries such as England simply do
not exist here, Spaniards are driven to living pellmell on
top of one another in a manner not seen anywhere else except in Arab lands. Hence the warmth and animation of
social life, but hence too, when disagreements arise, the

bitterness. Even the recent division of the contending parties into rich and poor can be called an accident of the age, since one has only to look at North Africa before the French occupation to find every little *ksar* or township divided against itself into Guelfs and Ghibellines, sniping at one another from behind walls, in a state of chronic civil warfare. History contains many sorts and kinds of explanations, and one may perhaps as well account for this state of affairs by a neurosis brought on by the dread of Nature as by a shortage of food or a lack of social justice.

Our visit to Zallaka over, we went to the Cathedral Square to have coffee. There it was again, this six o'clock quickening of the pulse, when the dull town wakes up to an hour or two of furious life! Once more we saw the well-dressed crowds ranging up and down the narrow street; once more they stopped at a certain point and turned back, to be succeeded by even denser crowds of working-class people. Hoarse amazonian women crying their wares, blind lottery sellers creeping along the walls like lizards, women so advanced in pregnancy that their stomachs seemed to point at one like cannons, men on crutches, girls with baskets, barefooted gypsies, workmen, soldiers. Then we arrived at the Plaza Alta and at the white, cavernous arcades, and climbed to the castle enclosure. A whirl of birds was circling in the air above it and on the broken arches of the ruins storks were standing with their sage fatherly look, sometimes rattling their beaks together in a quaint, Bruegelesque way or opening and shutting their wings with solemn symbolism. A crimson cloud, soft as a moth's wing, had spread over the eastern quarter of the sky and below it lay the river, shallow, divided into channels, winding now in pale sleeves, now in mirror-bright pools upon its shingly bed. A line of mules and horses was crossing it, for the men who had been digging for sand were going home, and the plain was turning from dark green to brown. Then the Angelus began to ring—with a noise like the beating of tin trays; the birds circle faster and lights begin to come out in the streets below. It is time to descend—the guardian is blowing a whistle—and as we do so by a rocky path we alight on some gypsy tenements that have been built among the ruins. Outside them on the ground a fire is burning, a man is hammering a copper pot, naked children scream, there is a glimpse of dusky breasts, while from the low doorways women with babies in their arms come scrambling forward and surround us, begging for alms. We escape. Through a broken arch of the castle we drop down and come out in the Plaza Alta. Here the lights have been lit. The crowds are eddying and turning like the birds in the air above. But, as we watch, a change is taking place: the street-sellers are leaving, the shoppers making for home with their purchases, the night population is coming out. Prostitutes lean lazily against the arches, soldiers with mute, lust-dulled faces stroll by, the taverns fill up. We press on. Now we are in the long shopping street among the middle-class promenaders. Flashes of eyes and teeth, ripple of voices, bursts of sudden laughter. Then we reach the square; a moment more and we are ensconced in the red plush seat of a café. We have seen Badajoz.

MÉRIDA

When, fifteen years ago, we saw Mérida for the first time, it was a summer evening. We had been driving all day across bare, waterless hills, drenched with heat and light, and as we came down to the river and saw the city spread out beyond it, the sun was setting. Cattle were standing in the shallow water or straying over the broad gravelly bed and a lurid red light fell on the Roman battlements and on the turrets bristling with storks' nests. I got the impression of a lost city, stranded far from civilization, in the remote and barren West.

This morning, April 7, as we got out of the little electric train that had brought us from Badajoz, the effect was totally different. The sun was struggling to come through a veil of mist, drops of dew hung on the grass and all the trees were bursting into leaf. It was, in short, spring, that unreal season, when Nature puts on for these sun-baked lands a brief charade, so that the vivid greens of acacias, planes, figs and elms seemed to be not ordinary leaves, but flags hung out to decorate a carnival. The small market place we passed was crowded with country folk and, as we walked down the principal street, we came on new types of people—tall weather-beaten men with broad hats on their heads and long whips in their hands and handsome, slow-paced gypsies, who told us that we were in the region of Spain which had given Mexico its *vaqueros* and the Argentine its *gauchos*. The ruins of Emerita Augusta, capital of Roman Lusitania, might stand around, but Mérida was no more than a small country town, given to cattle raising.

After leaving our suitcases at the hotel, we strolled down to the bridge over the Guadiana. On its sixty-four granite arches it crawled like a brown centipede over the river bed. The current flowed under only two of these arches, for this has been an unusually dry spring, but sometimes it fills the whole half mile of its channel with a brown turbulent flood. It is for this reason that, since its erection by Augustus, the bridge has been many times repaired.

As we stood in the middle of its narrow passageway, looking back at the town, we observed the figure of a man coming toward us. A small, lightly built man, neatly dressed, walking with a jaunty step and carrying a portfolio in his hand. As he approached, we noted his cheap tight overcoat, well-polished shoes, little black moustache and liquid, melting eyes. A smile came slowly over them as he recognized us, for this was of course our journalist policeman friend from Badajoz.

"We meet again," he said. "Bravo. I thought we should. I am on my way back to Madrid. I left my wife in a hotel in the town—she is too ill to get up. How are you?"

"We are very well," I replied. "But where are you off to?"

"To the slaughterhouse. You have heard of it, of course? It is the finest in Spain and has made the name of Mérida known from one end of the country to the other. It occurred to me that I might get some copy there. An article on the finest slaughterhouse in Spain—that would make a good front page in a Madrid paper! And then I thought I might slip in something in the local press too—visit of cele-

brated foreigners to a national monument. That would
sound well, wouldn't it, and would help with the railway
fare. Come along with me—you won't regret it."

"How far is it?"

"Just a stroll—say a couple of miles. By all accounts it's
a tremendous place. If you came, you could really be useful to me, you know."

"Very likely," I said, surprised by his new mood of
chirpiness and familiarity; in Badajoz he had been all
deference. "But I'm not interested in slaughterhouses."

"Ah, but this is much more than a slaughterhouse—it's a
packing factory too. And then wouldn't you like to see
yourself written up in the local papers?"

But I stood firm—a mistake, no doubt, for should not the
traveler accept every new adventure?—and we watched his
small, slight figure walking confidently on into the distance.

Had I then been wrong in assuming that our friend was
a police spy? Who could say? There are intermittent spies,
amateur spies, who work on a commission system as well as
regularly employed professionals. But his basic status was
clear. He was one of that army of floating waifs and strays
who pick up their living in a variety of manners. Chiefly
no doubt in his case—without excluding the possibility of
his getting from time to time some journalistic work—by
a hard-luck story. It is difficult to dismiss a man who forms
your acquaintance in the guise of a respectable journalist
and then, when you can do nothing for him, makes an appeal to your generosity. Spain is full of such rolling stones
—men who have lost their foothold in the safe niches of
society and wander about, gathering up the crumbs that

fall from those who have had better luck than themselves. One doesn't have to bring in the Arab past to see it as a land of nomads—ambulant lottery sellers and bootblacks, street vendors and touts, *contrabandistas* and commission agents, *cesantes* now in jobs and now out of them. And how else can people live? The Spanish economic system is like a game of musical chairs, in which there are only half as many seats as there are performers.

After lunch we went to see the basilica or convent church of Santa Eulalia, on the edge of the town. This Eulalia was a girl of thirteen who was martyred in the year A.D. 305 under the Diocletian persecution. Prudentius, the Spanish poet who flourished toward the end of that century, wrote a hymn in her honor in which he speaks of her church as "gleaming with white marbles, roofed with a gilt-coffered ceiling and having for its pavement a mosaic that is like a meadow crimsoned with many kinds of flowers." Her cult spread all over Spain and till the rise of Madonna-worship in the thirteenth century, which eclipsed the veneration given to the martyrs, her shrine at Mérida attracted many pilgrims.

We found, not the building described by Prudentius, but a fine thirteenth-century church with an *artesonado* ceiling. Two chapels, each entered by a low arch supported on heavy columns and capitals, were Visigothic, and fragments of the early basilica are said to be incorporated in the foundations. But the mosaics have vanished; perhaps they still lie covering the body of the child martyr underneath.

The parish priest, who was busy organising the *pasos* or

floats for Easter Week, showed us round. He told us that
he had been in charge of this parish for thirty-seven years
and that it was under his direction that the plaster had
been scraped off and the old ceiling and stonework exposed to view. It was also, I gathered, by his tact that the
church had been saved from desecration during the
brief period—a fortnight—in which the Workers' Commit-
tees had been in control. However it was not as a rule the
local people who wrecked churches but strangers coming
in from outside.

As we left, we noted outside the south porch a curious
edifice composed of the fragments of a Roman temple to
Mars and containing what is piously believed to be the
oven in which the saint was roasted. This, however, is not
the story that Prudentius gives. According to him, Eulalia,
after being hidden away by her parents in a country villa
(the place has recently been rediscovered) escaped and
trudged into Mérida, eager, like St. Theresa at a still
younger age, for martyrdom. Here she presented herself
before the city magistrates and, with the uncompromising
conviction of youth, poured out a furious harangue:

> *Isis, Apollo, Venus are nothing,*
> *the Emperor himself is nothing—*
> *those nothing because made with hands,*
> *this one nothing because he worships them.*
> *All worthless and all nothing.*

After this and a few sarcasms in the style of Left Wing
orators upon the pretensions of the Imperial Government
to benevolence and justice, she called, in the usual martyr's

formula of the day, on the executioners to cut, burn and mutilate her limbs: they would find it easy to destroy her body, but even their fiercest torments would not be able to reach her soul within.

Then the praetor, unable to refuse the challenge, ordered the executioners to begin their work; they tore her body with hot pincers, while she sang in her shrill child's voice a song of triumph. On this they plied the faggots round her and set fire to them. She died, and as she did so a white dove—it was her soul, *lacteolus, celer, innocuus*—flew out of her mouth and ascended to heaven, while a storm of snow fell and covered the ground. She had won, and the audience, moved by the thrill of her victory, burst into tears.

Tertullian, the African Trotsky of his age—for there is a certain analogy between the rise of Christianity and that of Communism—has described the effect that these scenes had on the onlookers. They were regarded less as a spectacle of pathos than as a contest between the flesh, representing the material world, and the spirit. "Sure that girl has a power we haven't got" would have been the comment of the good people of Mérida. "To make her trample on torments in that way, there must be something in that antisocial religion of hers." So the dove and the snowstorm were there, if only in people's minds. But today we are perhaps most likely to be impressed by the stupidity of the Roman authorities in permitting these public demonstrations that did so much to weaken the prestige of the state. And also by their essential decency. Horrible as these scenes must have been, they gave the fanatic the open test and trial he

required. We moderns do not do this. Our martyrs, who
are not children but mature men, die in lonely cells or
labor camps; their names are unknown to the world, their
fates undiscovered. Or if they are permitted to make a last
confession, it is only after they have been worn down by
methods that no one can resist into denying their own be-
liefs. Even the worst of authoritarian regimes have a
rough humanity, the result in part of their political in-
efficiency, which the totalitarian state lacks.

From the basilica of Santa Eulalia we went to the
museum. It is housed in an eighteenth-century domed
church which, because of the sense of space and air it gives,
is a pleasure to move about in. The Roman sculptures and
friezes, taken mostly from the theater, are above the usual
level to be found in the provinces; doubtless they were
carved by Greek or Roman artisans. However, Roman
sculpture, even at its best, is so dull and stereotyped that,
if we were not drawn to it by historical curiosity, we should
never look at it. The real treasure of this museum lies in
its collection of Visigothic sculpture, dug up from now
vanished churches. The more one sees of Visigothic art,
the more hopes it raises, and though these carved architectural fragments do not go beyond a crude imitation of the
new style that was growing up from the permeation of the
old Roman world by Oriental influences, they are all the
same strangely moving. Almost certainly they are the work
of Spanish artisans, with nothing Germanic about them
but the names of their rulers, and one will note that they
contain examples of the horseshoe arch which was a Visigothic rather than an Arab discovery. But how little we

know! Only two churches of certain Visigothic construction have survived to modern times, and though one of these, San Juan de Baños, near Palencia, is of surprising beauty, that is little to go upon. One is inevitably led to judge Visigothic architecture by that wonderful collection of miniature churches put up in Asturias in the ninth century; for although their date is later, their style is the same, and they show no new influences. This confirms an impression that sooner or later comes home to every traveler in the Peninsula—that though Spain is not a country of bold ideas or discoveries, there is yet a surprising quantity of artistic talent lying dormant in the various regions, which comes into play whenever the opportunity is given it.

The weather was warm and we were glad to sit in the open-air café that has been set up in the middle of the acacia-planted square under an awning. Here our chief entertainment was watching the storks. These odd birds are a great feature of Mérida. They nest for preference on Roman walls, aqueducts, and columns, but when they cannot get them they condescend to a church tower or to some projecting portion of a convent building. At a pinch they will take a town hall, but for anything modern, un-ecclesiastical, or unofficial they show a marked disinclination. Their manners are grave and dignified and it was amusing to watch a couple who had built their nest on a belfry in the square, just above the bells; when these rang, they stood up and slowly flapped their wings, as if in answer to a salute, and then sat down again. Once a horse became a Roman senator and it was, as Sterne would say, "a pretty fancy" that in Mérida the long vanished praetors, decurions and aediles might be enjoying a quiet prolongation of their existence in the form of these birds.

Of the Roman remains that crowd and clutter Mérida, the most famous is the theater. It is in good condition and has been intelligently restored. More beautiful, however, is the *alcázar* or fortress, which rises sheer from the river with its decaying granite stones and upright buttresses. Seen from the bridge, it makes an uneffaceable impression of strength and antiquity. Unfortunately, however, we could not enter it because it was temporarily closed to visitors. I regretted this the more because I remembered from my previous visit that it contains a Visigothic draw well, with a double flight of stairs leading down to the still water, which has a considerable fascination.

But how the archaeologists contrive to destroy the beauty of the places they excavate! I can remember Old Sarum when it was overgrown with yew and elder, as a place where the mind could lose itself in the dimness and uncertainty of the past. Then they dug it up and marked it out like a tennis court, and it became trite and commonplace. So it will soon be with Mérida. The value of most Roman remains is that they strike a note of age and vanished splendor which sets free the imagination, but the moment one stops to examine any particular ruin one is disappointed, because one can see that when it was new it had no more architectural beauty than a railway viaduct or a gas works. When they have been explored for the light they throw on history, they should be allowed to sink back into their natural state of decay.

One question that the visitor to Mérida is likely to ask is—why did the Romans create a city of this size and importance in such a waste? Mrs. Isobel Henderson, an expert on Roman Spain and the author of various learned articles on it, has kindly explained this to me. Baetica, which we call Andalusia, had been civilized for many centuries before the Romans came. With its old Iberian municipal system and its high standard of agriculture, it might almost be called a province of Italy. The East coast, too, with the Ebro valley had long been under Greek, Carthaginian and Roman influence. Since the center was thinly populated, there remained only the West which had not been Romanized. Of this the mountainous Northwest (the *Cantabrum indoctum iuga ferre nostra* of Horace's famous ode) was in Augustus' time incompletely subdued and therefore still under military rule, whereas Lusitania, the province comprising Portugal, Estremadura and the western fringe of Castile, had been subdued but not assimilated. That is to say, it lacked cities and its economy was pastoral rather than agricultural.

Mérida was therefore built by Augustus to be its capital and administrative center. Its immediate purpose was to provide homes and pensions for veterans; its larger purpose to develop the whole region and teach it the arts of peace and civilization. It was for this reason rushed up quickly, "like Mussolini's Ritz airdromes in the Libyan desert" as Mrs. Henderson puts it, without regard to expense or to its purely economic prospects. One may call it a gigantic propaganda stunt, intended to impress the cattle-herding natives with the grandeur of Rome and the advantages of accepting the way of life the Empire offered. Its actual position was determined by its being on the great North Road, the *Camino de la Plata,* that ran from Seville to Astorga; otherwise it should have been placed a little further to the west, near Badajoz, where there is more arable land.

Mérida retained its prosperity till the fall of the Empire, and the Visigoths made it one of their principal cities. Then in Arab times the rise of Badajoz, with its great plain and its stronger military situation, put it into the shade. The Reconquist completed its ruin: the city was handed over to the Knights of Santiago, who housed themselves in its Roman fortress, and its fields ceased to be cultivated. Soon the whole region was given up to the merino flocks of the Mesta. Today it has recovered and is for the first time in its history the small country town it is cut out to be.

Toward sunset, tired of sight-seeing, we walked out along the Roman bridge. It was crowded with men and women, mules and donkeys, returning to the town from the further bank. The water of the river was a pale, ethereal blue and on the broad expanse of yellow gravel on either side of it were women washing clothes in basins and spreading them out to dry, cattle standing idle with only their tails moving, and horsemen and muleteers giving their mounts a drink. Then behind these rose low green hills, almost crystalline in the clear light, and beyond them diminutive rock-crowned mountains, as blue and as high in tone as the mountains in a Patinir landscape. One never grows tired of the beauty of Spanish light and scenery.

On the further side of the bridge there are two *merenderos* or snack bars, where the people of the town resort when their work is over. *Radio Sevilla* blared out its droning *cante jondo* and the air had a faintly aromatic scent from the young poplar leaves that were unfolding. But the bridge could not be seen properly from this side, so we turned back to the town and took a lane leading along the other bank. Hardly however had we entered it when a boy whose acquaintance we had made at the café began calling us.

"Psst. Psst. Don't go along there! That's the *barrio de las mujeres,* the brothel quarter! Understand, the *señora* can't go along there."

We accepted the convention that a *señora* must not sully the natural purity of her disposition by looking at a prostitute, and my wife turned back. I however went on and after passing some girls taking the air in their dressing gowns by the stone parapet of the embankment (they enjoy the best view in the town), came to the end of the street and saw the long, crawling, black line of the bridge stretched out above the golden gravel and the blue water. Then the frogs began to croak in chorus, the crickets to chirp and another day in Southern Spain was over.

April 8

I HAVE made friends with the brother of the hotel proprietor. He is a pleasant, talkative man with a large mouth, small eyes screwed up in a perpetual good-natured smile, and glasses. Like all his family he is a convinced Monarchist. His father, he said, brought up six sons on a wage of 3½ pesetas a day and they always had enough to eat, but to live now on the same scale one needs thirty. Yet the agricultural wage is less than half that, besides being irregular. That is why, in spite of the higher rents, people are flocking into the towns. However to live well one has to have several jobs. He himself is a tailor in the afternoons, takes charge of his brother's hotel at night and makes a bit in his spare time as a land agent. He regards himself as lucky, especially as he pays a prewar rent. For the great majority of people life has become insupportable.

I asked him about the slaughterhouse. It seems that it is really an important enterprise. The owner, a young Galician, has been to Chicago to learn his trade and has installed in his factory the most modern machinery. He is also an enlightened employer. He pays good wages, rising to 30 pesetas a day, provides cheap and wholesome meals and insurance against sickness. For his technicians he has built a suburb of model houses, very pretty, with acacia walks and gardens, and bathrooms. What would Mérida be without him?

My new friend has a word which he uses continually—*una defensa*. Marriage is *una defensa*, knowing a trade is *una defensa*, getting on with one's landlord is *una defensa*. This word has, I think, its origin in the proverbial expression *defender el garbanzo*, "to defend the chick pea"—in other words "earn one's living." Anyhow it is typical. Life for the middle-class Spaniard is a continual war of defence against the encroachments of the State and the threats of unemployment and illness, which appear to his imagination as continually attacking and undermining him. In few countries is there so much economic insecurity.

One of the rituals to which the foreigner in Spain must adapt himself is the friendly stroll. Watch two men of the middle classes taking one. They walk ten paces and then, as the conversation warms up, stop and confront one another. Spaniards cannot converse, as the English do, with averted looks. They like to meet one another's eyes and watch the effect of what they are saying in one another's expressions. *Mal d'occhio,* evil eye, is thought to be a Mediterranean rather than a Northern superstition, but really it is the English who suffer from a collective fear of it; it is an instinctive belief of theirs that the human glance is dangerous. It is because Spaniards do not believe this that they regard it as permissible to stare at others and innocuous or even pleasant to be stared at.

Yet they show in other ways how much on their guard they are against one another. The whole of Spanish life, one may say, is organized in a sort of clan system. Within the clan—which consists of relatives, friends, political allies and so forth—all is warmth and friendliness; outside it all is distrust and suspicion. For this reason new acquaintances must be provisionally brought into the clan by the offer of bread and salt—in modern times, of a cigarette. Hence too all those pats on the back, those touches on the arm; they serve to give reassurance. It may be that this way of conducting social relations is the mark of a primitive or imperfectly organized society, but at least it avoids the English vice of indifference.

The morning being rather hot, we walked across the square to the parish church of Santa María. It is a medieval church, begun in the thirteenth century and added to in the fifteenth, with a short, broad nave and two aisles, off which open the usual side chapels crowded with the blaze and litter of baroque ornament. The windows, small, square, and closely barred, are placed high, just under the roof, so that the light, entering from above, scoops out the general configuration of the walls and vaulting, but leaves a dimness that satisfies the senses. Out of this one picks out with peculiar delight the tall clustered columns of soft granite, which, since they have only rudimentary capitals, one can follow up without any check to the eye till they break out like the petals of lilies into the three ribbed leaves of the stone vault. All the proportions of the building are designed to calm and satisfy—not pressed together into a high narrow passage like most French and English Gothic, but giving out round them a feeling of space and of the circulation of air. Thus, though quite modest in its scale, this church strikes me as being the most beautiful I have seen on this journey, excepting only the Mosque of Cordova. It confirms the impression I have often had before, especially when visiting the magnificent churches of Catalonia, that Spanish Gothic is an intrinsically finer style than French. The classic tradition of the South was antagonistic to the strained, soaring uprush of the other, which seems to aim at defying the forces of gravity rather than at producing a building which will be harmonious in its proportions and give the sensation of a hollow shell resounding with shadow and light. But of course the climate of the South was a factor in this, by making it possible to reduce the window space to a few small openings.

In fact the two styles, though they make use of the same idiom, are very different in their arms. Norman Gothic is romantic architecture: it is inspired by ideas of growth and forest vegetation, by new forces bursting into life, new classes and social patterns arising; it conveys the restlessness of people hurrying toward the future and thus foretells the age of the Industrial Revolution and the great spate of modern energy that has transformed the world. Spanish Gothic, on the other hand, expresses the old stationary world of fixed dogma and Oriental traditionalism: in its exterior aspect, the majesty of towers and upright buttresses and of buildings made to exist beyond time; in its interior, the plastic sense which is the gift of the East and of its brilliant pupil, the Mediterranean. It is an architecture made for those who, because they live in the present, attach a higher value to contemplation than to action.

But to return to Santa María, the baroque decorations of the chapels add a note of refined yet barbaric splendor to the otherwise bare interior. Every chapel delights with its carved and gilded *retablos,* its ecstatic Christs and Madonnas, its complicated plaster convolutions and dimly discovered, smoke-blackened paintings. One does not often see great art in these golden candlelit recesses, but what one does almost always discover is a high level of plastic skill and invention, a perpetual variety and an exuberant yet somehow always triumphant taste and design. It is in

churches such as these, unstarred by Baedeker and often
unknown to any guide, that the principal delights and sur-
prises of Spanish travel are to be found. How sad then that
over so large an area they have been wantonly gutted!

After lunch, as it was still too hot for walking, we took
a taxi to visit the so-called Lake of Proserpine, which is a
Roman reservoir lying some three miles outside the town.
Mounting a low rise, we came suddenly upon a wide
stretch of undulating country, covered with rocks, grass,
asphodels and a few scattered ilex trees. This is the beginning of the great sheep and cattle-raising region of Estremadura that stretches northward to Salamanca and west to
Portugal. Below, in a hollow, lay a blue lake, some half a
mile in diameter. So clear, so blue it looked among its
rocky margins that one would have said it was a lough in
County Clare or Connemara.

We stopped when we reached it and got out. Beside us
was the dam that blocked the valley—a long wall of finely
cut stones, strengthened with upright buttresses—a splendid
example of the builders' art and showing the beauty that
can be given to simple masonry. It looked as firm as if it
had been put up yesterday. Somewhere close by was found
the slab, now lost, that gives its name to the lake. It contained a curious inscription—asking, begging and demanding the Turibigensian goddess Ataecina Proserpina that
she would avenge the loss of certain clothes that had been
stolen: to wit, tunics, 6; mantles, 2; shirts, ? . . . and here
the slab broke off and the rest of this ancient Roman washing list was effaced.

Below the dam there stood a largish farmhouse with

various outhouses and other buildings, all in a state of utter
neglect and dilapidation. A few bedraggled children were
playing about, for a family of laborers lived here, and run-
nels of water that had leaked from the reservoir turned the
ground into a quagmire. But there was no sign of any of
this precious water being used for irrigation.

I asked the chauffeur who it belonged to.

"Once this was a cattle ranch," he said, "and a prosperous
one too, but when the late owner died there was a lawsuit
between his heirs, who were brothers and sisters, and a lot
of money was wasted. Finally the youngest son won it, but
as he lives in Madrid and has no need of the income because
his wife is wealthy, the place has fallen into its present condition. Now malaria has broken out and the house is uninhabited in summer."

"It's a pity another brother did not get it," I said.

"That would have made no difference," he replied, "for
the elder brother is in a bad way too. He inherited the best
part of his father's estate, but as he was the Conservative
deputy to the Cortes and a man of great influence in the
district, he omitted to pay taxes. Now the State has closed
down on him and he has been obliged to mortgage his
whole property to settle the fifty years' arrears that are
owing. All that is left to him is his *palacio* in the town,
where he lives on his wife's income. Great sympathy is felt
for him."

"Great sympathy!" I exclaimed. "Why?"

"Well, perhaps he has done some things he had better
not have done, but then, just think, he was a man of influence, a deputy! Everyone in that position did such things

in the old days. And then he has always been liked in
Mérida. Although he comes of a very old family, he has no
false pride, but talks freely to everyone. And today he is
more respected than ever because of the fidelity he has
shown to the King; that of course is why they came down
on him over the taxes. Why, only the other day I saw him
kneeling in the church with his arms stretched out in the
form of a cross—no light thing for a man of his age—in
front of the *Virgen de los Dolores*. 'Well, Don F.,' I said to
him, 'what's the trouble now?' 'I'm praying,' he replied,
'to the Virgin to bring the King back to Spain before I
die.' "

This chauffeur was an elderly man with grizzled hair,
rather silent, with strong and deep convictions. Brought
up in great poverty, the son of a herdsman, he had all his
life been a devout Monarchist. He showed no animosity to
Franco, whom he regarded as a good general, but had an
utter contempt for the Falange.

"Look at Spain today," he said. "The working man is
starving, the middle classes can barely stagger along. We
are approaching complete disaster. And everyone knows
the reason."

"And what is the reason?" I asked.

"Why, that the directing classes are robbing the country.
Where does the oil go, where does the corn go, if not into
their pockets? As you know, they are all Falangists. They
haven't a peseta to call their own when they obtain office
and within a year or two they have large cars, large busi-
nesses, large estates all over the country. There's no secret
about it. Everyone knows it."

"But haven't the politicians always been like this?"

"They have avoided paying taxes, given jobs to their friends—in short, protected themselves. Everyone must defend his own interests. But made fortunes out of the country—no. That, never."

The thing that the chauffeur most complained of was the recently instituted office known as the *fiscalía*. The *fiscales* are officers appointed by the State with the powers of the secret police. Their business is to unearth supplies of corn, oil and other foodstuffs that are being kept for the black market. To enable them to do this they have the right to search houses, arrest, and impose fines without any legal process or sanction whatever. But the worst feature of these inquisitorial proceedings is that the *fiscales* act on the information of delators whose names are never revealed. These delators receive a reward of 40 per cent of the value of what is discovered, so that delation becomes a prosperous business on which people thrive and grow rich. The result is an atmosphere of suspicion in which no one can trust anyone else.

"You should just see," he said, "a town when the *fiscal* enters it. As soon as he is recognized, the streets are emptied, the shops will not serve him and no one will speak to him. He is treated like Judas."

"But surely," I said, "the fact that these great powers have been given to the *fiscales* is a proof that the government is sincere in its desire to suppress the black market."

"The government perhaps," he said, "but the individuals who compose it, no. The black market would soon fizzle out if it was not maintained by an artificial system of scarcity. And in any case it gets its chief supplies, not from the landowner, but from the stores held by the syndicates and other official bodies."

We were sitting by the edge of the lake with our feet dangling over the stone wall that held in the water. There was not a breath of air to stir the surface and one could hear a partridge calling from the hills a mile away.

"Who does this lake belong to?" I asked.

"The State."

"Then why don't they use the water for irrigation?"

He shrugged his shoulders:

"What do they care about irrigation? They aren't even working on the canal begun by Primo de Rivera twenty-five years ago."

"You must remember," I said, "that they lack credits. To get things going again they need a foreign loan."

"I'll tell you a story," he said. "In this town there is a family who have lost all their money by gambling. Their clothes are worn thin, their larder is empty and they don't know where their next meal is coming from. Yet they own a large house full of pictures and furniture and even two or three old cars. 'Sell them,' their friends say, 'sell them. What use are they to you now?' So they make up their minds to sell them and send for the dealers. The dealers arrive. They go round everything and put their fingers into everything, and then they make their offer. But this offer doesn't please the owners at all. 'What,' they exclaim, 'that's all you'll give! Why, these things that have come down to us from our ancestors are worth twenty times more. We'd rather starve than let them go for less than their proper value!' So the dealers go away and the family returns to its crusts. And, believe me, it's true that they'd rather go on living like this than lose their belief that their possessions are of immense value. Now I've often thought to myself that this family is like the Spanish nation. We are proud, very proud. We think that we are worth a lot, and in the eyes of the world we are worth very little. So if some foreign nation were to come along and offer us a loan on reasonable terms—such as for example that we should put our affairs in order a bit—we'd drive them away from the door with insults."

"Yes," I said, "and then ask them to come round quietly to the back entrance."

He laughed, and we got up to go. The fish were beginning to make circles in the lake and the sun to descend behind the green hills of Portugal.

"Poor Spain!" he exclaimed as he started the engine. "What a state it's in! *Todo abandonado—todo abandonado.*"

On our way back into the town four civil guards passed us walking in file.

"Look at them!" the chauffeur exclaimed. "There are two of those gentry here for every working man. How can the country support such a load?"

However, when later on that evening I praised the car we had driven in, a man said:

"Don't you know? It's a police car. He hires it from them."

And it seems that, as private cars are scarce, this is a regular custom.

TALAVERA *and*
TOLEDO

OUR time in Spain was getting short. We should be obliged to pass through Estremadura, that region of beautiful towns, without stopping. A diesel railway coach was leaving next morning for Madrid, so, as this is the only rapid form of travel on this line, we decided to take it as far as Talavera and from there get a motorbus to Toledo.

Scarcely had we taken our seats when a man came up and addressed us in excellent English. He was the English master at the *instituto* or *lycée* of Mérida and a great Anglophile. He took an empty place beside us and in his company the time flew by rapidly.

A. had had one of those sad histories that are rather the rule than the exception in Spain today. He was Castilian of good family. His father, a retired colonel, had been shot in Madrid during the Civil War and so had his elder brother and eighteen other members of his family. He himself had spent the war in prison and owed his survival to his youth. But he was a man of great mildness of disposition and appeared to bear no resentment. Most of the murders he believed to have been due to foreign influence, and he gave as an instance of this the fact that his father had been shot by a tribunal of the G.P.U. in which the only Spaniard present had been an interpreter.

We came, as one always does in Spain, to the question of the high cost of living. His salary was 6,000 pesetas. He was able to live and support his family only because he had private means. As a point of comparison, an infantry officer gets with his allowances between 20,000 and 24,000 pesetas, and even on that finds it difficult to maintain his position if he is married. But then nearly half the national budget is spent on the armed forces and police and only one fifteenth on education.

Like so many of the middle-class Spaniards of today, A. was an admirer of English institutions and ways of life. At night he dreamed of green fields with herds of brown and white cows browsing on them and of a mild, red-faced race, much given to beer drinking, going quietly on their errands. I told him that if I were a Spaniard I should feel in the same way. I should grow tired of the disorder and irresponsibility of Spanish political life and crave for a little of the enlightened selfishness of the English. However, since I *was* English—I added—I found in Spain a kind of freedom and spontaneity that I missed at home. What in our country one gains in order and social justice, one loses in zest and vitality. And then have not Northerners always had to go to the Mediterranean to learn the arts of life? In these matters the English were still philistines.

"You think of us then as a primitive people?" our new friend asked.

"In some respects, yes," I replied. "As Mediterraneans, you are a people who have not yet been conquered by the pattern of industrial life with its crushing discipline. Outwardly you conform, but inwardly you resist and sabotage it. Then, as Iberians or Ligurians, or whatever the word for the aboriginal Spaniards should be, you are a family of spoiled children who every twenty years quarrel and break up the toys in your nursery. Besides this you have a certain aristocratic quality, a sort of pride in yourselves which is fortified by an Oriental stoicism; and it is this that makes you liked and esteemed wherever you go. It's a quality for which we English no longer have any word, but which you call *nobleza*."

"Yes, yes," said A. eagerly. "That is something on which we Castilians in particular pride ourselves. We are gentlemen. But how curious, is it not, that we two, meeting by chance like this, should both be people who envy the qualities of one another's nations! You a Hispanophile, I an Anglophile!"

"In the federal Europe of the future," I said, "we shall find it quite natural to have a second *patria* in some other European country—a *patria* of our ideals, of our superego. We shall each of us marry a foreign nation and those marriages, whether platonic or otherwise, will be the bond which will keep our federation of diverse speeches and races together. You and I, with our admiration of one another's countries, are the forerunners of this system."

"I like that idea," he said. "It's good."

As we moved swiftly along, a wild heath-like expanse rolled monotonously by beyond the carriage windows. We crossed the Tagus in its narrow trench and the country became more arid. At one point we put up a flight of giant bustards. Then the train drew into Plasencia station and, in accordance with the excellent custom of Spanish trains, waited for us while we had lunch. And, need I say it, that lunch was ten thousands times better than any lunch ever eaten in a British railway waiting room.

After Plasencia the train turned eastward along the Tagus valley. At first it ran through ilex woods; then the trees ceased and cornfields took their place. On our left lay a broad, hollow plain, green with young corn, and beyond it rose, as in Juan Ramón Jiménez's poem, the vast silent mass of the Sierra de Gredos, its summits glittering with snow. Toward four o'clock we reached Talavera de la Reina.

Talavera was the home town of Francisco de Rojas, the author of *La Celestina*, which is not only the first of European novels (it came out in 1499) but also one of the greatest. Rojas, who was a *converso* or converted Jew, was at one times its *alcalde mayor* or mayor. Later it was the birthplace of another eminent writer, the Jesuit Juan de Mariana (1536–1624), who wrote here his great history. But these antecedents have not prevented it from being today a disagreeable place and one of the few towns in Spain that one can call squalid. Its streets are dusty and badly paved, its buildings either ugly or insignificant and its whole layout aimless and straggling. Nor does one see whitewash. Coming up from the South, with its cult of civil elegance and formality, one is shocked by the indifference shown to aesthetic things and even to ordinary cleanliness. Talavera manages to combine the worst qualities of Castile and of Estremadura.

But the river Tagus is beautiful. A really great river, carrying ten times the volume of water of the Guadiana, it has the consistency and reserves of strength of Northern streams. Thus, in spite of the drought, it flowed in two broad channels that occupied more than half of its broad bed. Its color was a deep yellow—gold, when a poet looks at it—and its banks were lined with tall white-trunked poplar trees and bushes of giant tamarisk. The old bridge, low and many-arched, had been damaged by floods and a new, ugly steel bridge had been put up beside it.

We walked back through the dusty, aimless streets, passing the bare wall of the famous pottery factory. Considerable stretches of the Roman and Arab fortifications remain, including some mysteriously tall and massive towers; in any other town than this they would please one. Every fountain, we noticed, was surrounded by a group of a dozen or so women waiting their turn to fill their pitchers. There is no public water supply and I was told that in summer time, when the tap trickles slowly, the women queue for hours and even sit up all night. They bring out guitars and make it into a sort of social occasion. Yet there is abundant water in the Sierra Guadarrama not far away and the town is rich. The explanation is that for the last sixty years or so the municipal authorities have been corrupt and negligent.

We made our way back to the hotel hot and covered with dust. A tiresome wind had got up and, in these streets which are never swept or watered, vague eddies of dust and straw and waste paper were blowing and whirling about. The Angelus was ringing—a harsh, angry sound—and in the dingy café with its dark cracking walls, decorated with a paper frieze that showed a pattern of worm marks and hung with a flyblown portrait of Franco and colored posters of bullfighters, the loud raucous voices of unshaven men discussing a football match produced a mood of depression.

The traveler, alas, is at the mercy of his aesthic sensations. A fine evening, a seat under a plane tree, the smile of a peasant girl, the scent of orange flower, a view over mountains or river—and he feels at home. His country is not the land where his friends live, but the wider territory of beautiful things—the territory where, if one agrees with Stendhal, he collects those promissory notes of happiness which give a precious fraction of their value when they are pocketed. He is therefore continually subject to accidents. An ugly town, a rainy day, an unsympathetic hotel, and he is at once a double exile—equally far from his native land and from that ideal country which he has set out to visit. The only recourse left is a bottle of wine.

We had intended to go on next day to Toledo, but it was Sunday and there was no bus. To get through the time therefore we walked out to Nuestra Señora del Prado, the hermitage church which contains the local Virgin. Immediately after Easter a fair is held here which is known as *Las Mondas*. Although its ceremonies are no longer what they used to be, it is famous to folklorists as being a survival of the pagan festival of *Cerealia*. The characteristic feature is the procession of girls from the neighboring villages, carrying flower-decked baskets which contain small offerings to the Virgin; these are the *Cereris munda* of which Apuleius speaks in his *Apologia,* and which in his time consisted of objects which the profane must not see, such as phallic symbols, sprigs of vegetation and barley cakes.

Another ritual which has fallen out of use at Talavera, though it survives in various Estremaduran and Andalusian *pueblos,* is that of the Bull of St. Mark. A bull is caught, doped with wine till it has become gentle and paraded through the town under the name of the saint. Women and girls caress it with Pasiphaë-like gestures, and their future fate in love and childbearing are deduced from its response to their attentions. It is commonly believed that the bull becomes gentle because the spirit of St. Mark has entered into it—a view which we Northerners may find a little odd, because that spirit is entirely sexual. But St. Mark is really a thin disguise for Zeus. Another part of the ritual consists in the blessing of the cattle in front of the church and in the distribution of a ring-shaped roll of bread—the *rosca de San Marco.* I once lived in a village near Granada where this ceremony took place every year on April 25.

After lunch we took a car down the valley to Puente del Arzobispo. The weather was grey and a high covering of whitish, oyster-shell clouds made the empty landscape appear emptier than ever. On our left ran the Tagus with its line of poplars and willows and beyond it rose the arid hills of the Montes de Toledo. At Puente del Arzobispo there is an ancient bridge and here the river enters the *tajo* or trench from which it gets its name and in which it remains confined until it reaches Abrantes in Portugal.

We returned by the main Seville-Madrid highway. At Oropesa there is a magnificent castle of the Duques de Frias, which has been turned into a state hostelry. Here one can live in luxury and at moderate cost (60 pesetas a day) and look out on an immense sweep of corn lands leading up to the snow-covered Sierra de Gredos. These hotels of the Patronato de Turismo, which were founded by General Primo de Rivera, are a great boon to those travelers who wish to see Spain in comfort.

Our chauffeur was a short, ugly man with a habit of making a violent grimace whenever he spoke. He made no criticisms of the regime yet, like everyone else, was pessimistic about the present situation. Speaking of the Civil War, he said:

"Why call them Reds? Both sides were of the same color and both did terrible things. On our side and on theirs there were people who killed just like that—for pleasure."

But this was in his philosophical moments; in another mood he said, pointing to the Castle of Oropesa and making his largest grimace:

"The Reds were in such a funk when General Yagüe approached that they couldn't hold even a fortress like that. The mere rumor of a Moor within ten miles sent them scuttling off as fast as they could go. Yet this didn't prevent them from burning all the images and *retablos* in the churches or shooting fifty harmless people. They were men without guts."

"What sort of people did they shoot?" I asked.

"Mostly landowners. But they only killed the good ones. The bad had fled, and those who remained were those who had nothing on their conscience."

I gathered from him that, though this is a country of large estates, the land is well cultivated. Tractors and mechanical reapers are used, the farm hands are taken on by the year and little casual labor is employed. Every laborer is given an allotment and can buy corn and oil at cost price from the estate. His position therefore, in spite of the lowness of the wages, is decidedly better than that of the Andalusian *jornalero*.

We spent the evening talking to this chauffeur and his friends in the café. He introduced us to his elder son, a good-looking boy of eighteen who was learning French, English, and Italian all at the same time. In his spare moments he wrote poetry and one of his poems had been read aloud on the radio. His father was naturally very proud of him. But oh the cost of bringing up a family! Expatiating on this, he told me that he found 70 pesetas a day the minimum on which he could live and even then he only managed by concentrating on food and dressing badly. To earn so large an amount one had to buy most of one's petrol on the black market at three times the usual price, as the official ration was insufficient. One got it from farmers who did not use their ration. So profitable was this trade that there were some people who found it worth while to buy a tractor so as to sell their petrol coupons. Just as in the old days a family kept two or three cows and lived off their milk, so now they kept a tractor and lived off its petrol.

The subject of the stockyard at Mérida and its enlightened owner came up.

"Oh yes," said the chauffeur, "there is a new sort of employer about. At Navalcarnero there is one who has a cement factory, and the government encourages him by giving him contracts. He has put up model houses, schools and dining rooms for his workmen and he even, I think, provides insurance."

"But surely," I said, "there is a government insurance system for factory workers."

"Yes," he replied, "there is. But the trouble in this country is that, though we have good laws, no one observes them. The *Ley de Previsión* (Insurance Act), for example, is an excellent law, but look how it is carried out! Half the people entitled to insurance money don't get it, whereas others, who are not entitled to it, do. And so it has always been. We Spaniards are not like other races—we are bad, bad, bad. That's the truth of the matter."

Ever since I first came to Spain in 1919, I have heard this said again and again by people of all sorts and descriptions. And up to a point it is true: the Spaniards have no sense of equity. They live by a tribal or client system, which makes it a moral duty for them to favor their friends at the expense of the State and to penalize their adversaries. That is the first law of this country, and it was as much observed during the rule of the Republic as it is today. Three-quarters of the endemic revolutionary feeling in Spain is caused by it.

Our bus next morning started early—to be precise at seven o'clock. We staggered out of the hotel, still half dazed from sleep, and took the road to the ticket office. As we went into the street we passed women sweeping the dust from their doorways into the street and a few workmen on the way to the potteries. Overhead the still grey sky with its ceiling of oyster-shell clouds had a tinge of rose in it.

After buying our tickets, we went into a bar close by to

have some much needed coffee. Here an elderly man, who was drinking a glass of anise, engaged us in conversation.

"So you are on your way back to England?"

"We are."

"Does it take long to get to England by airplane?"

"Four hours."

"*Caramba!* Is that all? Only four hours!"

"That's all."

"And is England the next nation to Spain?"

"No, first comes France."

"And so to get to England you must pass over France?"

"Exactly."

"*Caramba!* Who'd have thought that? And as you pass you will see the French below you?"

"We will."

"Those would be the same French of—of—Napoleon?"

"Their descendants."

"*Caramba!* So you will see the descendants of the ones we defeated here and drove back?"

"That is so."

"And after that you will come to your own country?"

"We will."

"*Caramba,* who'd have thought that the world was so great!" Turning to the others, "Here we Spaniards sit and never go anywhere and these foreigners travel through all the nations and see everything! They know all there is to know and we sit here like brutes and know nothing. *Caramba!*"

The bus started. Beside us sat an old man with a face

wrinkled like a dry hillside, who wore a small beret on his head and a striped blanket over his shoulders. There was a quince-complexioned woman who was afraid of being sick, several peasant matrons in voluminous black, a couple of nuns and four or five commercial travelers with their boxes of samples. Still only half awake, we watched the soft grey cloths of the olive trees, the little red flames of the pomegranate bushes, the green gases of the hedgerows floating past us. Then we climbed out of the Tagus valley and the scene at once became harsh and dreary. Dry uplands planted with unpromising corn, no trees, castles on the horizon. "A mangy wearisome country" as Richard Ford describes it, and it lasted till we came charging down a ravine and saw Toledo on its hill before us.

We took rooms in the Hotel del Lino, an old hotel in a still older house. The pleasant proportions of the low-ceilinged rooms, the ample width of the doors and passages, the ancient, hard, lumpy beds and dated furniture evoked the ghosts of the Victorian young ladies who had once stayed here with their papas and mamas and sallied out into the sunny streets carrying silk parasols and the thick buff volumes of Ford's *Hand Book*. My own great grandmother had been one of these: here in the 1840's she had been courted by a young Irish colonel, who knew all about Spain because he had fought in the Carlist War, and a few weeks later ran off with him by post chaise, pursued as far as the Pyrenees by her indignant parents, who never forgave her for marrying a penniless soldier.

As soon as we had had some coffee we went to visit the Alcazar. This is a square barrack-like pile, rebuilt after a

fire in the eighteenth century, which stands up like a huge
ugly box in the middle of the city. Here at the outbreak of
the Civil War General Moscardó took refuge with I forget how many civil guards and military cadets, as well as
some women and children, and defended himself against
the attacks of the Republicans until he was relieved by the
Nationalist army advancing from Seville. It was a heroic
feat, and the beam of history has fallen on it and given it a
prestige not granted to the much more prolonged and
tragic defence of the Civil Guard in the hermitage of
Nuestra Señora de la Cabeza in the Sierra Morena. The
culminating horror was the blowing up of the building by
a mine a few days before its relief. The defenders, huddled
in the most distant of the cellars, escaped, but everything
else was left a ruin. Today the shell rises, gaunt and hid-
eous, above the somber roofs of the city and there it will
stay until a swing of the pendulum brings a change of feeling, for the intention of the present regime is to preserve
it as a national memorial. To house the military cadets
who used to live here, a large ugly barracks has been put
up on the opposite side of the river gorge.

The underground cellars where the garrison lived are
shown and we went in to see them. On the wall of General
Moscardó's headquarters there is a marble plaque, report-
ing a telephone conversation that took place during the
siege between the Commander of the Republican Militia
in the city and the General. The Commander rang up the
General to inform him that his son, a boy of seventeen,
would be shot unless he surrendered the Alcázar, and, to
make the threat more actual, brought the boy to the tele-

phone to speak to his father. The moving conversation that took place between them is recorded. "You must get ready to die," the General said, and the son replied, "Yes, father. I will." He was then taken out and shot.

Now this was not the isolated act of a fanatical militia-man. The Prime Minister, Largo Caballero, an elderly and respectable trade union leader, whose head had been turned by his sudden elevation to power, was in Toledo at the time and had taken personal charge of everything relating to the siege. He must have given his consent to this deed, which at any period in history would have been regarded as cruel and base. One could not have a better example of how profoundly revolutions corrupt those who take part in them.

And what was the effect of this heroic defence? Franco, hurrying to relieve the Alcázar, missed the chance of entering Madrid before the International Brigade arrived. Had Moscardó not defended himself, the war would have been over within a few weeks. In that case a civil government under General Mola and not a military dictatorship backed by the Falange would have been established. On the other hand the blowing of the mine not only failed to achieve its object, but destroyed much of the glass in the Cathedral and also the delightful Posada de la Sangre, where Cervantes had stayed and which was still in use as a peasants' inn.

After lunch we walked down by the Puerta del Sol to the Hospital de Afuera, on the northern outskirts of the city. It is a large, handsome building put up by Cardinal Tavera in 1541–1579 and contains an arcaded court, divided down the middle by a two-storied gallery, which is one of the finest things to be seen in Spain in the Italian style. Before the war this building was used as a hospital, but lately it has come into the possession of the Duquesa de Lerma, who has furnished one wing very splendidly with antique furniture. Visitors are shown over it and there are three good El Grecos.

The streets of Toledo are steep, the cobbles hard to the soles. One loses one's way in the maze of narrow lanes and gets tired. After some further explorations, therefore, we found our way back to one of the cafés in the Plaza de Zocodover, where we settled down to coffee, ices and buttered toast.

What historic events, I told myself, had taken place in this little market square! Here the Visigothic, the Arab, the Castilian kings of Middle Ages had come and gone. Here the Cid had come clattering up from the bridge on his charger Babicca, with his beard tied in a net so that his enemies should not pluck it, to submit his suit against his daughters' husbands to King Alfonso. Within a few hundred yards of its paving stones St. Theresa had sat and scribbled her letters, Garcilaso de la Vega had grown to manhood, Tirso de Molina, the creator of *Don Juan,* had spent his best years, the Archpriest of Hita, Spain's ebullient Chaucer, and St. John of the Cross, her greatest lyric poet and mystic, had languished in prison. Here too Lope de Vega had kept one of his mistresses, Cervantes had come escaping the boredom of his wife's family, Góngora had visited El Greco.

But, as every tourist knows, thoughts of this kind are a

mere rhetorical exercise. The historic imagination refuses to rise for such proddings. Only through books can one take flight into the past. And so we soon got tired of looking at this dull little square with its irrecoverable memories, all the more since it is never lit up, like the streets of Southern cities, by the animation of the evening *paseo*. We called the waiter and got up to go.

The best way to see Toledo is to forget about directions and town plans and follow any street that takes one's fancy. We set off and, perhaps because we were feeling a little tired, found ourselves walking downhill. As we descended, the houses got older, the inhabitants poorer, the lanes more twisting and narrow. The frying oil smelled more rancid and the ribs of the street dogs stood out more starkly. We were entering the Middle Ages and when we looked up we could see, like the turrets of an Arthurian castle, the rocky crest of the opposite face of the river gorge, and every time we saw it, it was closer to us and higher above us.

Suddenly a great sensation. We had come out on a little space by the edge of the water. A flat-bottomed boat was tied up there, a ferryman sat waiting in it, some steps led down to it. Near by a few sheep were feeding. In front the yellow current poured by between its narrow walls and beyond it rose the savage rocks of the further shore, dark and sunless, without trees or houses. All about us the light was failing, though when we looked up we could see that a fish-shaped cloud, that floated motionless in the center of the sky, had turned a deep crimson. As we stood looking at it, the ferryman beckoned to us and I had that sensation, so strange when it occurs, that at some time, I did not know

when, I had been here before. Yet it seemed also true that
we had come to a totally mysterious and unvisited place—a
combined image of the cliffs and rivers in Dante's *Inferno*,
the banks of Styx or Phlegethon as a new Marco Polo might
see them, pastoral and but vaguely inhabited, supposing
him to have come on them after the failure of belief in a
life beyond death had left them vacant and derelict. And
then I remembered where I had seen this spot before.
Once, after reading Dante, I dreamed that I had joined
an archaeological expedition for excavating the ruins of
the Christian hell which had just been discovered—its fires
long extinct with the decay of the faith that had created
them and its famous monuments covered over with ash and
sand—and this grey bank on the gorge of the Tagus, or
something like it, had been the place I had seen in my
dream.

For a short time we stood there, while the glow in the
cloud above us faded, then climbed up again in the half
darkness the slope we had so easily descended, and returned to our hotel.

Of the many buildings in Toledo that are worth a visit,
the only one which Baedeker double-stars is the Cathedral.
It is a thirteenth-century Gothic edifice, built to the plan
of French architects, but much altered later. I confess that
I find it disappointing. In every great building of the Middle Ages there is something to admire, but to my mind this
cathedral falls much below its reputation. There is a feeling of discomfort in the fact that the nave is too narrow for
its height and that the aisles are by comparison low and
squat. Then the Spanish habit of planting a choir in the

middle of the nave, like a church within a church, is particularly fatal to Gothic buildings, which are best seen in
long diagonal vistas. However as a museum the Cathedral
is unequalled. The splendid Flemish glass in the windows
(much damaged by the explosion at the Alcázar), the choir
stalls carved by Berruguete, the Renaissance *rejas* that en-
close the chapels, and the paintings by Juan de Borgoña
are all well worth looking at, while the treasury and
sacristy are crowded with precious and sometimes beautiful objects, among them several admirable El Grecos. I
must not forget either the collection of embroidered vest-
ments and other fabrics, which include a fourteenth-cen-
tury chasuble of rare beauty and two Moslem banners
captured at the battle of the Río Salado. Personally I find
these early fabrics, with their heraldic or maze-like designs, very moving to the imagination. The Orientals made
of pattern and decoration something that affects the sense
of sight like rhyme in poetry. Their abnormal sensibility
to small variations of light, color, and spacing enabled them
to create the sort of pattern which, by bringing out the
value of these variations, leads to effects that are on an
altogether higher plane of beauty than could be achieved
in the West. Thus an Oriental pattern becomes not a
string of identical things repeated, but a design in which
each separate element increases in some mysterious way
the potency of the others.

Three churches stand out above the many admirable
buildings in Toledo, and all of these are Oriental. The
first is Santo Cristo de la Luz, a small mosque built in 922
and altered by Mudejar architects to suit the purposes of

Christian worship. The other two are synagogues, built during the Christian occupation in pure Moslem style. The larger of these, Santa María la Blanca, is a building with five naves, divided by rows of pillars that support horseshoe arches. Lovely in its proportions and in its arabesques, it has, I think, been overrestored. The smaller is the Tránsito, built by a treasurer of Pedro the Cruel in 1366. Imagine an oblong box, seventy-six feet by thirty-one, bare in its lower part but with rich arabesque friezes running round the upper walls and above them an arcade pierced with small windows, which let in a subdued light through their lattices of carved alabaster. The roof is of coffered cedar, inlaid with ivory and mother-of-pearl plaques to bring out the complex pattern of the woodwork, and the sensation of cool delight and repose one gets on entering is a proof of what perfectly chosen proportions, enhanced by a contrast between bare walls and a richly decorated surface, can do for the spirit. In its general plan no interior of a religious building could be simpler, yet every time I have seen it I have felt an intense and peculiar emotion.

These arabesque patterns of the Moslems or Arabized Jews have a hypnotic effect on the mind which on second thought could well be called mystical. I have often asked myself why this should be so. Sitting in this synagogue today it occurred to me that it might be because, while the general design was too complex for the eye to follow out in detail, it gave one a feeling of certainty that a pattern was there and that the same leaf or scroll that one saw in front of one would reappear a little further on in the same context, and then a little further again and so again and again. The surface of the wall had the apparent complexity of Nature, yet everything in it—even the Hebrew writing which affirmed its purpose—was under the law of order and eternal recurrence. This gave a deep feeling of satisfaction and reassurance. For what else is mysticism but the sense of exultation given by the sudden perception that there is order and harmony where at first sight there appeared to be nothing but arbitrariness and confusion?

But, to leave buildings, what am I to say of Toledo as a whole? The impression, I confess, it makes on me is of a strange, dark, almost ominous city. Built on a bare rocky hill in a loop of the Tagus—a fortress if there ever was one —it has, through the greater part of its history, been the citadel not of the kings but of the Church. Here the most menacing religious power the world has seen held its state and from tortuous lanes and gloomy palaces stretched out its tentacles—sometimes for good and sometimes for evil. Under the weak Visigothic kings it showed its persecuting energy against the Jews to a degree not known in any country before Hitler (for example, in 633 it persuaded King Sisebut to order that every Jewish child should be taken from its parents, and a few years later that every circumcised male should be castrated) and in a later period it set up the Spanish Inquisition. Yet in between there was a tolerant interval. In the twelfth century, just after its re-capture from the Moslems, Toledo became a center of Arabic and Jewish studies—the place from which, with the help of Jewish interpreters, Greek philosophy was trans-mitted to the Western world. However this was not a

Spanish venture. It was effected through the influence of the French and Burgundian clergy who dominated the court and under the direction of a French archbishop, trained at Cluny. The Toledan clergy, conservative to the core, fought to maintain their old rites and customs.

A city then of priests rather than of laymen; an anthill in which the ruling ants were marked out by their large black thoraxes. This situation began under the Visigoths. The Church acquired immense wealth during this time and the bishops became potentates who reigned over wide lands and thousands of slaves. The archbishops of Toledo, metropolitans of Spain, controlled the kings by supporting them against their unruly nobles and then leading the nobles against them when they became too strong. Thus they got rid of King Wamba who had expressed the intention of taxing them—giving him, it is said, a drug that took away his memory—and by this helped to prepare the way for the Arab conquest.

Under the Moslems Toledo reverted to what it had been in Roman times—a provincial city. One of its archbishops, Elipando, lapsed into the Nestorian heresy, while others bore Arabic names such as Obaidalah ben Kasi. Then, on its recapture by the Christians in 1086, the wealth that the Moslems had taken from the Church began to pour back again, till in the seventeenth century no bishop in Europe except the Pope had higher rents than its archbishop. However the kings of Castile did not feel comfortable in so ecclesiastical an atmosphere and after a short residence left for good. The last great drama came in 1559 when Archbishop Carranza was arrested by the Inquisition on suspicion of holding Lutheran ideas on works and grace and kept in prison for seventeen years before his acquittal by a Roman tribunal. So fine had the line of theological orthodoxy become in Spain that they could indict a man who, when he had been confessor to Queen Mary in England, had burned Protestants. As in the case of the Russians today, the mere fact of his having lived abroad made him suspected.

Yet if this great concentration of ecclesiastical power in close alliance with that of the state seems to us Anglo-Saxons a sinister thing, it was certainly not felt so by the Spaniards of that time, who in all matters which in their view allowed of freedom of choice enjoyed a great liberty. Here, in her little Carmelite convent, St. Theresa lived and wrote and felt at peace, looking out over the brilliant red hills and the great sweep of the river, as it winds through flat fields before entering the gorge. She, a religious reformer, nurtured on mystical books that were now on the Index, occupied in a fierce struggle with hostile ecclesiastical authorities which ended in the prison and disgrace of her coadjutor St. John of the Cross, would yet have been amazed if anyone had told her that she lived under a theocratic tyranny. And what of El Greco, a foreign intellectual, born in the Greek Church and versed in doubtful Levantine theologies, who of his own free will lived in Toledo from 1577 to 1616 without any incident but a dispute with the Cathedral chapter as to whether the head of Christ should be painted six inches lower or higher than the heads of the thieves? These things should put us on our guard when we endeavor to estimate the popularity of the Communist regime in Russia.

El Greco—how this Greek pervades the town! There are four museums that contain his pictures and several churches. He is the newly canonized saint who brings the tourist pilgrim to the doors and fills the pockets of the tradesmen and hotel keepers. Yet how un-Spanish he is! That penetrating gravity, that intellectual refinement that one sees on the faces of his apostles and prophets is a thousand miles away from anything that has ever been conceived in this country. Look at his portraits of the apostles in the Greco Museum! They electrify us with their air of supernatural intelligence; their glance seems to have taken in the whole of celestial mathematics. Or see in the next room the *St. Bernard of Siena*, leaning a little to one side with softly abstracted gaze as though he were being drawn away by stealth to the things of another world. These faces are very different from those of the empty-headed and ecstatic monks of Zurbarán, as earthy in their origins as Sancho Panza. And then how cold and strange the light that falls on them and on all the figures in this Greek's pictures—the steely, morgue-like light of the visionary, who found no use for the splendid Spanish sun!

Yet it must be admitted that in El Greco's painting there is an affinity with Spanish things. The Balkan races possess certain qualities—austerity, a heightened attitude to suffering—that are characteristic of Spain too. We may suppose that he came prepared by his youthful upbringing to like this harsh and forbidding land—so different to pleasure-loving Italy—and that in Toledo, the holy city of churches

and monasteries, Mount Athos and Jerusalem combined,
he found what he needed to make him more intensely himself. To his adopted country he brought a visionary Levantine eye which revealed to him things that were indeed
there, but which the Spaniards with their intellectual
timidity and their self-punishing realism were incapable
of seeing or portraying. In this one might compare him
with George Borrow, who also found himself in Spain and
who wrote about his experience a book which, though no
Spaniard could have written it, is all the same Spanish.

The key to El Greco is his theological Byzantine mind
which informs his vision. Look for example at the small
Crucifixion shown in this museum. It comes, I believe,
from the Duke of Alba's collection and is not shown in the
Phaidon Edition, but for those who possess this, the two
Golgotha s now in the United States will give some idea of
it. It shows a cross standing up against a darkened sky, in
the immense solitude that stretches between earth and
heaven; on this cross we see a severe face and a long, con-
torted body. Yet it does not seem to be the death agony of
a man that we are witnessing, but a theological fantasy—
the kind of suffering that might be supposed peculiar to a
dying god. The human aspect of Christ, which was first emphasized by Giotto and which has been the subject of every
Crucifixion painted since his time, has been completely
transcended by the supernatural one.

Here then, one might say, is a picture that carries one
straight back to the days when the Christian dogma about
the Trinity was being formed, when those arguments about
the sameness or unsameness of the Son's substance with

that of the Father, that are so meaningless to Western minds, were real and important. But these dogmas upon the nature of the Trinity are precisely those which make up the central core of belief in the Greek Orthodox Church —the point round which all the ceremonies of its cult revolve. The Byzantine mind likes to emphasize the remote and timeless aspect of the Christian mysteries—the power of the sublime figures who stand on the golden walls of the apses and cupolas, all with their faces turned toward the worshipper, and the supernatural or magical knowledge and wisdom that continually emanate from them. This, expressed in the language of Italian baroque painting, is what we find in El Greco: in all his representations of the holy figures we are conscious of a Gnostic tinge. Man is saved not so much by right conduct or by blind faith as by a visionary knowledge of the divine things, imparted through the sacraments, and grace comes down from above not to move the heart but to enlighten the mind. That is the classic attitude of the race that produced Plato, Plotinus, and Dionysius the Areopagite, and when we look at El Greco's pictures and observe the faces of his saints and apostles and still more that of Christ himself, we shall see that they are filled with the power and the plenitude that come from perfect knowledge.*

* Joachim of Flora, the abbot of a Cistercian monastery in Calabria in the twelfth century and the author of a famous prophetic book, declared that the highest gift possible to a Christian, that of *spiritualis intelligentia,* was better preserved in the Eastern Church than in the Western because the Eastern Church had a special devotion to the Paraclete. *Latinus populus ad honorem Filii . . . electus est. Graecus ad honorem Spiriti Sancti.* This remained true in El Greco's day.

I need not say that this is a very un-Spanish attitude. Few Spaniards, we may be sure, except the Platonist Luis de León, have ever regarded the enlargement of the intellect as the chief reward of the blessed on their entry into paradise. It may be interesting therefore to consider in which of his pictures El Greco most nearly approached popular Spanish taste. Pacheco, the father-in-law of Velázquez, held him to be an extravagant painter who refused to follow the rules—that is, the classical system set up by Raphael—but declared that he was the best painter of St. Francises of his time. This must have been the general opinion too, for El Greco painted more pictures of that saint than of anyone else. Now St. Francis was the prime enemy of what El Greco cared for most in religion: by the emphasis he laid on the humanity of Christ, he put an end to the Byzantine spirit in Western Europe. One can call him the creator of the popular medieval Christianity, which reaches its apex in Thomas à Kempis' *Imitation of Christ*—a book which still had a great vogue in Spain in the painter's time. And so we see that in his most-copied pictures of that saint, El Greco paints a plebeian type, gazing in front of him with a sort of hungry rapture such as we find in Zurbarán's ecstatic monks. That is to say, a figure whose sanctity was based on the very un-Byzantine notion of the imitation of Christ's sufferings, a man of love rather than of vision and for that reason especially suited to appeal to popular devotion. While therefore we may agree with Pacheco that these pictures are very fine, we cannot fail to see how different they are in intention to the terrifying *St. Bartholomew* of the Greco Museum, the serene *St. John the Evangelist* of the Prado or the sublime *Madonna Caritatis* at Illescas. No doubt had El Greco been working for a Greek church, he would have consigned St. Francis to the lower walls, while placing most of his other pictures on the dome or vault. Decidedly he was a painter of what are called in books on Byzantine art "the upper zones."

It is often forgotten that El Greco is one of the greatest of portrait painters. Indeed I do not believe that in depth and subtlety of psychological perception any painter has equalled him, though obviously several have excelled him in the purely painterly qualities. Look for example at his portrait of Don Diego de Covarrubias, the bishop-statesman, which hangs in the hall of the Greco Museum. Like most of his best heads, it was painted when he was over sixty and, since Don Diego had died long before, either from memory or from another picture. In the same way the fine portrait of Cardinal Tavera, which is in the Hospital de Afuera, was painted from a death mask. But El Greco's great psychological endowments are perhaps even better displayed in those representations of apostles and saints and divine figures, in which he steeps a face in the expression of a single, all-absorbing state of mind. The most immediately striking of these is the St. Bartholomew I have already alluded to and for which I suspect that he took his model from a lunatic asylum. The power conveyed by this apostle's glance—it is a power derived from supernatural knowledge, since in Byzantine theology all spiritual power proceeds from such knowledge—freezes the blood. Or one may take one of his many representations of Christ.

This psychological penetration shown by El Greco when taken in conjunction with his visionary power and with the feverish turmoil and exaltation of his large canvases naturally calls to mind Dostoevski. The resemblance is too obvious to need illustration. But let us also note the important differences. El Greco's mind is finer and more delicate. This, I think, is because in Dostoevski sin and repentance—those very earthy states—constitute the sources from which the spiritual activity of his characters spring. But in El Greco's later pictures we have got beyond this. Evil, if it ever positively existed, has fallen away and we are left with those glorified beings who are depicted as ascending into or ceaselessly gyrating about a timeless world, which lies far above in space. Even the Crucifixion, which supplies the energy for this movement of ascension as a dynamo supplies power and light to a metropolis, is a cosmic event which, if in one sense it takes place on earth, in another reaches out through creation. Even Toledo, which he was so fond of painting, is no longer in his pictures Toledo, but Jerusalem.

As an illustration of this let me take that superb *Assumption of the Virgin*, which hangs in the San Vicente Museum and is one of the last pictures he painted. The Virgin is rising through the air above the painter's city, surrounded by angels and angelic choirs, and with the Paraclete in the form of a dove suspended above her head. The speed of her ascent, which is spiritual as well as material, has elongated her body and also the bodies of the angelic figures who are bearing her company. As they rise, we get from the oblique views of their limbs, from the receding planes of their faces, from an indescribable something about their averted heads and necks, a feeling of evading, eluding, turning away, bidding farewell, as though the world with all its sorrows and delights could be left behind by a simple inclination of the neck, without struggle or regret. This sort of diagonal movement into the picture space is observable in most of El Greco's larger canvases and bears such a characteristic accent—so different from anything in ordinary baroque painting—that it does not seem to me extravagant to see in it the expression of a religious or mystical attitude. The true life, one might say, lay in gently averting one's gaze from this world toward the light which came from another—that light which, when once seen in a vision, could never be rejected. In realizing his vision through his art, El Greco no doubt felt, like Blake later, that he was working out his salvation as a Christian.

For the last time, on the evening of the 12th, we went for a stroll through the town. What a rabbit warren its streets and houses and churches make! Like Fez, it reeks of the Middle Ages; like Lhasa, of monks. Yet the thing that most impressed me on this occasion was the proximity of the bare, rocky hills beyond the river gorge. Walking in narrow, crooked lanes, one suddenly catches sight of a crest of rock so close in the clear plateau air that one im-

agines one could throw a stone onto it. That harsh, waterless sierra, with its iron-colored boulders looks as if it rose
from the end of the street. Toledo, one says to oneself—
though it is not quite true—is a fortress built in a desert.

ARANJUEZ and MADRID

As we rode on a bumpy, jolting train up the Tagus valley, I opened the morning paper. It told me that in the Sierra de Avila, some thirty miles away on the left, a wolf hunt was in progress. The wolves, it seems, have been more than usually troublesome this year, coming down to the villages and killing the sheep and cattle, so that to get rid of them it had been decided to have a large *battue*. A doctor called Montoro had organized it, five thousand volunteer guns and beaters were taking part, and a film company was filming it. A couple of days later I read the result: no wolves had been shot; the total bag was two foxes.

The train was leaving the open cornfields of La Sagra and entering an irrigated region of gardens and tall trees. Then, with much bumping and rattling, it slowed down and pulled up; we were in Aranjuez. We got out and took a very ancient horse bus to the hotel.

Aranjuez is the Spanish Versailles: everything in it speaks the language of pleasure, formality, and the eighteenth century. The town is laid out in broad parallel streets and wide parade-ground squares, around which stand in neat rows the lodgings of the palace servants. Beyond are the villas of the nobility. And all these streets, squares and villas are shaded with spreading plane trees.

The Palace is a rather dull building with some charming rooms, decorated for the most part in the Pompeian style of 1770. Two of them, the Queen's dressing room and the

Porcelain room, are particularly lovely. The latter is so called because it has its walls and ceiling faced with white porcelain, out of which stand raised figured decorations in a Chinese style in green, blue and rose. Long mirrors inserted in the walls give their endless series of reflections and the result is the setting for a Ronald Firbank story about a princess of perverse and inconsequently naughty tastes.

The Palace windows open on a parterre that is planted with exotic shrubs and trees, and beside this flows the river. At the further end it passes over a weir, and it is the sudden change of level that creates all this fertility. When I was last here in May 1934, the water came down in a rushing, splashing flood that filled the whole garden with its sound. But today there is silence. Every drop has already, before reaching this point, been taken off for irrigation and the bed of the river below the weir has become a chain of green and stagnant pools, fit only for frogs to croak in. I felt that I had never before realized the terrible intensity of the drought.

Beside the river and below the Palace lie the gardens of La Isla, where the famous nightingales of Schiller sang. But in Don Carlos' time there were no trees—it was his father Philip II who planted them—and if we let our imaginations wander to the eighteenth century, we have to remember that Spain did not produce a Louis XV. What the royal family was like one may see from Goya's portraits. Yet the place seems contrived for a Watteau or a Fragonard. Nowhere else in the world do planes, elms, and poplars reach so extreme a height, and in the long avenues and vistas converging on statues and in the clumps and thickets scattered with flowering shrubs, one has the ideal garden of the eighteenth century.

That night we went for a stroll down the avenue of gigantic planes—it is more than three miles long—that skirts another and larger garden—that of the Príncipe. The moon was full—is it not always full at Aranjuez?—and the tall blotched trunks rose into an interlaceage of thin branches and of leaves that had not yet spread to their full extent. No nightingales could be heard, though we had listened to one earlier that afternoon, but instead there were cuckoo-voiced owls, called in Spanish *cuca,* that answered one another with a ringing musical note. When these calls ceased, not a sound could be heard; the moon itself, with the brightness of its light, seemed to be making the silence. We ended our walk with a glass of beer and a dish of fresh strawberries at the café by the bridge.

The broken springs of a Castilian bed do not tempt one to lie long, so we were up early. In the cool air, under the tall trees, walking was pleasant. We followed the avenue we had discovered the previous night as far as the small palace known as the Casa del Labrador. This is a building put up in 1803 by Charles IV and his queen, María Luisa, in imitation of the Petit Trianon at Versailles. After going over it and deciding that its Empire furniture was vulgar and tasteless, we set out to walk back through the Jardín del Príncipe.

I recommend all serious dendrophiles—that is, all lovers of trees—to come to Aranjuez. Till they have been there they can have no idea of what a tree can do. Planes in these gardens reach twice the height they reach in London and elms, growing in a loose, graceful form not seen in Northern countries, shoot up to a hundred and fifty feet. Besides these there are North American trees such as liquidambars, hemlocks and horse chestnuts, while the *flor de amor* or judas tree startles one among the undergrowth with its vivid magenta note. The causes of this stupendous growth are a deep soil, a hot sun, and water. All these gardens are irrigated and the temperature in August sometimes reaches 115 degrees in the shade.

How pleasant this little town is with its formal arcaded streets and its shady gardens! To walk in their green labyrinths after traveling for so long through red and yellow steppes was delight indeed. Yet, though this place is only thirty miles from Madrid and has a good train service, few people come here. And of these still fewer spend the night. Is the reason for this the traditional Castilian hatred of trees? (Like the Chinese, the Castilian peasant is a furious dendrophobe.) Or does it lie in their aversion to a foreign sort of amenity—pleasure grounds laid out by kings who had French taste? Or is it simply that, in a land where money is scarce, they cannot afford it? Whatever the reason, we took the morning train to Madrid.

On arriving at the Estación del Mediodía we found the traffic across the city held up by one of the Holy Week processions. There was nothing to be done but to go to a hotel near by, which an Englishman whom we had met at Toledo had recommended to us. It turned out to be just what we had feared—one of those large international businessman's hotel where one lives badly at considerable expense. The lounge smelled of varnish, the dining room had sham oak paneling, the waiters were sulky, and the food tasted as if it had been flown over that morning from England. Some elderly compatriots of mine at the next table were thoroughly enjoying it. Had not every dish got bottled tomato sauce poured over it? Were not the ices made with real custard powder? I heard one of them confiding to the other that she had never imagined Spain could be so homely.

After so much traveling it is pleasant to be in Madrid again and to have nothing to do but sit in the shade and drink the excellent Spanish beer and coffee. The weather is hotter than it usually is in this month: even at seven o'clock one finds oneself crossing the street to avoid the sun, but the *fond de l'air* is cool and there is generally a fresh breeze at midday. No wonder, for this city stands at more than two thousand feet above sea level.

Coming from the South, the first thing that strikes us when we walk in the streets is the sibilant sound of the Castilian accent. There is a continual subdued hissing as from snakes. But listen not for sounds, but for words. Then one will hear, like shots fired off at intervals, a stream of *no no no nada nada nada*. These people seem to be always refusing or rejecting something. If the language of Provence used to be known as the *langue d'oc* and that of France as the *langue d'oïl* and that of Italy as the *langue de si*, then decidedly Spanish should be called the *langue de no*.

Good Friday in Madrid is like any other holiday: the bars and cafés are crowded with a cheerful noisy population and the streets are packed with men and women in their Sunday best. Many of the girls wear the traditional penitential costume—a long skirt of black satin or watered silk that reaches to the ground, a high comb with a mantilla laid over it, and a rose or carnation in their hair. With this goes a heavy black rosary which they carry in their hand and a prayer book with a silver clasp. But there is nothing devotional in their manner: they trip gaily along with their *novio* by their side, a little overconscious of their fancy dress and finding their skirts awkward to manage. One has to go to Seville or to look at elderly women to see the mantilla and the long skirt worn properly.

The best way of enjoying the fine weather and the crowds is to go to the Parque. Here one may sit under the trees in one of the open-air cafés and watch the endless, leisurely procession of people moving past. How lovely are the women with their splendid, eloquent eyes and vigorous heads of hair and fine carriage! The girls are a perpetual delight, but the older women fascinate me too with their handsome features and their air of dignity. Only in Rome or Florence does one see as many beautiful ones. But if Italian women have better figures and faces of a finer oval, they have decidedly less character and expression.

The Spanish girl places her accent a little differently from the English one. Her face, her hair, her hands, her gestures, her gait are the matters she gives most attention to. Every evening promenade or *paseo* is a school of deportment and flirtation, but it is a national school in which the movie stars do not, as in England, serve as models. The gait or carriage is the most important thing; Spanish girls carry themselves wonderfully. But even in this there have been changes. In Madrid, at least, the art of walking, or rather pacing, in very high-heeled shoes has declined. There is no longer time or space today for the mannequin steps in which their mothers showed off their qualities. They have gone out with the horse carriage.

Yet Spanish girls do not dress well. Their clothes are either homemade or cut by cheap dressmakers, instead of being bought ready-made or cut to Vogue patterns. The long skirt and short coat, which are being worn this year in London and Paris, are never seen and their tightly corsetted waists (all Spanish women corset madly) are put into cheap English-type cardigans, which they call "Rebeccas." The colors too are ugly and badly matched. So awkward and provincial is the general effect that one cannot help feeling that they need some Worth or Paquin of their own race to show them the way they should go. The old national costume was very successful in concealing their bad points—short legs and stocky figures—and in bringing out their good ones. It is a pity that nothing has been thought out on the same lines, but in a modern style.

Yet look at their faces, their necks, their shoulders and hair, and all this will be forgotten. They give a great deal of time to their hair and their make-up, and this time is not wasted. And then there are those large brilliant eyes with their clear whites which can throw a signal as far as one can throw a tennis ball. English girls use their eyes much less deliberately. But what strikes the foreigner most is the fact that they are so conscious of their beauty. They sail along, buoyed up by the admiring glances that follow them, without any of the doubts and hesitations that affect even beautiful girls in England. They know that they are there to be looked at and that men exist simply in order to look at them. For this reason they allow themselves in conversation a range of facial expressions from vigorous pouts to broad grimaces such as in less attractive girls would be thought unbecoming. A heavy frown, which no English girl would dare to be seen with, is part of their regular armory.

With all this life and animation there goes a great deal of warmth and good humor. Quite obviously the relations of the young with the other members of their family are often happy and unconstrained. And they love children. It is a common sight to see a well-dressed young man playing with a child or making faces at a baby without any feeling of embarrassment. One does not see much shyness or timidity, however much their novelists may write about it. In short, an old-fashioned society—early Victorian or Second Empire, but beginning to crumble and break down.

But if the first impression one gets of Madrid on an Easter holiday is of life and happiness, one must not suppose for a moment that everyone is enjoying himself. The immense majority are engrossed in the problem of making both ends meet. One has to see Spanish life from the inside to realize how very difficult that has become. Yet in this fine city and climate, where people like to take their pleasures in public, the forms of happiness are perpetually open to the eye, as at a fair. And all are in the race. The prospect of enjoyment is continually there, dangling before the eyes, ready at a moment to drop into the lap of even the poorest in the form of a winning lottery ticket. It is only the old who know that they have lost. One of the curious and pathetic things about these old in Spain is the way in which they contract and shrink. At every step one sees old women who are so thin and light than one feels that a breath of air might blow them away. These women are never cheerful. A look of settled melancholy has dropped like a death mask on their faces and they sit motionless on a bench in the park or in some dull corner of a room without any change of expression passing over them, as though they were ferns or plants. Another sort have that round-eyed expression of terror that one sees in Goya's portrait of the Infanta María Josefa in the Prado. But all without exception are sad, and not only, I think, because they are poor and lonely and shattered by some tragedy proceeding from the Civil War or from the repression that has followed it—although, heaven knows, there is cause enough in these things for misery—but because they cannot forget that the possibility of happiness has passed. In this country where youth and vitality are everything, they are the totally defeated because their strength has gone and their days are counted and told.

But all the same what a dramatic city Madrid is! The moral sense may often be shocked by the contrast between riches and destitution, but one will be stimulated in spite of oneself by the feeling for life. Spaniards throw themselves into both pleasure and pain more openly and wholeheartedly than do other races. They run avidly after the one and when they have lost it, they make something of the other. One imagines that in limbo there are few souls of Spanish origin, for the greatest evil to them is numbness or loss of feeling. And of course the great vicissitudes they go through leave a residue on their faces, which is all the more noticeable because their features are prominent. The expressions one sees on people over fifty are often extraordinary.

We moved today to a hotel in the Gran Vía, where we pay 50 pesetas a day *pension,* have a private bathroom and get tolerable food. Just half the price of last night's lodgings. This hotel offers no luxuries, but has a gay and friendly atmosphere; its clients are chiefly young people— students, foreigners, actors and so forth. During the afternoon, as we were crossing the town, we ran into two processions; in one of these the Virgin was carried in front and the dead Christ followed in a glass coffin behind; in the other there was a *paso* of Christ being scourged by the soldiers. In both of these the place of honor was given to a detachment of the city police, who have the reputation of being the toughest of the four different sorts of police in this country.

That night we went to see another and much larger procession. The crowds were very dense, but mounted policemen kept lanes in it, so we struggled forward up the Calle de Alcalá in the hopes of getting a near sight. Before long we saw a large unwieldy object, lit up like a Christmas tree with hundreds of candles, come tottering slowly down the Gran Vía towards us. Then the crowd became denser, knots of people began to shove and push and my wife was almost thrown down. I put out both arms to hold her up and when she was on her feet again I found that my purse, which I kept in my trouser pocket, was gone. It contained nearly thirty pounds. No doubt it was fitting that the thieves, whose patron saint had suffered on the Cross on that day, should reap some advantage, but for me the blow was a severe one. We went back to the hotel in a state of great depression, without waiting to see any more catafalques.

In the hotel where we are staying there are a number of French girl students. They offer a strong contrast to the Spanish girls. Not one in seven of them is pretty, but they differ greatly among themselves. They have less animal vitality, but their mental processes are more complex. They have a greater range of feeling and character because they have a modern self-consciousness. The truth is that the Spaniards are a simple race in comparison to the English and French. As in their climate and scenery, the halftones appear to be left out. Or is it that, like music written in an unfamiliar mode, we are unable to take in all the complexities? This seems to me the more probable hypothesis. The deep melancholia, the religious obsession, the abysmal emptiness and nothingness that one so often sees graven on their faces are of a different kind to anything that one sees elsewhere in Europe. And what of the strange blood lust that, as the Civil War and the Carlist War and the Napoleonic War all show, comes over them on particular occasions—that morose, half sexual, half religious passion in which they associate themselves with Death and do his work for him? Yes, they have their own brands of cruelty and delicacy and melancholy and extravagance, which are often as difficult for us to see with our daylight-fed eyes as is a nighttime landscape.

For there are two sides to the Spanish soul correspond-
ing, as it were, to day and night. The daylight Spaniard is
the man one sees—sociable, positive, capable of great
bursts of energy and animation, often rather eighteenth
century in character and not very imaginative. In his ordinary conduct he is rather a simple person, as one can tell
from a glance at Spanish literature. It contains no Mon-
taignes, Racines, Pascals, Rousseaus, Constants, Prousts,
Blakes, or Shakespeares, though it has a Cervantes. Its
complexity, when it has complexity, lies as a rule in certain poetic overtones or in the arabesque-like manner in
which it treats its material. The other side of the Spanish
nature one does not see, because it rarely shows itself
clearly on the surface. But one can easily divine it, for it is
its silent welling up into the consciousness that gives to
Spanish things that strange and unaccountable accent
which everyone recognizes. I call it the night side of the
Spanish soul—though I might equally well call it the seventeenth-century side—because it is associated with thoughts
of death and contempt for life.

Menosprecio de la vida, disdain for life! That phrase is
like a bell that tolls its way through Spanish history. The
Spaniards are great destroyers. Is it their pride—the *orgullo*
for which they have always been famous—that makes them
so despise all the detail and humdrum of daily life? Nothing
is good enough for them—that is the first stage of their immense egoism; in the second stage nothing is any good at
all, since life and the world do not last forever. *Todo o
nada.* Everything or nothing. It is this attitude that has
made both Spanish fanaticism and Spanish mysticism.

The Spaniards are great realists—that is what we are always told. Certainly they see things minutely and objectively. But this reality hurts and wounds their pride; too often they look on life as if it were their enemy. And it is precisely the cruelty and precision of their vision (consider Goya) that throws them back into themselves with the desire to transcend what they see. Hence their nobility, their generosity, their extravagance. They have to vanquish their own meanness, exceed and outbid their own egos. To a *caballero* other people's opinions do not matter, for other people scarcely exist, but to have a good opinion of oneself —that is what is important. So Philip II built the Escorial and lived in two small rooms. He erected the largest palace in the world to flatter his pride, and then to flatter it still more turned it over to the monks and built a royal *pudridero*, where he and his descendants might slowly rot in black, unornamented marble coffins. Don Quixote, dismayed by the dullness and insignificance of his life, imagined himself a knight-errant and then proved to himself that he was noble indeed. Under the veneer of a nineteenth-century character, one will very often find in modern Spaniards the deep stamp of the Counter Reformation.

How quickly the time passes in this brilliant sunlight, in this handsome, well-built but perhaps monotonous city where everything is made for ease of life! Our time is spent in drifting from café to café, drinking coffee in one, eating an apricot ice in another, then having a glass of *manzanilla* and some potato crisps before lunch and in the evenings ringing the changes on beer and anise, with black olives and those large prawns called *gambas*. In between we visit the Prado and the museums (among which I must signal out a private museum, the Instituto Valencia de San Juan with its fine collection of pottery, tapestries, embroideries and so forth) call on a friend, or turn over the art books in the excellent German bookshop on the Castellana.

As we move about we look at the passing faces, so lovely or so deeply marked—either preternaturally solemn with the leaden solemnity of Spaniards or else more than usually gay and animated. The bald are more bald, the obese more obese, the thin more cadaverous, the one-legged more limbless than in other countries. From this generalization I except the young men, who do not stand out. Till he is thirty the Spanish male tends to be a tailor's model of a man, with too much animation and too little character. Then, as he enters middle age, his head begins to swell till by the time he is fifty it is huge and massive—a lion's head which his short legs and body seem too meager to support. Seated they are full of dignity, walking they tend to be ungainly—Roman senators as their portrait busts portray them, without the nobility bestowed by flowing togas. Yes, Roman. The Roman Empire left more of its essential stuff in Spain than in Italy: the coarseness, solidity, stoic strength of character of that great imperial people form the understructure of Spanish life, on the top of which has been built an edifice of an entirely different sort—a fretted skyline of Oriental minarets and battlements that make up the tight and well-defended fabric of pride and honor. This sense of honor, or rather of self-esteem or *pundonor,* is one of the things one cannot be an hour in Spain without noticing. It is what prevents one from sharing a taxi or

paying for a theater ticket or buying a drink; if one happens to be in the company of a Spaniard. It is a liberating
and ennobling quality which, even if it does not go deeper
than good manners, does much to raise the tone of social
life.

Pleasant though Madrid is at this season, the tourist
would probably not wish to linger in it if it were not for
the Prado. Here, in a gallery that is just the right size, one
may see a large number of masterpieces so freshly preserved in this smokeless mountain air that they look as
though they had been painted yesterday. One can have
only a feeble idea of the magnificence of Spanish painting
if one has not visited it; almost the whole work of Goya, for
example, is to be found there. And then there is the superb
collection of Titians and Tintorettos, Roger van der Wey-
dens and Rubens, not to speak of a host of lesser Flemish
and Italian painters.

The Titians are of every period, from his two Venuses,
where one still feels the touch of the spring-like Renaissance air, to his *St. Margaret* and his *Danäe*, where the age
—that of the Council of Trent—has become June-like and
sultry. Then there is the equestrian portrait of Charles V,
in which, much repainted though I believe it has been, one
feels a richness of worldly experience and a mastery of all
the varied resources of art such as can scarcely be matched
by any other painter. Finally there is his self-portrait,
painted in extreme old age, in which he seems to go beyond
anything he had previously done. But the Prado has other
very great portraits to show. Rubens' painting of Marie de
Médici is one of his finest pictures, while Raphael's *Young*

Cardinal staggers one by the quantity of life and reality which it contains.

The Goyas will be the greatest sensation for the traveler who has not been to Spain before. Of all painters he is the most approachable, because his combination of irony and raciness with a lovely surface of paint is easily appreciated even by those whose feeling for art is moderate. One might call him the greatest of journalist painters, in the same sense in which Voltaire is the greatest of journalist writers: marvellously quick in eye and mind and swift and incisive in brush strokes, yet when compared to the supreme masters of his art, a little superficial. The etchings and crayon drawings, however, show another side—a fantastic, visionary eye and a power of finding new and surprising compositions that in their speed and variety of improvisation evoke the daemonic art of Picasso. Certainly he caught the look of Spain. He was not only the painter but the novelist of his age, and as one travels about the country one sees his types and gestures still alive today.

Velázquez, however, is a Spanish painter who attracts me more because he is enigmatic. His pictures do not reveal themselves, as Goya's do, at the first glance. People say, "He was just an eye," but he did not, like Goya, use his eye to see things, but to look through them. What his feelings about the world may have been we do not know, for, as Roger Fry said, he dwells entirely in the realm of pure vision and seems utterly indifferent to the symbolic or emotional meanings of the things that he paints. Now such an attitude in painting, even when judged by the light of modern practice, is extraordinary and in fact the impression his

pictures make is often, I think, more deeply disturbing
than even that made by Goya's war etchings. Here, for
example, is the representation of a head—say that of
Philip IV or of an Infanta—and it is obviously a perfect
and complete likeness of the original. Yet this likeness is
not the point of the picture at all; it is so far even from
being the point that it strikes one as being a little uncanny.
Velázquez is looking through the unity of the object we
call the king's face at its material composition, and in this
he finds a play of light and color which he conveys, by very
delicate and mysterious means, to his canvas. But, it will
be said, this is just what the Impressionists were doing
with cruder means. I do not believe that this is really so,
for although they claimed to be putting down only the impressions of light and color that struck their retina, one
may see that in fact they by no means rejected the vital and
emotional content of the objects they were painting. Velázquez, on the other hand, seems deliberately (though no
doubt unconsciously) to undermine the reality of the material objects he paints and to substitute for them a loose tex-
ture of light and color which removes them to some other
more tenuous world of pure aesthetics. And at the same
time, because the visible appearance or similitude of the
things we know is still there, he makes us feel, sometimes
in a rather shocking way, their emptiness and nothingness.
Such detachment from the values of ordinary life is surely
unprecedented.

One must call Velázquez the disillusioned painter of a
melancholy and disillusioned age. All his later pictures
show an aristocratic form of *menosprecio de la vida,*

disdain for life, and a flight from actuality that has some
analogy with the more dogmatic flight that has seized on
painters today. One can compare him to Góngora, whose
long, beautiful and obscure poem, *Soledades,* though by no
means sad, shows a similar escape into the world of pure
aesthetic values. By the time—twenty or thirty years later
—that Velázquez was painting his great pictures, the
shadows that hung over Spain had sensibly deepened.

Before leaving this painter I would like to single out
two of his pictures: one of these, the *Villa Médici Gardens,*
painted in Rome either in 1630 or in 1650, is the greatest
landscape in Spanish art and especially interesting to us because it leads straight to the French landscapes of the nineteenth century; the other is a small Crucifixion, discovered
in a convent during the Civil War, and previously unknown. It is painted with a most un-Velázquezlike intensity of religious feeling.

Some Spanish painters are poorly represented in the
Prado. For the primitives one must go to Barcelona and
Valencia; for Zurbarán, who is not sufficiently known outside his country, to Guadalupe, Cadiz, and Seville. And
where are the moderns? I am told that in the whole of
Spain there is not a single Juan Gris, Miró, or Picasso.
This is surprising, because Spain is the country that produced the Conquistadors, and what else are contemporary
painting and poetry but colonial adventures—heroic at-
tempts to explore and cultivate new regions of the mind,
where the climate is so inhospitable that it seems doubtful
if human nature will be able to establish itself?

Madrid, unlike London, is a real capital. Here this great

dusty, barren land, with its poverty and its tedium and its
insoluble problems, throws up a city that is splendid, spacious and entirely made for human life. Everyone in it either
has money or is pretending to have it. The shops are full of
luxury foods, every few yards there is a café or a tempting
bar, the streets and parks are crowded with people who
seem to have nothing else to do but to stroll about. Everything that could remind the people of this city that their
land is poor, their villages wretched, their agricultural
workers clothed in rags and starving is spirited away. Life
is for display and for enjoyment. Youth is a time for pleasure. No reminders of the starkness of the national situation
must be allowed. And so all those who can somehow raise
a few pesetas throw themselves into the dance and think of
little else but women and bulls and cards and endless, endless conversation. We English do not live like this because
our cities are sad and sordid places, our food Lenten, and
the pressure of work on us remorseless, and so it would be
hypocrisy for us to throw stones at those who do. But we
can note the result. Spain is being gambled away every
night by these idle, money-seeking classes who profess to
govern it, just as in Regency times young lords used to
gamble away their ancestral estates. Money, money, money!
By hook or crook money must be found to pay one's debts,
to incur new ones, to breathe in deeper and deeper
draughts of this intoxicating life. And so the racket goes
on. One must condemn the process, but if one has ever
been young or had a taste for pleasure, one must not in
honesty be too severe on the perpetrators.

On the last evening of our visit to Spain I chanced on a

situation that, trifling and insignificant though it was, seemed to me to sum up the condition of this country. The Café María Cristina is the largest, most expensive café in Madrid. Every afternoon its spacious ground floor and upper floor are filled with a well-dressed population. In the basement, however, there is a dark, mysteriously lighted region, encumbered by billiard and ping-pong tables, where young men and boys play for small stakes from morning to night. In the darkest and most confused corner of this, under a staircase and among a litter of beer bottles and empty soda-water bottles, is a gents' lavatory, or as Spaniards say "retreat"—a horrid cupboard, whose doors do not fasten, whose plug does not work, and whose walls drip with a continual, oozing moisture. Just outside this— invisible till one has accustomed one's eyes to the gloom— sits a little old woman on a chair. She has nothing to do but to open the door, which is always open anyway, and to provide those who ask for it with paper. In return for such services she takes any coin that may be offered her. This is the income on which she lives and since the café pays her nothing, I doubt whether she earns more than 3 pesetas a day. But she has a post, she has an income, and she thinks herself lucky.

My last observation on Spain—though it might have been my first—is on the subject of women's hair. The strength of Spanish women appears to lie, like Samson's, in this feature. Those great jets of wiry locks that spring like cascades from their heads and then are washed and brushed and combed and dressed and set and scented and rubbed up with brilliantine to rival the shine on their

shoes and the gloss on their pupils, are the index of the
huge animal vitality of this race: a vitality that would be a
little crude and monotonous if it had not so often imposed
on it a peculiar sort of refinement and melancholy. All vital
races feel keenly the existence of the antivital principle; it
haunts them more persistently than it does the busy,
phlegmatic, vaguely worrying English. Those great
draughty halls of the mind in which the Spaniards habitu-
ally live make it difficult for them to keep out the facts
of life or to dope themselves with petty activities. As a
lampwick feeds on oil, so they feed on a secret store of
melancholy, which even their family affections or their
zest for pleasure cannot dry up entirely. Thus their lives
are like sermons by Jeremy Taylor, with the last phase always in view: the narrow box, the niche in the wall, the
train of mourners; the turn of the key in the heart's lock
which will shut their thoughts within them forever.

April 19

THE time has come to leave. As we drink our
coffee, we read that the drought has broken over the greater
part of the country. On our way to the airdrome a few
drops of rain fall and thus we leave Spain as we found it—
with high, purplish clouds spreading like enormous hands
over the sky and the dry tableland below waiting like a
woman on a bed for the expected moment to come.

Then we are in the air. Instantly we are over uninhabited
country. The earth below us is magenta red, for the corn
that covers it is too thin to hide the color of the soil. Then

come mountains and rivers and after them more mountains, till we reach the sea and so leave the great spread ox-hide, as Pliny described this peninsula, behind us.

Yet it seems that we have not left Spain after all. It continues to travel along with us in our minds, affecting and lighting up by its contrast everything that we see. Here is England below us. Neat as a kitchen garden and of a piercing macaw-like green. Then the scale increases, increases, goes on increasing . . . we are down. A thin rain is falling, there is a smell of mackintoshes.

We climb into a coach to drive through the London suburbs. Here my Spanish sensibilities begin to rage and protest. The ugliness and anarchy of this great sprawling city, grown up like a miners' town on the banks of the Yukon, appalls me. Can a civilized people really live in this low squatters' settlement? Yet as the rain lifts, I become aware of the April light, as it falls on the elm trees with their young pointed leaves and their black, silky branches and stems. London is ugly and haphazard, I tell myself, because the English are not a race of city dwellers: they are countrymen who are trying to pretend that they are camping here provisionally.

But what is a traveler, fresh from the dramatic features of the Madrileños, to say of the people? As we pass through the packed and sordid streets, I see all about us a throng of plain, rounded faces that lack the distinction of real ugliness. Faces like puddings that seem never to have desired or suffered, smooth vegetable faces, placid cow-like faces, lightly creased and rippled by small worries. Yet there is kindness and good humor in their little bird-like eyes,

there is a sense of reassurance in their soft, creaking Cock-
ney tones! My Spanish-conditioned faculties tell me that
this is a sensible, fair-minded, humorous people. But not a
beautiful or a dynamic one.

It takes time to readjust oneself. After three days I am
still half a foreigner. What I feel most is the absence of the
sense for leisure. In London there is the dreadful scramble
to get about, the grime, the crowds, the discomfort and in-
convenience and ugliness of everything put up by human
agency. In other places, the Germanic neatness and fussi-
ness. Our mania for "raising the standard of life"—by which
we do *not* mean eating better food, or having well laid-out
cities, or places to sit and to talk in, or the freedom to eat
and drink when we want to—is making us the prisoners of
our conventions. Seen through Mediterranean eyes, we
English are a cautious, fussy, elderly-minded people, living
without large ideas among a litter of temporary expedients,
far too taken up with the problems our muddle creates for
us to have much faculty left for practicing the arts of life.

The sun had sunk as I said this to myself and in the
country lane I was following the slow English twilight was
stealing on. Somewhere among the treetops the doves were
cooing; perched by their nests on the tall elms the rooks
were cawing, while across the fields came the notes of the
blackbirds, sweet and prolonged. Then they ceased, and
the countryside sank into its thick silence.

What, I asked myself, continuing the interior dialogue
that had obsessed me since my return, what is England?
Intellectually and aesthetically it is a rabidly self-destruc-
tive country. For three centuries its famous men have been

THE FACE OF SPAIN

at work, destroying the sense for pleasure, poisoning the wells of faith, draining away spontaneity, impoverishing the language and the literature. All in the name of truth and utility. From Locke to Hume and from Bentham to Ayer our philosophers have been flattening out the hills of the mind and robbing us of our most precious dimension. From Swift to Huxley our writers have been giving us private tuition courses in self-hatred. We do not dramatize sin because we are not Christians—or if we are Christians, because we belong to the Pelagian sect—yet our bad conscience about ourselves has seeped into our souls and perverted our natural appetites.

There is then the class aspect. Our peasantry and artisans once had a culture, as have those of all the European nations. They knew how to cook, to eat, to converse, and to enjoy their leisure. But by the destruction of our countryside through the Enclosure Acts and the driving of its inhabitants into the slums of the industrial towns, this culture was torn up and they were reduced to a rootless, amorphous and disease-ridden mass. Now that they are, quite properly, rising to the surface and invading the old, more or less educated classes, they bring with them nothing but a few moral notions founded on the ethics of the football field and the boxing ring.

Yet, I thought to myself, things are not really so bad as they appear on the surface. The pressure of ideas which has destroyed the traditional pattern of our lives (utilitarianism has been the most pernicious of them) has generally been exerted in the name of a sacred principle—that of liberty, the right of everyone to live by his inner light.

Thus at the same time that we have been enslaved by our doubts and scruples and herded by them along the dustiest of beaten tracks—that of nineteenth-century materialism—we have in other directions been freed. And this has had two admirable consequences: the first is that we English have developed a stronger sense of responsibility than any other people; the other is that our social pattern has acquired complexity and diversity. In comparison to it, the pattern of Spanish life, at first sight so seductive in its sharpness and vigor, may well appear obvious and monotonous.

For who can sum up or describe this country? Our lives are hushed and private and shut in by laurel hedges with spotted leaves. Our thoughts are obscure and muffled and not to be conveyed in speech or writing. Our philosophies consist of doubts and ideological solvents, but fantasy colors our daydreams. Neurotic guilt makes us live in fear of one another and in hiding from ourselves. Then so great is our dread of the future that, like people who cannot bring themselves to make their wills, we refuse to plan our cities. We refuse to commit ourselves to anything beforehand, in case we should wish to change our minds. With the obstinacy of the born procrastinator, we camp in the present, because that is all we are certain of. Yet when some threat to our existence crops up, we forget our dithering and fight to the last ditch. What else does this mean but that we are all Hamlets, or that Hamlet is the type of Englishman as he is never found in real life—the Englishman undressed?

Darkness had come on as I walked and the last noises of

the village had died away. The stars came out faintly as
if wrapped in overcoats, their eyes peering dimly and
apologetically through the blackness as though they were
English too. A bat fluttered round me, a mouse in the
hedgerow squeaked.

If then, I continued, the pattern of English life, seen from
outside, seems soft and shapeless, our minds damp and
hesitating and our pulse slow, we are all the same, under
our protective covering, an adventurous people, forever
feeling our way in new directions, without form or rule to
guide us but secure in our own instinct for what is right
and fitting. Moreover, though we differ much among ourselves, our sense of national cohesion is so strong that it
allows each of us to steer by his own compass. Without a
peasantry and without a city life, camping in a landscape
that has been wrecked by an industrial tornado, we are
necessarily barbarians in our lack of culture, but in the
art of getting on together we are supremely civilized.

The cars passed by, lighting up the hedges and then
throwing them back into the blackness. The air was heavy
with faint animal and insect sounds. One had the impression one could hear the grass growing. Yes, for all its mossi-
ness of mind and its grey philistinism and its dread of
reality, this was a country worth belonging to. It was
mysterious, it was complex, and it was decent. One could
anyhow say, as Orwell had done, that it was a country
whose people did not kill one another. Coming as I had
from Spain, that was something.